Muzzleloader Hunting

Then and Now

Muzzleloader Hunting

Then and Now

TOBY BRIDGES

Dedication

This book is dedicated to my special partner in life–Deborah Jean. She makes life worth living and today's hectic world a whole lot easier to tolerate. Her love, support, and encouragement are the driving forces behind everything positive in my life.

Front cover images: Toby Bridges   Back cover images: Toby Bridges
All interior images by Toby Bridges unless noted otherwise.

Published by: Woods N' Water, Inc.
Peter and Kate Fiduccia
P.O. Box 550
Florida, NY 10921

Printed in the United States of America
10 9 8 7 6 5 4 3 2 1
ISBN: 0-9722804-9-9

Table of Contents

Introduction

Depending on whose figures one chooses to quote, there are now estimated to be between three million and four million muzzleloading shooters and hunters in the United States and Canada. And the majority of these "frontloading aficionados" have joined the ranks during just the past two decades. Chances are that those of you reading this book are part of that majority.

Since the 1956 introduction of the first modern-made reproduction muzzleloading rifle, the Dixie Gun Works' .40 caliber "New Squirrel Rifle," the variety of modern manufactured muzzleloaded rifles available to today's shooter and hunter has grown into a mind-boggling selection. There are now literally several hundred different muzzleloading rifle models and variations to choose from, and while such a selection may make it more difficult than ever to pick just the right rifle, this array of frontloaders does make it possible for a shooter to end up with the ideal muzzleloader for his or her need, purpose or taste.

Through the following chapters of this book, you will discover that the only thing that has remained constant in muzzleloading has been change.

Interest in hunting with a muzzleloading gun has never been greater. And neither has the selection of both traditionally styled and modern-design frontloading rifles, whether for big game or an enjoyable morning of squirrel hunting.

Through all of the first six hundred years that muzzleloading guns have been in existence, ingenious minds worked diligently to improve the efficiency of various early ignition systems or to increase the stopping power of a muzzleloaded rifle—whether it was being used to hunt large game or stop an enemy.

When Turner Kirkland traveled to Belgium during the early 1950s, seeking a gunmaker to produce his new manufactured Dixie Gun Works muzzleloader, what he ended up with was a very representative copy of what has come to be known as a "Kentucky Rifle." Dixie offered the rifle in both flintlock and percussion ignition, and only in .40 caliber. The need at that time was for a sound, solid and well-made muzzleloader of suitable caliber for the slow-growing crowd of historically minded shooters who could no longer find a trustworthy one hundred- to one hundred fifty-year-old original that would stand up to the rigors of everyday shooting. And almost as soon as that rifle hit the U.S. market, the evolution of the muzzleloader took off again, at almost the same point where it had ended a hundred years earlier, with the advent of breechloading cartridge arms.

The author's introduction to muzzleloading was purely accidental. It happened on the first day of the 1963 Illinois deer season. That was my second year to hunt deer, and even though I had not tagged a deer the first season (at age thirteen), I went home knowing that I would forever be a deer hunter. Now, Illinois is one of those "shotgun states" that do not allow the use of center-fire rifles. I had heard that a hunter could use a rifle of muzzleloaded design, but back then I did not know anyone who even owned a muzzleloader.

Opening morning of the 1963 season broke frosty and cold. I had worn just about every piece of warm clothing I owned, including a heavy navy-surplus wool coat. About mid-morning, the sun began to warm things up, and I slipped the heavy coat off and laid it on one of the logs near the top of the old bulldoze pile I had chosen for my stand. I had just about settled back down when suddenly a big doe popped out of the thick timber and was running at me at full tilt. As she shot by at forty yards, left to right, I swung on her with the bead of the old Steven 12-gauge double and let fly with the right barrel. In my excitement, I had totally forgotten that the barrel printed the big one-ounce rifled slugs nearly eighteen inches to the left, and I shot right behind the deer.

Before I could get off the second shot, the doe was gone. But forty yards behind her was a young button buck, and when he ran past in almost the same spot, I swung on him and touched off the left barrel . . . and fortunately the left barrel tended to print a little to the right. Still excited, I once again forgot that the barrel shot about twelve inches to the right . . . just the right amount of built-in lead to put the slug a little forward on the shoulder. At almost the instant the gun sounded, the young whitetail rolled, but got right back up and headed down the side of the ridge. I grabbed two slugs from my pants pocket, reloaded and was in hot pursuit.

Nearly a half-mile down the wooded valley, the deer slowed. I was able to ease within sixty or so yards, and took another shot. A miss! The deer ran another quarter-mile, then stopped once more, and this time I moved to within forty yards and shot again. Another miss! And when I went to reload, it immediately dawned on me that all of my other slugs were in the pockets of that wool coat still lying on top of the bulldoze pile nearly a mile away.

The deer was still standing in the same spot, apparently hit hard. I was contemplating going back for more slugs when someone shouted from the side of the ridge. I looked up to see another hunter walking toward me. Cradled in the crook of his right arm was the first muzzleloader I had ever seen, other than in photos or in movies. Later, I would realize that it was an original .58 caliber Remington "Zouave" rifled-musket dating from the Civil War. It didn't take me long to accept the hunter's offer to let me put in a finishing shot with the frontloader. From forty yards, that big, patched soft-lead round ball dropped the young buck where it stood. And that one shot would change the way I hunted deer for the rest of my life.

The following spring I was given a Dixie Gun Works catalog, and the long-barreled percussion "New Squirrel Rifle" caught my eye. To meet the need for a bore size that was better suited for hunting deer and other big game, Dixie Gun Works had upped the bore-size of the rifle to .45, which seemed huge to me at the time. Just before my 14th birthday that summer, I dug out my cache of hard-earned trapping money and ordered one of the muzzleloaders, forking out a whole $79.50 for the rifle. By the time deer season rolled around that November, I had the muzzleloader shooting inside of four inches (actually near the point of aim) at a hundred yards. The second morning of the season, I took an eight-pointer at almost sixty yards. And after being hit, the deer went only about a hundred yards before going down. I've been a muzzleloading hunter ever since.

Dixie's "original" .40-caliber version of their reproduction Kentucky Rifle had proven to be an accurate and very economical muzzleloading rifle for National Muzzle

The booming whitetail deer population is very likely the number one reason why hunting with a front-loaded gun has become so popular these days. The seasons offer additional hunting opportunities.

Loading Rifle Association competition (and other local or regional matches), as well as informal plinking. But the bore-size left a lot to be desired when it came to big-game taking performance. The tiny ninety or so grain patched lead .390 inch round ball simply could not be driven fast enough by charges of black powder to generate the energy needed to bring down a whitetail much past thirty or forty yards. And the bore size was simply too large for use on small-game like squirrels and rabbits.

Still, a growing number of states began to offer special "muzzleloader only" or "primitive weapons" hunts for deer and other big game, plus more and more of the "shotgun only" states began to allow the use of a muzzleloaded rifle as well. It was the need for better performance on big game that caused Dixie to move the bore-size of the first reproduction rifle up to .45 caliber. Plus during the 1960s, we saw the introduction of other modern manufactured muzzleloading rifles also built with the hunter in mind. It has been the needs of the hunter that have pretty much dictated nearly every change or trend in muzzleloading since.

By the mid 1970s, both the patched round ball and .45 caliber bore-size had lost a lot of favor among serious muzzleloading big-game hunters. The slightly larger and better performing .50 caliber rifles were in vogue. And instead of loading and shooting a simple patched sphere of soft lead, hunters were turning to heavy elongated bullets for the added knockdown power they delivered. Muzzleloading was quickly becoming a true hunting sport, and by the early 1980s, it was clear that those who clung to strictly traditional ways, guns and loads were destined to become the minority in this shooting sport.

Through the 1960s and 1970s, whitetail populations across the country began to explode, and by the mid 1980s, game departments were looking at every possible management tool at their disposal to try to keep herds in balance with the habitat available. Up until then, the muzzleloader hunting seasons had been pretty much considered niche or specialty seasons, with low harvests. Not many game managers had taken these hunts seriously enough to consider them bona fide harvest tools. But as the guns and loads continued to evolve, the success rates of muzzleloader hunters also improved dramatically. And it was during the mid to late 1980s that the evolution of the modern muzzle-loaded hunting rifle truly shifted into *accelerated metamorphosis!*

The combination of a modernistic in-line percussion ignition system and a brand-new plastic saboted bullet system definitely set the stage for just about all future muzzleloader development. Both saboted projectiles and in-line ignition muzzleloaded rifles were nothing new. They had been around for a couple of centuries. Saboted projectiles had been shot out of muzzleloaded cannon long before the Civil War, and there are several surviving specimens of flintlock in-line ignition systems. What made the combination of the two the trend setter of this sport since 1985 were the vast improvements that had been made to both concepts.

Whether it was the in-line ignition muzzleloader or the saboted bullet that made the biggest impact on what hunters are loading . . . shooting . . . and hunting with today

Muzzleloader Hunting

is actually irrelevant. These two innovations hit the market within a year of one another, with the saboted muzzleloading bullet concept first offered in 1984 and the "improved" in-line ignition rifle coming to market in 1985. From that point on, the two have had a continuing influence on one another's further development.

Of course, it was Muzzleload Magnum Products of Harrison, Arkansas, that developed the tiny plastic cup-like sabot that allows shooters to load a wide range of jacketed and non-jacketed *pistol* bullets into slightly larger diameter muzzleloading rifle bores. And it was Modern Muzzleloading of Centerville, Iowa, that managed to incorporate the features today's hunter wanted—all the bells and whistles—in a sure-fire, easy maintenance in-line percussion ignition system. While it took five or six years of convincing shooters how well the combination of the two

Today's modern in-line rifles and saboted bullet loads deliver accuracy and energy without the horrendous recoil, making the sport appeal to all members of the family.

performed on game, then another ten years of getting twenty or so states to change regulations that prohibited the use of the guns and saboted bullets, today nearly ninety percent of all muzzleloading hunters rely on an in-line rifle of one sort or another. Close to eighty percent of all muzzleloading hunters now use a saboted bullet to harvest the game they are after.

During the two decades since these ideas were put into production, modern in-line rifles have just kept getting more and more modern, and so have the saboted bullets most are now shooting. When the Knight MK-85 first hit the market in 1985, the rifle featured a one-turn-in-forty-eight inches rate of rifling twist. This is the same rifling pitch that Thompson/Center Arms had established as ideal for shooting the big, heavy and long "Maxi-Ball" conical bullet the company developed right along with their stylized, contemporary version of the "Hawken" half-stock rifle. That rifle and hard-hitting bullet were the number one combination used by muzzleloading big-game hunters through the 1970s and into the early 1980s. However, it didn't take long to determine that the rate of rifling twist was simply too slow to deliver optimum accuracy with the saboted pistol bullets. By the end of the second year of production, the Knight MK-85 sported a much faster one-turn-in-thirty-two inches rate of twist. Then, just a couple of years later, the twist was stepped up to a still faster one-in-twenty-eight inches rate of twist. And the latter has become something of a standard among today's .50 caliber "sabot-shootin'" in-line rifles.

As muzzleloading hunters have continually sought higher velocities and greater game-taking energy levels with their in-line rifles and saboted bullets, the hotter powder charges have demanded a lot from the polymer materials used to make the sabots. Fortunately, Muzzleload Magnum Products and several other sabot suppliers have stepped up to the plate with sabots that are far superior to those available only a couple of years ago. Many of today's hotter loads, shot out of some of the more advanced .50 caliber in-line muzzleloading rifles, are now topping 2,300 f.p.s. at the muzzle—while the makers of several "Super" .45 in-line rifles are now touting 2,600 f.p.s. with hot powder charges and light saboted bullets.

In recent years, there has been a move away from shooting the big jacketed and non-jacketed hollow-point pistol bullets that the sabot system was originally built around. For the most part, these bullets have been designed for reloading handgun cartridges like the .44 Remington Magnum or the .45 Long Colt. And out of a six- to ten-inch handgun barrel, most loads for these cartridges rarely top 1,400 f.p.s. (except the .454 Cassul). Even with a charge of just one hundred grains of Pyrodex "RS/Select," most saboted bullets will leave the muzzle of a twenty-four-inch .50 caliber in-line barrel at 1,600 to 1,700 f.p.s. With some of the hotter 150-grain charges of Pyrodex or Triple Seven Pellets,

The special archery seasons have lured many hunters to become "two-season" hunters. The new muzzleloading seasons offer a bona fide third season opportunity.

velocities with a saboted 250-grain pistol bullet can top 2,000 f.p.s. Quite frankly, these bullets were never designed to be shot at such speeds. Still, the vast majority of hunters who switched to saboted handgun bullets early on found that they did perform far better than a simple pure-lead round ball or bore-sized conical bullet.

With the quest for higher velocity and more knockdown power also came the desire for more range. Unfortunately, big hollow-pointed handgun bullets like the 250- or 300-grain Hornady XTP or the 260-grain Speer JHP are about as aerodynamic as a thrown brick! The blunt frontal shape and volcanic-sized hollow-point nose of some bullet designs guarantee that the projectile will shed velocity and energy quickly, and with the loss of speed comes considerably more bullet drop at extended ranges.

Truly performance-minded muzzleloading big-game hunters these days are making the switch to saboted bullet designs that feature a sharp spire-point tip for a higher ballistic coefficient and vastly improved aerodynamics. When pushed from the muzzle of some current in-line models at 2,300 to 2,400 f.p.s., some of the loads that utilize the new sleeker projectiles will drop just four to five inches from one hundred to two hundred yards, compared to the ten to fourteen inches of drop with the older, slower loads that utilized the hollow-point pistol bullets.

Most of you who have hunted with a muzzleloader since the introduction of the in-line rifle and saboted bullet have probably loaded and shot primarily with either black powder or Hodgdon's Pyrodex, a substitute for black powder since the mid 1970s. These two powders have been the mainstay muzzleloader propellants since the mid 1980s. Now and then since, new "black-powder substitutes" would show up on the market for a few years, then kind of disappear. The only other successful muzzleloader propellant to be marketed has been Triple Seven, which was introduced in 2002. It is also a product of Hodgdon Powder Company.

Triple Seven, which is available in loose-grain and pellet form, is significant in two regards. First, it is a black-powder substitute that does not contain sulfur in its chemical make up. The powder is considerably cleaner to shoot and less corrosive to the bore and other metal surfaces. Second, this propellant delivers top-end velocities that can be twenty to twenty-five percent faster than with equal measurements of black powder or Pyrodex. Many .50 caliber in-line rifle shooters are getting 2,200 to 2,300 f.p.s. velocities with "magnum" charges of Triple Seven and light saboted bullets.

As you can see, nostalgia has gone right out the window and top game-taking performance is the number-one concern of today's muzzleloading hunter. The changes in this sport since the 1960s are chronicled with the muzzleloaded guns I've hunted with since 1964.

The load I shot in my first .45 caliber Dixie long rifle consisted of seventy grains of FFFg black powder behind a tightly patched 128-grain .440 inch round ball. That load would consistently give me a muzzle velocity of about 1,900 f.p.s. But due to the light weight of the tiny ball, the energy produced at the muzzle was just 1,025 f.p.e. The poor aerodynamics of the lead sphere also meant that it would slow quickly, and by the time that ball got to a hundred yards it would hit a whitetail with a mere 300 f.p.e. Hardly a potent whitetail load.

Like so many other muzzleloading hunters, during the early 1970s I made the switch to a .50 caliber Thompson/Center Arms percussion Hawken rifle. The load I chose was one hundred grains of FFg black powder and the big 370-grain bore-sized "Maxi-Ball" conical bullet. This load would get the bullet out of the muzzle at around 1,420 f.p.s., generating more than 1,650 f.p.e. At 100 yards, the load was still good for more than 1,200 foot-pounds of whitetail-taking energy.

In December of 1985, I was the first kid on my block to get a .50 caliber Knight MK-85. The serial number on that rifle was just No. 31, meaning I was most likely one of the very first people in the state of Illinois to own one of the new in-line ignition muzzleloaders. The load that shot well for me out of that first Knight rifle was basically the same as just outlined for my old .50 caliber Thompson/Center Hawken rifle. Remember, that early in-line still had a turn-in-forty-eight inches rate of twist. But when I first started shooting one of the rifles with a faster turn-in-twenty-eight inches twist, I went to either a saboted 250-grain .452 inch Hornady XTP or a saboted 260-grain .451 inch Speer JHP. With a 100-grain charge of Pyrodex "RS/Select," the rifle and load would give me right at 1,640 f.p.s. at the muzzle, with close to 1,500 f.p.e. At 100 yards, the load would still deliver right at 1,000 f.p.e. to the target.

When I later moved up to a .50 caliber Knight DISC Rifle, I went to loading three of the 50-grain Pyrodex Pellets (150-grain charge) behind one of the saboted all-copper 250-grain Barnes Expander MZ bullets. The load would get the bullet out of the muzzle at just a little over 1,900 f.p.s., with right at 2,000 f.p.e. Down at 100 yards, this one would take out even the largest whitetail with nearly 1,300 foot-pounds of retained energy.

In recent years, I've done some of my muzzleloader big-game hunting with the new Savage Model 10ML II—the first commercially manufactured muzzleloader designed and built to be loaded and shot with modern smokeless powders. One load that performs relatively well out

The number of muzzleloading hunters in the country today is now about equal to the number of bowhunters. Game departments have discovered, however, that the special muzzleloader seasons tend to contribute more to overall game management plans due to a higher success rate.

Muzzleloader Hunting

of this rifle is 44 grains of VihtaVuori N110 loaded behind a special protective sub-base and a saboted 250-grain .452 inch Hornady SST poly-tipped spire-point bullet. This one spits the bullet out of the muzzle at an astounding 2,350 f.p.s., with right at 3,100 f.p.e.! Out at a hundred yards, the load is still good for nearly 2,200 foot-pounds of wallop. In fact, all the way out at two hundred yards, this load still hits big game with just over 1,500 foot-pounds of knockdown power.

My forty plus years of muzzleloader hunting have pretty much spanned the development of modern muzzleloading in the 20th century, and now the 21st century. I wouldn't even consider going after deer-sized game with the rifle and load I used

In some states, more than 100,000 hunters now participate in the special muzzleloading seasons, causing game departments to make muzzleloading a big part of their standard hunter-education programs.

confidently back in the mid 1960s. Stealing a line from an old Bob Seger song, often "I wish I didn't know now what I didn't know then."

Muzzleloading has been the fastest changing of all shooting sports over the past fifty years. In the following chapters of *Muzzleloader Hunting: Then and Now,* we will look at the guns, loads, loading practices, cleaning techniques, hunting opportunities and even some of the tactics used by muzzleloading hunters—past and present. In order for today's muzzleloading hunter to fully appreciate the equipment he or she is using, it's important to know how it was developed and why. The information shared on these pages should broaden every muzzleloading shooter's and hunter's knowledge of the sport. And the more anyone knows about muzzleloading, the easier it is to master the challenge of getting top performance from any frontloaded gun—traditional or modern.

—Toby Bridges

1

Why Hunt with a Muzzleloader?

In today's modern, *high-tech* world, it seems kind of irrational that so many hunters have taken to hunting with slow-to-load, *old-fashioned* muzzle-loaded guns. Still, more than 200,000 muzzleloading hunters head for the deer woods during the special muzzleloader season every December in Michigan alone, while in Tennessee and Virginia as many as 150,000 in each state now rely on a muzzleloaded rifle to hunt whitetails. Even larger numbers of deer hunters in Ohio and Oklahoma now do some of their deer hunting with a rifle of muzzleloading design. In Colorado, as many as 80,000 elk hunters annually submit applications for the 40,000 or so muzzleloader elk tags offered each fall, and many of these hunters do so for four or five years in a row just to build the *preference points* required to be eligible for obtaining a muzzleloader permit for one of the premier hunting units in that state.

Let's face it, the interest in hunting with a muzzleloader continues to grow with each new season. And thanks to the number of hunters who are now picking up a frontloaded rifle for the first time, muzzleloading has remained one of the healthier segments of the shooting sports for most of the past two decades. While muzzle-loading gun sales have sort of leveled off during the past few years, between 300,000 and 400,000 *new* muzzleloaders are still manufactured in or imported into the United States every year. So, why have so many hunters turned to muzzleloading for at least some of their hunting? The answers may not be as surprising as most would think.

To better understand why today's hunters continue to take to muzzleloading in record numbers with each new season, let's take a look at how and why muzzle-loader hunting managed to get started in the mid- to late- 1900s in the first place.

Then...
Except in a very few remote regions of Appalachia, muzzleloading had pretty well died out in this country by the end of the 19th century. Here and there in the mountainous regions of Tennessee, Kentucky, North Carolina, West Virginia and a few other rural eastern mountain states, small pockets of muzzle-loading shooters continued to fan the embers of this ancient shooting sport. For a few, it was simply the challenge and enjoyment of shooting the guns from our past.

Muzzleloader Hunting

For others, especially through the Depression years, the old guns were all they could afford in order to keep game on the table to feed a hungry family. And it was from this very small nucleus of likely only one thousand or so muzzleloading shooters that the sport as we know it today got its new lease on life.

During the early 1930s, muzzleloading got a little boost with the establishment of the National Muzzle-Loading Rifle Association, headquartered in the small southern Indiana town of Friendship. It was the "officially sanctioned" target competition of this small organiza-

During the 1960s and early 1970s, many shooters were drawn to muzzleloading as a living link to relive the past.

tion that first began to attract new muzzleloading shooters from around the country. Through the '30s, '40s and early '50s, a few of these shooters were fortunate enough to own hand-crafted custom muzzleloaders with new bores. However, the majority had to rely on original guns dating from the 1700s and early 1800s, and the limited number of originals still capable of target quality accuracy surely restricted just how many new shooters turned to muzzleloading.

It was the birth of the modern *reproduction muzzleloader industry* during the mid to late 1950s that made the sport available and affordable to tens of thousands of new shooters nationwide. As the ranks of muzzleloading shooters continued to grow rapidly on into the 1960s and early 1970s, more and more companies began to cater to this new market with an ever-growing variety of new-made muzzleloading guns. By 1970, the National Muzzle-Loading Rifle Association had grown to around twenty thousand members, and most were shooting competition with newly manufactured muzzleloading guns.

It was inevitable that the larger the number of shooters who found themselves bitten by the *black-powder bug,* the more likely that a good percentage of them would also want to hunt with the old-fashioned frontloaders. When Dixie Gun Works introduced the very first reproduction muzzleloader back in 1956, not one single state offered a *"muzzleloader only," "black powder"* or *"primitive weapons"* big-game season. Quite a few states did allow the use of a muzzleloader during the general seasons back then, but the establishment of special seasons devoted solely to muzzleloading hunters did not begin until the early 1960s, with the majority of the seasons we now enjoy taking root during the 1970s and early 1980s.

Nostalgia played a significant role in game departments establishing these first muzzleloader seasons. These special hunts offered the muzzleloader hunter a unique opportunity to head afield with others sharing a common interest to experience hunting deer and other big game with a muzzleloaded gun design from the past. It was a chance to relive history.

Keep in mind that back then whitetail populations were just truly beginning to recover from the all-time low levels of the 1930s and 1940s. In a number of states with an open season for these deer, the hunter often could not hunt both the modern gun season and the muzzleloader season. To restrict over-harvesting of the fragile resource, game departments occasionally made the hunter choose—to hunt either the regular firearms season . . . or the special muzzleloader season. Most would not give up the tradition of hunting with family and friends during the general deer season. Consequently, the early muzzleloader seasons were slow to gain new participants.

Through the 1970s and 1980s, big-game populations began to explode everywhere. Not just the number of whitetails, but the numbers of other game such as elk and pronghorns as well. To both expand hunting opportunities and keep herd sizes in balance with forage and habitat, many game departments became more

Nostalgia for America's colorful past was once the primary reason for the growing interest in muzzleloading.

Muzzleloader Hunting

Game departments are now faced with controlling an ever-growing whitetail population, and states have established new muzzleloader seasons that appeal to the hunter looking for more time to hunt or to harvest bonus game.

liberal with annual harvest limits and the number of different seasons in which a hunter could participate. Both bowhunting and muzzleloader hunting benefited greatly from this new bounty of big game, and the number of hunters participating in the special seasons began to skyrocket during the early to mid 1980s.

During the early 1960s, muzzleloading shooters and hunters in the United States likely numbered between 50,000 and 100,000. By 1970, that number had grown to around 500,000. And thanks to the growing opportunities to hunt with a muzzleloader and the greatly expanded variety of well-built modern copies of original muzzleloader designs from

A small percentage of muzzleloading fans continue to hunt with guns of old-fashioned design, such as the .50 caliber Dixie Tennessee Mountain Rifle used by this hunter to fill a doe tag.

the past, it is estimated that there were as many as 1.5 million muzzleloading gun fanciers in this country by 1985.

The challenge of mastering a firearms design from the past is often credited with being the initial reason why early shooters turned to muzzleloading during the 1950s and 1960s. Some shooters simply take pride in developing a good load that will consistently hit the intended target with a high degree of accuracy. Even so, the real driving force behind why so many turned to muzzleloading from about 1970 on can just as easily be credited to the establishment of the muzzleloader seasons and to the new hunting opportunities they created.

Now . . .
Muzzleloading has not only been one of the fastest growing shooting sports, it has also been one of the fastest changing. This is very evident with the design and style of muzzleloader preferred by today's hunter—who can no longer be called a *black-powder hunter.* No longer is nostalgia the driving force behind why a modern-day shooter and hunter turns to muzzleloading, and hasn't been for most of the last twenty years. Today's muzzleloading shooter is a hunter who simply has turned to muzzleloading to enjoy more time in the deer woods, and today the concern is more on rifle and load performance than whether or not the muzzleloader carried accurately copies any rifle from the past.

The muzzleloaded rifle that deserves credit for changing the way big-game hunters look at muzzleloaders was the modern in-line percussion ignition Knight MK-85. Now, this wasn't the first rifle of in-line ignition design. Back in the early 1970s, I had the opportunity to do some shooting with a unique modern in-line percussion rifle known as the Eusopus "Pacer." Then in the mid 1970s I hunted some with the handy Harrington & Richardson break-open "Huntsman." Both of these "in-line" percussion ignition rifles offered all of the sure-fire ignition possible with the first Knight rifle. The H&R Huntsman was even more weatherproof than the far more successful Knight in-line that was introduced nearly ten years later. Then, during the early 1980s, another in-line rifle known as the Michigan Arms "Wolverine," complete with No. 209 primer ignition, showed up on the market, predating the MK-85 by at least a couple of years.

So, what kept these three very innovative and modern in-lines from becoming the success that was eventually enjoyed by the Knight in-line design? Well, it was a combination of several reasons, but the failure of these three guns to make the same impact can mostly be credited to one major design flaw in all three. They were all offered with a slow rate of rifling twist, designed for shooting the old patched round ball. By the mid 1970s, serious muzzleloading hunters were quickly moving away from the round

The majority of today's muzzleloader-hunting crowd tends to favor modern sure-fire in-line ignition hunting rifles like the stainless steel Knight MK-85 pictured here.

ball as a big-game projectile, switching to more effective conical hunting bullets.

When William "Tony" Knight brought the MK-85 to market in 1985, the rifle was also offered with a relatively slow one-turn-in-forty-eight inches rate of rifling twist. Fortunately, Tony realized the newly introduced sabot bullet system offered the modern day hunter a better selection of bullet designs, diameters and weights to choose from, and quickly stepped up the rate of twist in order to tap the accuracy and game-taking performance of the sabot system. The company (Modern Muzzleloading, Inc.) made several changes in rifling twist before settling on a one-turn-in-twenty-eight inches, which has become something of an industry standard. The faster sabot-shooting rifling twist, combined with added features like an easily removed breech plug for cleaning, a double safety system and short *center-fire rifle-like* overall length, made the MK-85 a real success. (More on today's best selling in-line rifles in the next chapter.)

The Knight MK-85 and the other modern in-line ignition hunting rifles that quickly followed also made it easier than ever to mount telescopic sights on a big-game muzzleloader. The receivers of these rifles came pre-drilled and tapped for readily available scope bases, allowing anyone to install their own scope without any real gunsmithing at all. And with a quality scope, these sabot-loaded modern in-line wonders have proven deadly accurate and lethal on deer and other big game.

The extremely modern looks and enhanced performance of the modern in-line rifles has ruffled the feathers of many traditional muzzleloader fanciers. Quite a few of those who prefer to shoot and hunt only with a muzzleloader of historical design openly voice their opinion that this old sport has definitely gone too far too fast. This group, however, continues to be more and more the minority when it comes to the overall number of muzzleloading hunters. Today, they represent only about ten per-cent of all muzzleloading shooters. Still, they do continue to make up the bulk of the memberships of many state muzzleloading organizations, and these organizations do help steer the development of many muzzleloader hunting regulations.

Fortunate for the ninety percent of muzzleloading hunters who now tend to like some degree of technology working for them when after big game, state muzzle-loader hunting regulations have been among the fastest changing hunting regula-tions in the country. Most of the changes that have been made over the past couple of decades simply reflect the desires of today's muzzleloading hunter. Or, at least the majority of them. Today, in-line rifles can be used in every state . . . saboted bul-lets are legal during all but only a small handful of muzzleloader seasons . . . and telescopic sights are now permitted in nearly seventy-five percent of all states.

To meet the quest of most modern muzzleloading hunters for faster bullet speeds, more knockdown power, flatter trajectory and greater effective range, muzzleloading gun and loading-component makers continue to introduce superior

Muzzleloader Hunting

products. Just 20 years ago, a muzzle velocity of 1,700 f.p.s. with a saboted bullet was considered shooting at the outer edge of muzzle-loader performance. A number of rifles and loads available today can get muzzle velocities of 2,300 to 2,400 f.p.s. with ease. And the better the performance possible with a rifle of muzzle-loading design, the more this sport has appealed to the serious big-game hunter who demands optimum performance from whatever he or she hunts with.

Earlier in this chapter, I mentioned that back when the first muzzleloader seasons were established in America

Hunters from both the center-fire rifle and bowhunting ranks have flocked to hunt the muzzleloader seasons—either for the challenge or the opportunity.

during the 1960s, most game departments were worried about too much hunting pressure on deer populations that were just bouncing back from near extinction in some states. Today, a majority of these same game departments are faced with a different dilemma. Throughout much of the whitetail's range, there are now simply too many deer and we're not harvesting nearly enough of the animals.

Back in 1964 when I borrowed another hunter's original .58 caliber Remington *Zouave* rifled musket to put in a finishing shot on my very first whitetail, there were only about 100,000 deer in my home state of Illinois. Today, the "Prairie State" is home to nearly a million whitetails. Far more deer are now killed on the highways by automobiles and trucks every year than were harvested by hunters in Illinois during the 1964 firearms deer season.

Fortunately, many states in the same predicament of having more deer than they feel comfortable with have now discovered that a bona fide *"muzzleloading season"* can prove to be a bona fide *game management tool.* In those states where the muzzleloader hunts are structured to give hunters a reason to go afield with a muzzleloading rifle, 100,000 to 200,000 muzzleloading hunters are now harvesting 30,000 to 50,000 whitetails annually, significantly helping to keep the herd in balance with the habitat. In many of these states, one deer out of five or six are now taken with a muzzleloader. Such incentives to participate in the muzzleloader season can mean the opportunity to harvest bonus game, perhaps a longer season to hunt, or a season scheduled during the prime hunting period of the fall—such as just prior to the general firearms season. States with a progressive management plan learn to make muzzleloading a beneficial part of their overall program. Both the game department and the hunter benefit greatly from such seasons.

Unfortunately, a few states still have not figured out how to make their muzzleloader seasons work for them, and they treat such hunts as unimportant novelties. I'm ashamed to admit that my home state of Illinois has one such game department. The Illinois Department of Natural Resources doesn't have a clue how to benefit from a true muzzleloading season. Muzzleloading hunters in this state really get the shaft. Sure, they can use their muzzleloaders during the two "shotgun seasons," but when it comes to a "Muzzleloader Season," it's a token offering at best. The muzzleloader hunt is a three-day season (Friday, Saturday, and Sunday) the weekend after the second shotgun season, which is a four-day season. There is no incentive to hunt the muzzle-loader season, and not many Illinois residents do. In a state known for big, quality

Today, one whitetail in five or six that are harvested every fall is now taken with a gun of muzzleloaded design. Outdoor writer Wade Bourne is shown here with a good late muzzleloader-season buck.

Muzzleloader Hunting

whitetails, the Illinois Department of Natural Resources can only muster between 6,000 and 8,000 muzzleloading hunters statewide, and the muzzleloader season does little to reduce the high number of deer being killed on the highways.

Next door in Iowa, they schedule two muzzleloader seasons. The first is a week-long hunt in late October. The second season runs for two weeks, from about Christmas to around January 10th. This state is home to about 400,000 deer, and 25,000 to 30,000 muzzleloading hunters harvest around 15,000 whitetails every year. Many hunters, especially the nonresidents, opt for the late season, when the cold and snow forces the deer to feed. Some dandy bucks are taken at this time of year.

Muzzleloading has evolved into its own unique activity. It has matured into a true hunting sport, and for the most part, today's muzzleloading hunter isn't all that concerned about re-creating past hunting methods. These hunters do want their own "special" muzzleloading season, but instead of attaching historical ties to the challenge, they simply want an opportunity to harvest deer and other big game with a gun of muzzleloading design. And they want to take the game as cleanly as possible. In other words, they now want a little technology working for them to harness all of the accuracy and knockdown power a muzzleloading rifle can muster. ■

2

Choosing a Muzzleloader Big-Game Rifle

Then . . .

Through the ages, muzzleloading shooters have often had to consider many factors when choosing the muzzleloader they would carry. In Europe, where the firearm originated sometime early in the 14th century, the scarce availability of the various early ignition-type muzzleloaders was perhaps the strongest factor influencing the first three hundred years of firearms existence.

The earliest frontloaded *hand cannon* were pretty much in use through the late 1300s by the major military powers of Europe. Even so, most fighting was still done with swords, lances and the old bow and arrow. As the name implies, early hand cannon were small cannon-like tubes attached to the end of a short pike or pole. Stuffed with a haphazardly measured amount of early black powder and crude projectile, the small cannon was then pointed somewhat in the direction of the opposing force. The soldier would then reach forward with a piece of burning rope or *match* and ignite a small amount of priming powder poured into a small priming hole or vent on the top of the barrel.

Most surviving specimens of original hand cannon feature a bore of about one inch in diameter or slightly smaller, and are quite crude in design and workmanship. As could be expected, accuracy was poor at best, especially since very few had any way of actually aiming the early firearm. The projectiles loaded into these small handheld cannons were often as crude as the arms themselves, and were generally somewhat round iron or bronze balls close to bore size. However, it is known that some hand cannon were fired with projectiles that were nothing more than round stones.

Few soldiers were trained to use these early firearms, and when one went down to an enemy arrow or the slash of a broad sword, few others would pick up the hand cannon and resume its use. Since the earliest hand cannons were often crude castings of dubious materials, it's very likely that many literally exploded when fired.

The widespread use of firearms by the military did not begin until the mid to late 15th century, after the firearm had been significantly improved. While the early *matchlock* muskets of the time still relied on a simple piece of burning nitrated rope for igniting a charge of priming powder, which now usually rode in a shallow pan alongside the barrel, muzzleloaders of this period did feature a stock that allowed the gun to be fired from the shoulder. Plus many of these big-bored muskets sported sights of one sort or another, giving the shooter some control over just where the shot was going.

It was during this period that the predominately used projectile became a soft lead ball, usually patched with thin cloth to better harness the power of the burning powder charge and to keep the projectile in place over the charge of black powder. It is very likely that a shooter purposely harvested the very first head of big game with a firearm with one of these early shoulder-fired muzzleloaders. While the matchlock muskets of the late 1400s and early 1500s were primarily military arms, the wealthy landowners and nobility of the time began to rely on such arms to harvest big European game, such as the red stag and wild boar.

The one major drawback of the matchlock was the burning rope or match needed for ignition. Early designs often required the shooter to manually lever the end of the burning match into the priming pan, while improved designs actually incorporated a spring-powered serpent, or hammer, that could be cocked upward, then mechanically dropped into the priming pan by pulling a trigger. Still, ignition was reliant upon a piece of nitrated rope that had to be kept burning at all times.

Appearing sometime during the first quarter of the 16th century, the so-called *wheellock* was the first muzzleloader ignition system that was fully capable of producing its own fire for ignition. This system relied on an intricate, complicated and often delicate internal lock mechanism that would drive a spring-powered wheel. Around the outer edge of this tempered steel wheel would be a series of serrations.

To operate, the shooter would turn the lock mechanism with a separate spanner. The wheel would lock in place, then a piece of iron pyrite, held in the jaws of a movable *cock,* or hammer, would be positioned to ride on the serrated surface of the wheel. When the trigger was pulled, the wheel would spin and the contact between the pyrite and serrated surface of the wheel would create sparks, which in turn would ignite a small amount of priming powder in a shallow pan adjacent to the position of the pyrite. Some of the fire from that priming charge would travel through a tiny vent hole to reach the primary powder charge in the barrel.

Ignition with this system was relatively positive. Even so, wheellock arms were not very widely used or manufactured for one primary reason: They were extremely expensive to produce. The mechanism relied on dozens of precisely fitting internal parts and was easily made unserviceable due to broken and worn parts, or heavy fouling that had gotten into the mechanics of the lock work. Not many wheellock

If a shooter feels compelled to shoot and hunt with a traditional styled front-loader, then a choice must be made between early flintlock or later percussion ignition.

arms were employed by the military, but an ignition system that no longer relied on a piece of burning rope to fire the gun appealed to wealthy hunters. For that reason, many surviving specimens from the 1500s and early 1600s are ornately adorned with ivory, gold, and silver inlays, representing the status of the noblemen who could afford these early muzzleloaders.

Early in the 1600s, several different variations of the flintlock ignition system began to be produced in France, Germany and Spain. A few of these early *flint and steel* lock mechanisms had some of the working parts positioned on the outside of the lock plate. However, by the middle of the century, gunsmiths all over Europe were producing true flintlock-ignition smoothbore muskets, fowlers and rifles. And these quickly became the hunting guns of the common hunter.

It was the simplicity of the flintlock that made it such a success. Internally, the lock mechanism consisted of only a few parts—namely, a mainspring, tumbler, maybe a bridle, a sear and a sear spring, plus a few screws. Externally, the common flintlock mechanisms featured a hammer that gripped a small piece of flint, a pan for holding a charge of priming powder, a combination frizzen and pan cover, plus a spring for applying tension to the frizzen. Just about any competent gunsmith could reproduce and replace any part of this simple ignition system. Even the average shooter could replace most parts, and often carried spare parts just in case.

Operation of the system was equally simple. Once the rifle had been loaded, the shooter simply pulled the hammer back until the tip of the sear locked into the *half-cock notch* of the tumbler. The frizzen was then flipped forward to expose the pan, and a few grains of fine black powder poured into the shallow trough. The frizzen was then pulled back to cover the priming powder and the hammer pulled rearward to lock up in the *full-cock notch* of the tumbler.

When the trigger was pulled, the hammer would be pushed forward by the mainspring, causing the sharpened edge of the flint to hit the hardened surface of the frizzen. Then, as the flint continued to push the frizzen forward, it scraped away a minute amount of steel from the surface, resulting in a shower of sparks. Ideally, some of these sparks would fall into the pan and ignite the priming powder—and some of the flash would find its way through the vent hole leading to the powder charge in the barrel—and the muzzleloader would fire.

Surprisingly, with locks of the best quality, ignition with a flintlock was fairly *sure-fire.* Refinement of the flintlock took only a few years, and for the next two hundred years it became just about the only used ignition system wherever muzzleloaded firearms were carried, including the new American colonies.

In the early 1800s, the flintlock ignition system was replaced by a system that relied on a simple tiny copper cup that contained a small amount of an explosive compound known as *fulminate of mercury.* This cup was slipped over a hollow tube-like arrangement known as a nipple. When the cap was struck by a flat-faced hammer, the resulting fire from the compound shot through the hole running through the nipple and into the powder charge in the barrel. The percussion ignition system proved to be the most reliable of all muzzleloader ignition systems, but lasted roughly only about fifty years before being replaced by modern breechloading cartridge firearms.

Some of the earliest European explorers to set foot on North America carried late military styled matchlock guns. However, when early immigrants first sailed to America, they brought with them the flintlock arms that were commonly used in their homelands. Most European flintlock hunting rifles of the early 1700s featured large bores, often .62 to .72 caliber. When loaded with hefty charges of black powder and a patched round ball that could weigh upwards of five hundred or more grains, these guns were capable of delivering a mighty blow to game as large as brown bears, red stag and wild boar of five hundred pounds or more. Far from ready sources of powder and lead, early American riflemakers quickly developed a new breed of muzzleloading rifle that featured a significantly longer barrel with a smaller .40 to .45 caliber bore. And by the end of the Revolutionary War, the world had a new respect for the deadly accurate American longrifles that came to be known as *Pennsylvania* or *Kentucky rifles.*

Shooting powder charges that were one third the weight of charges used in early European hunting rifles, and a soft lead ball that often barely weighed one hundred grains, the long barrels of these rifles allowed the loads to reach higher velocities. With those velocities came energy levels great enough to harvest the occasional whitetail needed for food . . . or to stop an enemy. Plus these smaller-bored rifles could be loaded with still lighter powder charges and used to pot a mess of bushy-tails or take an obliging wild turkey without destroying too much edible meat.

Few settlers would travel far from their homes without a long-barreled Kentucky rifle in hand. It was a wild land, and danger, both human and animal kind, often lurked just back in the shadows. As these adventurous individuals began to expand into still more remote regions, the small bores of the uniquely American longrifles allowed them to carry a sufficient supply of lead and powder.

It was the supply of such necessities that first slowed expansion of the American colonies westward. But once the exploration and settlement of the wilderness beyond the Appalachian Mountains began, it wasn't long before the next generation of adventurers was looking up the Missouri River—wondering what lay farther upstream. And the huge plains grizzlies, powerful elk and plentiful bison they encountered demanded a muzzleloader of larger caliber than the typical eastern longrifle.

Two brothers by the name of Jacob and Samuel Hawken established one of the more famous gunmaking operations that catered to this need for more knockdown power. The muzzleloading rifles produced at their St. Louis shop were often .52 to .56 caliber—and built with a heavy-walled octagon barrel that could handle massive 150-grain (and heavier) charges of black powder. Such charges would get a 200- to 250-grain patched round ball out of the muzzle at velocities of almost 2,000 f.p.s., generating a whopping 1,800 to 2,200 foot-pounds of wallop. Within the effective range of the patched round ball, these rifles and loads would deliver twice the game-taking energy and stopping power possible with the long, slender .40 to .45 caliber eastern rifles.

Through the 1830s and 1840s, shooters began the search for a projectile that was more efficient than the old patched round ball. In the U.S. and Europe, a number of different *conical bullet* designs became popular, especially among muzzle-loading big-game hunters looking for a projectile that delivered more punch at extended ranges. However, quite a few different elongated bullets failed to win over shooters, primarily due to the difficulty of loading. Even so, some of these bullets, such as the hexagonal Whitworth bullet, proved extremely accurate.

Muzzleloader Hunting

In 1854, British gun designer Sir Joseph Whitworth was granted a patent for his unique hexagonal bore and mechanically fitted bullet. The flats of the six-sided polygonal .451-inch bore spun with a one-turn-in-twenty inches rate of twist in order to properly stabilize a length 1.32-inch long 530-grain bullet. The rifle was extremely accurate. In fact, during testing by the British War Office in 1857, the accuracy of the Whitworth rifle and bullet proved far superior to any other rifle tested at the time. The long, mechanically started bullet and hexagonal bore were capable of punching an unbelievable four-inch group at five hundred yards, while the rifle that produced the next best accuracy could only keep shots inside of two and a half feet at that distance. That rifle was the .577 caliber Enfield *rifled musket.*

Except for very limited use by both North and South during the Civil War, the deadly accurate Whitworth saw no other major military use. The odd-shaped bore was costly and time consuming to machine, the bullets had to be more precise, and the use of the mechanical starter simply took too long. Military tactics of the time relied more on a line of infantrymen delivering a large volume of fire than on pinpoint accuracy. Easy loading rifled muskets like the Enfield and the American .58 caliber Springfield muskets became the mainstay of the World's military powers during the late 1850s and early 1860s.

The standard service load for both the British and American muskets during the *War of Northern Aggression* (a.k.a. the Civil War) consisted of just sixty grains of FFg black powder loaded under a very loose-fitting hollow-based conical projectile known as the *Minié bullet.* Named after the French captain who developed the design, this bullet often weighed upwards of five hundred grains and was sufficiently undersized that, in a relatively clean bore, a soldier could practically thump the butt of his musket on the ground and the bullet would fall down to set on top of the powder charge. Even when the ramrod was needed, it took little effort to "seat" the projectile over the light charge of black powder.

The Minié bullet was designed with a deep, hollow-cupped base. When the powder charge ignited, the rapid expansion of the gases produced would force the thin, soft-lead skirt of the base into the rifling, creating the necessary gas seal and bullet-to-bore fit. Surprisingly, these big-bore muskets would prove to be extremely accurate, and even when pushed by such a light powder charge, the big heavy conical bullets could literally knock a man off his feet at two hundred yards.

The Civil War marked the last major military engagement in which muzzleloaded guns saw widespread use. Toward the end of the conflict, faster loading breechloading single-shot and repeating cartridge rifles replaced the slow-to-load muskets. Even so, many a homeward bound veteran made the trip with his old service rifled musket

Someone just getting into muzzleloading today has a lot of choices to make. First and foremost is whether to go traditional or modern.

thrown over his shoulder. And for the next several decades following the war, many head of big game were taken with the big-bored surplus muskets by those who simply could not afford one of the new Winchester, Marlin, Colt-Burgess or other similarly styled lever-action repeating rifles that put an end to muzzleloader production in this country.

Today's muzzleloading shooter looking to own and shoot an authentically styled muzzleloader from just about any period of the past will generally find several models to choose from. Companies like Dixie Gun Works and Navy Arms have done a remarkable job of re-creating, or having re-created, a tremendous selection of high-quality reproduction muzzleloading guns. Dixie Gun Works even currently offers very well-made copies of early English

Many early traditional rifles were rifled with a slow rate of rifling twist, strictly intended for shooting a patched round ball. This custom copy of a circa 1840 percussion "Hawken" rifle features a one-turn-in-sixty-six inches round ball rate of rifling twist.

and Japanese matchlocks. These two companies, plus the Italy-based Davide Pedersoli manufacturing firm, now offer nostalgia buffs extremely accurate copies of ornate flint and percussion Kentucky rifles, plain Tennessee mountain rifles, both early British and French flintlock muskets, stylish late percussion target rifles, an outstanding selection of mid-1800s percussion military muskets, flint and percussion English sporting rifles, fast-handling percussion double rifles, half-stocked "Hawken" hunting rifles, single- and double-barreled shotguns, a wide variety of percussion and flintlock handguns, and much, much more. Plus, a few companies, like Thompson/Center Arms, now bring to market a well-built selection of contemporary "traditional" rifles that offer the old-fashioned look, enhanced by a few modern features for improved performance.

Many of these guns can serve a dual purpose, providing the shooter with an authentically styled muzzleloader from the past for use both during historical reenactments and for hunting. When of appropriate caliber and stuffed with an adequate load, just about any of these guns are capable of taking game cleanly. Some of the following chapters will detail the guns and loads that are suitable for hunting both large and small game, plus take a look at loading techniques for optimum accuracy and performance.

Now...

For the vast majority of modern-day muzzle-loading hunters, nostalgia is now the last thing on their minds when looking for a new or first muzzleloaded big-game rifle. Muzzleloading is now a very performance-driven sport, and the game-taking effectiveness of the rifle and load is now the primary focus of the hunter looking to take deer and other big game as cleanly and humanely as possible. One thing is for certain, the rifles and loads now carried by these

A lot of different reproduction guns have come and gone since Turner Kirkland introduced the first modern-made copies during the mid 1950s. Shown here is an over/under double .50 caliber percussion rifle once offered by Harrington & Richardson.

hunters are a far cry from the long, slender Kentucky rifles of the late 1700s or shorter half-stock "Plains" rifles of the early 1800s. What they are is deadly accurate and hard hitting!

The Knight Rifle

The modernistic muzzleloader that can truly be credited with starting the in-line percussion-ignition rifle craze was the Knight MK-85, introduced in 1985 by rural Missouri gunsmith William "Tony" Knight. Now, this was definitely not the first muzzleloader of "in-line" ignition. Although rare, original in-line percussion-ignition systems date back to the early 1800s. And 20th-century produced rifles of this type were offered during the early 1970s and 1980s, before Tony Knight ever machined his first prototype. What the MK-85 represents is the first such percussion-ignition system built with all of the bells and whistles desired by the modern-day hunter.

William "Tony" Knight, here with a nice Missouri buck, is credited as the "Father of the In-Line Rifle Industry."

I first spoke with Tony on the phone in the winter of 1985. The more he described his new concept, the more it appealed to me. Then, during the spring of 1986, I drove to northern Missouri to turkey hunt with Tony Knight, and to do some shooting with the man behind the idea. By the time I headed home with a couple of muzzleloaded gobblers in the cooler, I had gotten to know Tony pretty well. During my five days of hunting with him and shooting each afternoon, we had decided two things—both the in-line ignition system and the saboted bullet concept were definitely the direction this old sport would eventually take.

The idea for the first Knight MK-85 began during the late 1970s, when a few of Tony's friends turned to muzzleloading in order to enjoy a few of the special "muzzleloader-only" seasons, especially for elk in Colorado. These were not veteran muzzleloading shooters, but rather hunters looking for added hunting opportunities. Most had never even loaded a muzzleloader before.

After a few hunting trips, they began to complain to Knight about how their rifles would misfire in bad weather, or how cumbersome a ten-pound muzzleloader became when packed all day at ten thousand feet. Then there was the concern about only a half-cock notch as the safety when traversing such rough terrain. That's when custom-gunsmith Tony Knight began to design the next generation of muzzleloading hunting rifles.

The MK-85 evolved over the course of a couple of years. The end result was the muzzleloader that would set the stage for practically all future muzzleloader development. Appearance-wise, the Knight rifle looked far more like a modern cartridge rifle than a muzzleloader. It sported a short, fast-handling twenty-four-inch barrel that gave it exceptional balance. The stock had the typical pistol grip and contours of a modern hunting rifle stock, and came with a rubber recoil pad.

But what really set the MK-85 apart from any other muzzleloader on the market at the time was the well-thought-out in-line percussion action, built with a high-quality adjustable Timney trigger and side-mounted safety. Additionally, the patented Knight design incorporated a second safety in the form of a large, knurled, nut-like arrangement that could be turned forward and backward on the rear of the plunger-style hammer. When this safety was threaded forward on the hammer, it would bottom-out

The very first prototype of the Knight MK-85, the rifle that began the modern in-line rifle craze.

on the rear of the receiver, preventing the face of the hammer from falling far enough forward to strike the capped nipple.

The breech plug of the Knight MK-85 threads directly into the rear of the barrel. This positions the nipple (and percussion cap) in the same general area as the primer of a cartridge in the chamber of a center-fire rifle. When the stiff coil mainspring of the Knight design forces the plunger-style hammer forward to strike the percussion cap, the resulting fire flows directly through the nipple and to the powder charge in the barrel. The flame travels just a fraction of an inch, providing spontaneous ignition. The straight-in approach of this ignition system also eliminated corners or angles where condensation or oil from a previous cleaning could accumulate, making the MK-85 far more *sure-fire* than any traditional side-hammer rifle.

A feature that immediately appealed to hunters, who were often faced with cleaning both harvested big game and a dirty muzzleloader the same evening, was the removable breech plug of the Knight design. In seconds, the hammer . . . nipple . . . and breech plug could be removed from the rifle, making it easier than ever to give this muzzleloader a quick, easy cleaning following a successful day in the deer woods or session at the range.

The first change that Knight made to the MK-85 was to go to a faster rate of rifling twist. The first several hundred of the rifles produced in Tony's garage-based gun

Knight's MK-85, early production model shown here, incorporated many modern features the muzzleloading hunter immediately liked, including a positive safety system and a removable breech plug.

shop featured a relatively slow one-turn-in-forty-eight-inches rate of rifling twist. Thompson/Center Arms had popularized this rifling twist with the company's widely used half-stock "Hawken" model, designed to give relatively good accuracy with either the patched round ball or the conical bullet the late Warren Center had designed right along with the muzzleloader, the T/C "Maxi-Ball." However, Tony realized that to tap the accuracy and performance of the new saboted bullet system developed by Del Ramsey of Harrison, Arkansas, Modern Muzzleloading, Inc. would have to step up the rate of twist. In late 1986, the company went to a snappier one-turn-in-thirty-two inches rifling pitch, and in 1988, Knight went to a still faster rifling twist of one-turn-in-twenty eight inches. The latter rate of twist quickly became a standard among many modern in-line rifle makers.

Traditional muzzleloading hunters hated the modern design of the MK-85, and the manufacturers of traditionally styled muzzleloaders hated the thought of losing sales to such a modern concept. As expected, they teamed up to fight the legalization of such *hi-tech* rifles and saboted bullets. But the stage had been set,

Modern in-lines and equally modern projectiles go hand-in-hand. When shooting open expanses such as this, the saboted bullets shoot faster, flatter and retain energy better at extended ranges.

and the modern-day hunter only looking to get into muzzleloading for additional hunting opportunities liked what he saw. As hard as traditional shooters and traditional muzzleloader manufacturers tried, they could not change the future of the sport. It took a lot of work to reverse poorly directed muzzleloading regulations and to promote the modernization of this nearly seven hundred-year-old shooting sport, but the time had come. Within five years of the MK-85 appearing on the market, a number of other muzzleloader manufacturers also jumped on the bandwagon

This modern-day muzzleloading hunter has added a bit of technology to his traditionally styled percussion rifle—a scope.

and began producing in-line ignition designs of their own. Most had fought the modernization of the sport, but when it was clear that the change couldn't be stopped, many were quick to capitalize on a growing new muzzleloader market.

I, for one, would like to say, *"Thank you Tony Knight!"*

New Designs

By today's standards, the once-advanced design of the MK-85 is now somewhat *outdated technology.* In 1996, Remington Arms Company sort of shook up the shooting world with the introduction of their Model 700 bolt-action center-fire rifle in an all-new muzzleloading version, dubbed the Model 700ML (blued) or MLS (stainless). Just eleven years after the introduction of the Knight in-line rifle, muzzleloaders of that design had already overtaken the market. Easily seventy plus percent of the muzzleloaded guns sold in this country at that time were of in-line ignition.

Remington wasn't content to simply jump into this market with just another plunger-hammer in-line muzzleloader. Instead, the company brought muzzleloading shooters a big-game frontloader built with many of the features they were already familiar with . . . and which were also found on the Model 700 center-fire line. Now, it wouldn't be exactly true to say that the new Remington muzzleloader is built with the same receiver and bolt as the cartridge models. To do so would require buyers to complete a B.A.T.F. Form No. 4473 and go through the same background check as required when purchasing a modern cartridge gun. Instead, Remington did utilize some of the same internal-bolt construction, but in a design that does not feature locking lugs, an extractor or ejector, or a regular firing pin for that matter.

The in-line Model 700ML/MLS bolt comes with a flat-faced hammer surface for igniting percussion caps. The bolt is also designed for relatively easy take-down for cleaning. And the lock up is accomplished by pushing the bolt handle down into a machined recess in the rear of the receiver.

What the Remington Model 700ML/MLS brought to an entirely new breed of muzzleloading hunter was a great-handling hunting rifle in a familiar bolt-action package. The advantage of the bolt-action ignition system was faster lock time, and with the special weather shroud snapped in place at the face of the bolt, the Remington muzzleloader was more weatherproof than the open-ignition plunger-hammer in-line rifles.

Not to be outdone in this latest round of in-line rifle development, Knight Rifles (Modern Muzzleloading, Inc.) countered with the introduction of the still more advanced DISC Rifle—the designation standing for *Disc Ignition System*

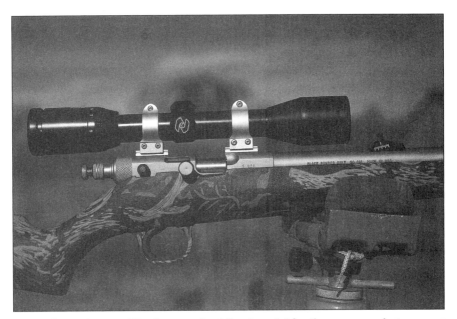

The Knight "Magnum Elite," was a short-lived model for the company, but was one of the very first "bolt-action" muzzleloaders, leading to the development of the very popular Knight DISC Rifle a few years later.

Concept. Here was a novel new "bolt-action" that didn't work like a typical bolt-action. The shooter simply lifted the bolt handle, which would cam the front of the bolt rearward, exposing a half-inch or so wide slot between the bolt face and the rear of the breech plug. A small plastic disc, containing a No. 209 shot-shell primer, was then inserted into this slot. When the bolt handle was pushed downward, the face of the bolt would cam forward to sandwich the disc between the bolt face and flat rear surface of the breech plug.

The extremely short hammer throw of the DISC Rifle resulted in exceptional lock time, and the

Outdoor writer Dave Richey with the very first head of big game ever taken with a Knight DISC Rifle—a muzzleloading record book-class pronghorn dropped cleanly at about one hundred and fifty yards with a saboted bullet.

use of the plastic primer carrying discs sure made this one of the easiest in-line rifles on the market to prime, or cap. Even though Knight's newest design broke from the plunger-hammer design that had started the in-line industry, the DISC Rifle still featured the patented Knight double-safety system.

The company first offered the new rifle in 1997, in .50 caliber only. However, I was fortunate enough to hunt with one of the first two prototypes through the fall and winter of 1996. Tony Knight hunted with the other. In September of that year, I took the very first bull elk ever taken with a Knight DISC Rifle. I was hunting the Wasatch Range of eastern Utah with friend and outfitter Fred John, owner/operator of Wasatch Outfitters, of Morgan, Utah. On the last evening of my hunt, we managed to get a half-dozen bulls fired up and bugling back at every seductive cow call that Fred and I made. Finally, I quit calling and my partner slowly crawled back up the side of the ridge, calling as he went.

Two bulls started working up in my direction. I watched as the larger 6x6, probably a good 340-class bull, eased across the side of the ridge out of muzzle-loader range. The other, another 6x6, came up a bulldoze cut directly at me. At just fifteen yards, the elk stopped and looked down in the direction of the other bull. When he did, he offered an easy, impossible-to-miss neck shot. My saboted 300-grain Barnes Expander MZ, pushed by 110 grains of Pyrodex "Select," caught the elk perfectly, literally dropping the bull where it stood. That fall, I also took several pronghorns and several whitetail bucks with the same rifle, only shooting the lighter 250-grain Expander MZ.

In recent years, Knight has done some redesign work on the DISC Rifle and renamed it the DISC Extreme. The rifle now features a more conventional bolt that is drawn rearward to allow the shooter to drop in a slightly longer *"full-plastic jacket"* that is the primer carrier. An earlier fault with the original DISC Rifle was that quite a bit of fire was lost due to the less-than-gas-pressure-tight seal of the disc between the bolt face and breech plug. The new and longer primer carrier of the DISC Extreme is more completely enclosed by the bolt face, eliminating the loss of fire. The company now offers the rifle in both the popular .50 and in .45 caliber, plus an all new .52 caliber.

Note:

Knight Rifles also still offers models built with the simpler plunger-style hammer, very similar to the original Knight MK-85.

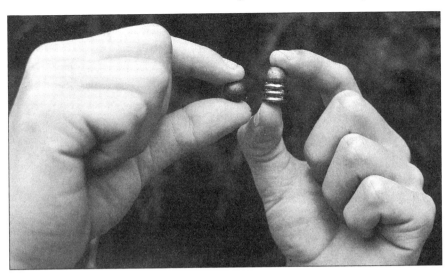

Both of these projectiles are for a .50 caliber rifle. The big T/C "Maxi-Hunter" at right would maintain velocity and energy much better out at about one hundred yards than the patched round ball out at about one hundred yards.

The hot No. 209 primer ignition of the Knight DISC Rifle and later DISC Extreme models results in more positive ignition of the powder charge than possible with the standard No. 11 percussion cap. The hotter flame also means more complete consumption of heavier powder charges. And it was the efficiency of the Knight DISC Rifle primer ignition that first popularized the use of "magnum" 150-grain Pyrodex Pellet powder charges, which are now favored by a large number of muzzleloading hunters who seek optimum range and knockdown power.

Back through the late 1980s and early 1990s, I worked hard to get a saboted 250- or 260-grain bullet out of a modern .50 caliber in-line rifle at velocities of around 1,700 f.p.s. It usually took a 120-grain charge of Pyrodex "P" to get the job done. Thanks to vastly improved loading components, especially tougher sabots and hotter powders, those shooters who are now loading 150-grain charges of either Pyrodex Pellets or Triple Seven Pellets consistently get modern saboted bullets like the 250-grain Hornady SST out of a .50 caliber primer-ignited in-line rifle at velocities right at 2,000 f.p.s.—and with exceptional accuracy. Some are now shooting lighter bullets of around two hundred grains at velocities exceeding 2,200 f.p.s. At these velocities, more aerodynamic bullets like the SST, Barnes Spit-Fire and the Precision Rifle "Dead Center" bullets exhibit very little drop from one hundred yards to two hundred yards. In fact, a 260-grain .40x.50 "Dead Center" bullet that leaves the muzzle at 2,000 f.p.s. will drop only about four inches between one hundred and two hundred yards thanks to its exceptionally high .376 *ballistic coefficient.*

Muzzleloader Hunting

Other great No. 209 primer-ignited bolt-action in-line muzzleloading rifles include the White "ThunderBolt" in .451 or .504 caliber; the Traditions Lightning Series E-Bolt 209 in .45 or .50 caliber, and the Winchester Muzzleloading X-150 in choice of .45 or .50 caliber. Shooters looking for something other than a rifle of bolt-action design may opt for the break-open Thompson/Center Arms "Encore .209x50 Magnum," the same company's top-selling "Omega" drop-action, or the Knight drop-action "Revolution." The latter was offered in .50 caliber only at the time of this writing, while the two Thompson/Center rifles were being offered in .45 or .50 caliber. Plus there are a dozen or more other great No. 209

Thompson/Center Arms' break-open Encore .209x50 Magnum Elite has often been touted as the "World's Most Powerful .50 Caliber Muzzleloader." It was more than enough for this Iowa buck.

primer-ignition muzzleloaders to choose from, all able to produce 2,000+ f.p.s. velocities.

Just about every time there has been a major improvement in the design or performance of today's modern in-line rifles, there has been some opposition from one group or another that feels muzzleloading has simply gone too far too fast. Often it is simply among concerned muzzleloading hunters, who feel that game departments might curtail the special seasons if the guns keep performing better and better. Then there are those in the game departments who often question the added range of today's guns. And there are shooters who just oppose something new coming along to make obsolete what they already own.

When Savage Arms introduced their .50 caliber Model 10ML back in 2000, there was also considerable opposition. You see, here is the first commercially manufactured muzzle-loaded rifle that's been designed to shoot modern smokeless powders. However, this time the brunt of the opposition to the ultra-modern design has not really been from the shooting public, but from other major muzzleloading

Round ball . . . conical . . . or saboted bullet? Any would do the job, as long as the hunter knew the maximum effective range of the powder charge and projectile being shot.

rifle manufacturers who fear having the performance of their non-smokeless rifles compared to the new Savage frontloader.

The concern of other muzzleloader makers was that shooters would be tempted to load smokeless powders into other non-smokeless muzzleloaders, or shooters would accidentally overload the Savage 10MLII with the hotter powders recommended.

Dixie Gun Works vice president Hunter Kirkland with a pronghorn buck he dropped with a patched round ball load at about eighty yards.

29

Muzzleloader Hunting

And there have been several instances of loads that produced higher-than-safe pressures in this gun, resulting in damage to the rifles. Still, the rifle has slowly begun to overcome some of the early opposition. Muzzleloader shooters who have gone to the present Model 10ML II enjoy slightly better velocities than with 150-grain Pyrodex Pellet or Triple Seven Pellet charges, with far less recoil, no corrosive fouling, flatter trajectories and a smoke-free shooting environment. All of this with a powder charge that costs less than twenty percent of what it costs to get similar performance with a compressed pellet black-powder substitute charge.

Old-Fashioned . . . or Ultra Modern?

Combined, the variety of modern reproduction guns available and the selection of modern in-line ignition rifles that now make up the best sellers, give today's muzzleloading shooter and hunter several hundred different guns to choose from. Making that choice has never been harder . . . but getting just the right gun for your wants or needs has never been better.

Before you ever start looking for the rifle of your dreams, first sit down and make a "Must-Have" list. On that list, write down everything that you demand in the muzzleloader you plan to hunt with—including everything you plan to hunt with the rifle.

Just thirty years ago, the patched round ball was the most widely used muzzle-loader hunting projectile, and was effective at close range. However, it quickly lost favor among serious big-game hunters looking for more knockdown power.

Some younger or female muzzleloading hunters cannot tolerate a great deal of recoil. Lighter saboted bullets still offer plenty of performance on game, but without the pain.

One of the first things you should decide is the type of projectile you intend to hunt with. It takes an entirely different rate of rifling twist to get the best accuracy from a patched round ball than it does with a bore-sized conical or saboted bullet. Keep in mind that a round ball is spun by rifling that the ball never touches. The patch must seal the bore to contain the gases produced by the burning powder charge, plus it has to grip both the ball and the rifling adequately to transfer the spin of the rifling to the ball. A .45 caliber or larger rifle that features a rate of rifling twist that is too fast (generally faster than one-turn-in-forty-eight inches) will make getting great accuracy with a patched round ball next to impossible—with heavy hunting charges, anyway. Then, on the other hand, a bore with rifling that does not spin fast enough will fail to properly stabilize a conical bullet in flight. This is just one of the factors that will determine how well your rifle and load shoot.

Many of the following chapters of this book will help you get the absolute best performance from whatever muzzleloader you choose to hunt with. There are many variables in load development that offer no compromise. Other factors the shooter may have some control over. But when it comes to the style of the rifle you choose, or the features that make it special to you, those decisions are entirely up to you. If you buy a rifle purely for aesthetic reasons, then you'll have to settle for whatever performance it is capable of producing and accept whatever limitations of that performance. However, if you buy one of today's top-performing in-line models, you'll just have to accept that it will never look like the rifles carried by Davy Crockett or Jim Bridger. But when you make a clean killing shot on a trophy-class whitetail buck at two hundred yards, you'll quickly forget about this rifle's modern looks. ■

Before Buying Your First Muzzleloader

When looking at muzzleloading for the very first time, someone new to the sport is faced with making a lot of deci-sions. The accompanying chapter does much to share what it takes for any muzzleloaded rifle to be effective on game as large as the white-tailed deer, and still larger game.

Many first time muzzleloading hunters make the unfortunate mistake of buying a rifle purely on the aesthetics of the rifle. In other words, they buy the rifle simply because of how it looks. And if that rifle is to be used for hunting, the *looks* of the frontloader do very little in the way of performance.

The logical first step to selecting an effective muzzleloading rifle is to first choose a caliber that's capable of generating the necessary level of energy for cleanly harvesting big game. Step two would be to study the efficiency of the different hunting projectiles, and to know their limitations. And the third part of the selection process should be to narrow down the choices to only those rifles that are rifled to produce optimum accuracy with the chosen projectile that will deliver the degree of performance that you personally are willing to accept, or which hunting regulations may allow.

The style or appearance of the rifle should be the last criteria for selecting a muzzleloaded big game rifle. However, the patient hunter who does the homework and shops hard should be able to find exactly the muzzleloaded rifle of his or her wishes. There is currently a great selection of traditional round ball and conical bullet rifles, and a tremen-dous variety of modern in-line ignition rifles in a wide spectrum of price ranges, plus a few so-called hybrid models with traditional looks and a fast-twist bore for shooting modern saboted bullets. And if a hunter still cannot find the exact rifle and styling desired, there are literally thousands of custom muzzleloading rifle makers coast to coast ready and willing to build whatever you want or need.

3

Muzzleloader Projectiles

Then...

For nearly five hundred years after the first appearance of the muzzleloaded firearm, the simple round ball reigned as the most widely used projectile wherever the early guns saw military service. Accuracy was once secondary to a soldier's ability to deliver a large volume of fire. Consequently, easy loading of a simple projectile was vital to getting off two to three shots per minute during the heat of battle, and a loose-fitting paper or cloth patched round ball was considerably easier to load than a projectile of any other shape or design.

Keep in mind that early firearms were almost entirely developed for use by the world's growing military powers from the mid 1300s on through the late 1700s. During that period, ingenious minds continually worked to improve the quality of firearms mechanics and develop ignition systems that were significantly more *sure-fire* than earlier designs, but until the early 1800s, very little was done to come up with a projectile superior to the simple round ball. Many of the earliest projectiles were nothing more than round stones, while others were made of cast iron or bronze.

The development of the firearm was a product of the *Renaissance* just as much as the literature of William Shakespeare or the art of Leonardo da Vinci. The period marked the birth of the *modern man.* In fact, some of the earliest-known drawings of the *wheellock* ignition system were done by none other than Leonardo, an engineer by trade who just happened to have a passion for art.

As more and more armies began to lay down the crossbow and the bow and arrow in favor of muzzleloaded muskets, widely known as *fusils,* lead projectiles became standard issue. Improved technology made it easier to extract the soft, easy-to-melt metal from the raw ore. Thanks to a relatively low melting point, lead could be taken from solid to molten by the heat of a campfire. Many soldiers of the period were issued a mold with one or more round ball cavities, and during a lull in the fighting, these early musketeers could often be found melting lead in small cast-iron pots and pouring round ball projectiles for the next day's battle.

When rifling grooves began to appear in muzzleloader bores (around 1500), they were, at first, cut into the metal to keep black-powder fouling from accumulating so quickly that it became impossible to load a tight fitting *cloth-patched* round ball after just a few shots. While it's doubtful that the grooves did much to alleviate loading problems, shooters quickly discovered they did tend to make early muzzle-loaders (matchlock and wheellock) more accurate. By the end of the 1500s, true *rifles,* with grooves that spiraled, were being produced all across Europe.

Shooters discovered they could precisely place their shots at longer ranges. However, they also learned that the more attention they paid to the consistency of the load, the greater the consistency of their accuracy. This meant using the same volumes of black powder, always loading the proper diameter of lead ball, and using patching material that was of sufficient thickness and strength.

Still, even with the refinement of the flintlock-ignition system through the late 1600s and the 1700s, military leaders of the period continued to arm soldiers with smooth-bored muskets. These could be loaded quickly and easily dozens of times with a drastically undersized soft-lead round ball without worry of heavy powder fouling in the bore. On the other hand, the American flintlock *hunting rifle* began to develop in a different direction.

Early on, muzzleloading shooters realized that the larger and heavier the ball, plus the heftier charge of powder loaded under the soft-lead sphere, the harder it would hit its intended target—whether it was an enemy soldier or a huge wild boar, red stag or bear. Smooth-bored military muskets of the 1600s and 1700s typically were of large bore-size. The French Charleville muskets were .69 caliber, while the famed British "Brown Bess" flintlock smooth-bores were .75 caliber. Likewise, most early European muzzleloading big-game rifles were of large bore-size, many of .60 to .72 caliber loaded with patched round balls that could weigh as much as five hundred or more grains.

Early muzzleloading gunmakers in the American colonies broke from European gun designs and began building rifles with long slender barrels that were of considerably smaller bore-sizes. Rifles of .40 to .48 caliber were very common, and made more efficient use of lead and powder that were often in short supply, especially in the vast wilderness regions during the mid to late 1700s. The American long rifle became world renowned for its accuracy. And with a 100- to 130-grain patched round ball loaded with sixty to seventy grains of fine black powder, these rifles were more than adequate for harvesting game as large as the abundant white-tailed deer, and warding off dangers of the human kind.

As the East became more "civilized" and settled, Americans turned their attention to the vast lands that lay to the West. When the Lewis and Clark *Corps of Discovery* headed up the Missouri River to places unknown to the white man, they took with them the first official U.S. military rifle . . . the .54 caliber Harper's Ferry flintlock.

Despite the relatively large bore-size of this rifle, and the 230-or-so-grain patched round ball used in the rifle, the light standard service powder charge of just 60 grains of FFg black powder often proved inadequate for some of the really large game these adventurers were to encounter. More than one incident with the fierce plains grizzly nearly cost the lives of expedition members.

Perhaps it was the questionable performance of the Harper's Ferry rifle and load during this three-year adventure that set the stage for future muzzleloading big-game rifle development in this country. By the time the percussion-ignition system was fully developed by the mid 1920s, large bore .52 to .56 caliber rifles, such as those produced by Samuel and Jacob Hawken in their St. Louis, Missouri, gun shop, had become famous for the knockdown power they produced with 140- to 160-grain charges of FFg black powder behind patched round balls of two hundred to two hundred and fifty grains. (The Hawken Shop commonly cut and provided a round ball mold of appropriate diameter for each barrel they produced.)

Birth of the Conical Bullet

Noted gunmakers in Great Britain and continental Europe truly refined muzzleloading guns during the late 1700s and early 1800s, and did experiment widely with improved projectile designs. Most efforts still centered on the round ball, resulting in everything from a "belted" ball to oblong-shaped ovals. And these generally required very specialized rifling. However, the development of the true conical muzzleloading bullet enjoyed its beginning in the United States.

As early as 1835, elongated projectiles known as the *"sugar-loaf"* or *"picket"* bullet began to win favor among American riflemen. These early conical bullets were somewhat odd in shape, featuring a round base (much like the curvature of a round ball) and a frontal shape that tapered to either a sharp *"spire-point"* or a slightly flattened tip. They still required the use of a patch to seal the bore and transfer the spin of the rifling to the projectile. Unfortunately, the rounded base meant that the bullet could be easily canted in the bore during loading, destroying any chances of accuracy. However, a *percussion rifle* of the period that had been precisely built with the proper loading accessories often proved extremely accurate,

This circa 1850 long-barreled half-stock percussion rifle is an excellent example of the accurate "bullet rifles" available by that time. These rifles often had twists as fast as one-turn-in-eighteen to twenty inches, for stabilizing bullets of a length two or more times their diameter.

and could increase the effective range (and accuracy) of the rifle two- or threefold.

The problems encountered with loading early conical bullets were quickly overcome, and by the late 1840s and early 1850s, true cylindrical bullets, and specially rifled muzzleloaders for shooting such, had completely replaced the older projectile designs. Gone for the most part were the rounded bases, replaced with a flat base (or hollow-cupped base) that sat squarely on the powder charge. The *improved conical muzzleloading bullet* was generally two- to four-times longer than it was in diameter, allowing the body of the bullet to be very cylindrical. This eliminated chances of the bullet canting in the bore, and provided more contact with the rifling.

One of the more revered elongated bullets of the mid 1800s was the design of English gun fancier Sir Joseph Whitworth. In 1854, he was granted a patent for an unusual hexagonal-bore rifle and mechanically started bullet. In .45 caliber, the Whitworth bullet was 1.32 inches in length and weighed in at 530 grains. During one demonstration, the rifle and bullet proved to be capable of printing four-inch groups at five hundred yards. However, the rifle-and-projectile system was expensive to make, and fouled easily. It failed to win over sportsmen looking for good accuracy with a relatively easy-to-load bullet.

Probably the best-known conical bullet of the 1800s was the big hollow-based Minié bullet dating from the Civil War. Named after the French captain who invented it, the Minié was a military design. Big percussion .58 caliber *rifled muskets* were the arms predominately used by both the North and the South. More than three million of the guns were either produced in this country or imported from Europe. As often as not, the outcome of any battle depended on which side could fire the greatest number of rounds. Consequently, the shoulder arms of the infantry had to be capable of being loaded easily—and quickly!

The Minié design sure made loading easy. Here was a big five hundred-grain bullet that was around .005-inch undersized, that could be pushed down the bore of an American .58 caliber *Springfield* or .577 caliber British *Enfield* rifled musket without any resistance whatsoever. When the standard 60-grain service charge of black powder was ignited by one of the big-winged musket caps, the burning gases would expand the thin, soft-lead skirts of the hollow base into the rifling, forming a very effective gas seal. Surprisingly, some of these big, single-shot muzzleloading muskets were extremely accurate. Even so, it was the sheer volume of fire possible with such an easy-loading system that resulted in the exceedingly high number of deaths on the battlefield. In all, more than 640,000 Americans died during the conflicts of the Civil War; more than during World War I and World War II combined.

The Civil War was the last of the *"Old Wars"* and the first of the *"New Wars."* It was the last large-scale conflict in which muzzleloading guns played a significant role, while also being the first war in which modern *breechloading cartridge* firearms also saw widespread use. Sportsmen had also pretty much abandoned frontloading guns as well, readily turning to more efficient and easier-to-load cartridge guns. Still, for the next forty or so years, a handful of dedicated long-range marksmen continued to use and further develop some of the most accurate muzzleloaded target rifles and bullets ever known. And some of this knowledge was carried over into the modern reproduction muzzleloading guns that became popular once again during the last half of the 1900s.

Round Ball or Elongated Bullet?

Like the muzzleloading marksman of the mid 1800s, the modern-day muzzleloading shooter looking for a bit of tradition in the rifle and load used for hunting can choose between using a patched round ball or conical muzzleloading bullet.

However, the rifle itself will dictate the choice.

It takes an entirely different rifle to get the best accuracy from either of these projectile types. The round ball relies upon the tight fit of the patch material in the rifling to grip the soft-lead ball and produce the desired accuracy. The ball itself never touches the rifling that

This patched ball is ready to be short-started into the bore, then seated with the ramrod.

spins it. The patching must be of sufficient thickness to be compressed into the grooves of the rifling, helping to form the necessary gas seal when the powder ignites, while at the same time transferring the spin of the bore to the projectile as the patch and ball travels down the bore at relatively high velocities. If the ball fails to be properly spun by the patch material and rifling, accuracy suffers.

Typically, a true *round ball rifle* for use on big game (.50 or .54 caliber) will feature lands and grooves that spiral with a rate of twist that results in one complete revolution of the ball in sixty to seventy-two inches. Such slow rates of twist allow the ball to be pushed down the bore with hefty 90- to 120-grain charges (depending on caliber) of black powder, Pyrodex or Triple Seven at muzzle velocities that can exceed 2,000 f.p.s. If the rifling spins with a rate of twist that is too fast, the patch and ball can resist following the grooves of the rifling, and exit the muzzle without being properly spun. Even modern reproduction rifles with a one-turn-in-forty-eight inches rate of rifling twist may not shoot a patched round ball accurately, not with honest hunting powder charges anyway.

It is also extremely important that round-ball projectiles be made from nothing but soft, pure lead. In addition to filling the grooves of the rifling, the weave of the patch material must also grip the curved surface of the ball. Round balls that have been cast from hardened lead, such as old wheel weights, may prove too hard for the patching to grip. Also, the harder the lead, the less it tends to *obturate* (flatten slightly) in the bore at the moment of ignition. This resistance to the pressure exerted at the rear of the ball by the

The only way to make a perfect sphere of lead heavier is to make it bigger. Here a .440-inch ball, left, is shown next to a .530-inch ball.

burning powder charge helps to seal the bore and force the patching to do its job.

Being two or more times longer than in diameter, bore-sized conical muzzle-loading bullets need the extra spin of a faster rate of rifling twist to stabilize the long bullets in flight. Modern conical bullets like the Thompson/Center Arms "Maxi-Ball" or Hornady "Great Plains Bullet" are two times longer than their diameter. Loaded into a bore with a turn-in-sixty-six inches rate of twist, these bullets will not be properly spun or stabilized. The result is often a bullet that *keyholes* on the target, or in other words a bullet that hits the target sideways. Many successful conical bullet shooters today have found that with most of the more current bullet designs, rifling that spins with a turn-in-thirty-two to a turn-in-forty-eight inches tends to produce the best accuracy. Just keep in mind that the longer the bullet, the faster the rate of twist needed to properly stabilize the bullet in flight. Back in the 1850s, Sir Joseph Whitworth relied on a super fast turn-in-twenty inches to get exceptional accuracy from a 530-grain .45 caliber bullet that was right at three times longer than its diameter.

The majority of today's modern conical muzzleloading bullets rely on slight engraving of the rifling during loading to keep the projectile in place over the powder charge. Thompson/Center's "Maxi-Ball" features a band at the nose that's several thousandths of an inch oversized . . . Hornady and Buffalo Bullet Company both rely on a couple of narrow bands and knurling slightly larger than the land to land measurement of the bore . . . and the Lee Precision REAL Bullet (Rifling

Engraved At Loading) is cast with a series of slightly oversized bands. The soft lead used in these bullets is easily engraved by the rifling when the projectile is started into the muzzle by moderate pressure on a short starter. Then it can be easily seated over the powder charge with the ramrod.

Since the early 1990s, White Rifles has been marketing a line of modern in-line ignition rifles designed primarily for use with the

The Thompson/Center Arms "Maxi-Ball" conical bullet was one of the more popular hunting bullets of the late 1970s and early 1980s. The expanded "Maxi" was recovered from a big mule deer buck taken at about one hundred and forty yards.

company's own line of conical bullets. Their system relies on what is often referred to as *slip fit* projectiles, which are slightly undersized. The big White *PowerPunch* conical bullets, weighing four hundred to six hundred grains, literally fall down the bore, or at most require a very minimal push on the ramrod.

Whether a lead conical muzzleloading bullet requires light engraving of the rifling during loading, or makes little if any contact with the rifling as it is pushed down the bore, all fit relatively loosely by the time the bullet is sitting atop the powder charge. Lead has no memory. In other words, once the rifling cuts into the oversized bands or surface features of some bullet designs, all resistance with the bore is lost. These bullets are totally reliant upon obturation to fill the grooves of the rifling and seal off the burning gases of the powder charge when the trigger is pulled. In recent years, a growing number of conical bullet fans have been making the switch to a design that is something of a combination of old and new technology. These conical bullets feature a plastic gas seal (cup) attached to the rear of the bullet to help keep the slightly undersized projectiles in place over the powder charge. However, it is the slight flattening (obturation) of the soft-lead projectiles that actually fills the rifling and seals the bore at the moment of ignition. The design, which has been sold as the "Black Belt Bullet" and the "Power Belt Bullet," loads easily, stays in place over the powder charge and produces very good accuracy.

If you are just now considering the purchase of a traditionally styled muzzle-loader for hunting, first decide the type of projectile you intend to hunt with, then buy a muzzleloader with the rifling that gives the best performance with that type of projectile. If you fully intend to *NEVER* shoot at big game beyond one hundred yards, then the patched round ball just may be the only projectile you ever need to hunt with.

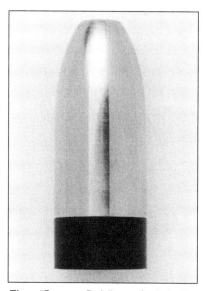

However, once ranges extend beyond one hundred yards, even a .50 or .54 caliber rifle loaded with a heavy powder charge just doesn't maintain enough energy with the round ball.

The "Power Belt" conical bullet design incorporates a "snap-on" plastic gas seal base that doubles to help hold this bullet in place over the powder charge.

On the other hand, a conical rifle of the same caliber can easily deliver one of the big bullets with twice the remaining energy at one hundred and fifty yards than the soft-lead ball has at one hundred. In the chapter on "Load Data," this book will detail the velocities and energy levels of loads with these traditional projectiles.

Now . . . Except among the very traditionally minded shooters who

make up just four to five percent of all muzzleloading hunters today, the patched round ball has become a thing of the past. Likewise, the big, heavy, bore-sized lead conical bullets also continue to see less use from one season to the next. Present-day muzzleloading hunters who have taken to the ultra-modern in-line ignition rifles are now using a projectile system that's every bit as modern as the frontloaded rifle they now carry for deer, elk, bear or any other species of big game.

The muzzleloaded projectile of choice these days is the plastic-saboted bullet. Close to eighty percent of all muzzleloading hunters in the U.S. and Canada now rely on saboted bullets of one form or another to harvest the game they bring home.

While saboted projectiles have been around for ages, once seeing widespread use out of muzzleloaded cannon, the system so many of us now use was the brain-child of an Arkansas muzzleloading hunter by the name of Del Ramsey. Back during the early 1980s, he began his search for a *"better"* muzzleloaded hunting projectile than the ineffective round ball or the hard-recoiling bore-sized lead conical bullets. Then it dawned on him that a great selection of bullets already existed: the tremendous array of jacketed bullets offered for loading .357, .44 and .45 caliber handgun cartridges. Fortunately for today's muzzleloading hunters, Ramsey also owned a small plastic injection-molding company and designed a simple plastic cup that would allow these bullets to be loaded into and shot from .45, .50 and .54 caliber muzzleloaded big-game rifles.

Predating the introduction of the Knight MK-85 in-line rifle by about a year, Del Ramsey established Muzzleload Magnum Products and began to market his sabot system in 1984. It was a combination of the ultra-modern Knight rifle and MMP sabot system that set the stage for muzzleloader hunting as we now know it.

When Ramsey first offered the MMP sabots, his best-selling sabot was for loading a .429- to .430-inch diameter (.44) bullet into a frontloading .50 caliber bore. And right behind that sabot in popularity was one designed for loading .451- to .452-inch bullets in a .50 caliber rifle. Back then, the selection of jacketed bullets for the popular Remington .44 Magnum handgun cartridge was much better than the bullet offerings for .45 caliber handguns, like the Colt .45 ACP or the .45 Long Colt. Fortunately, the growing popularity of big .45 handguns like the .454 Casull has resulted in an expanded selection of the slightly larger-diameter bullets.

Many experienced sabot users have found that when the bullet diameter is kept as close as possible to the bore-size, shooters tend to enjoy greater accuracy. In other words, saboted .45 caliber bullets (.451- to .452-inch dia.) will generally produce tighter 100-yard groups than saboted .44 caliber (.429- to .430-inch dia.) bullets out of the popular .50 caliber in-line rifles.

The thicker plastic sleeves of a sabot designed to shoot a .429- to .430-inch bullet from a .500-inch bore will tend to take a little longer to open up and peel back away from the bullet than the thinner sleeves of a sabot for shooting a slightly larger .45 caliber bullet. And the longer a sabot sticks with the bullet, the more it can affect down-range accuracy. When shooting sabots from a .50 caliber rifle, the sabots for .44 caliber bullets can usually be found about fifteen yards from the muzzle. The sabots for shooting the .45 bullets will normally be laying on the ground just ten or so yards from the muzzle, indicating that these sabots do indeed open up more quickly and peel back away from the bullet faster. Occasionally, an individual .50 caliber rifle may show a preference for saboted .44 bullets, but the norm is that the .45s will turn in the best accuracy.

The barrel on this older Traditions "Lightning" is marked to indicate that the gun has a one-in-thirty-two inches rate of rifling twist. Newer models feature one turn-in-twenty-eight inches.

One way to look at the plastic sabot is to consider it a modern patch. Its role is basically the same as that of the cloth patch used with a round ball. The sabot must grip both the rifling of the bore and the cylindrical jacketed bullet, and transfer the spin of that rifling to the bullet before the two exit the muzzle of the rifle. The fit of the bullet in the sabot, as well as the fit of the sabot in the bore, are both critical. If the bullet fits inside the cup of the sabot too loosely, or if the sabot/bullet combination is too undersized, accuracy and performance will suffer.

While the patched round ball tends to turn in its best accuracy when loaded into a bore rifled with a slow one turn-in-sixty to seventy-two inches, saboted bullets prefer something snappier—quite a bit snappier. Depending on the actual length of the projectile being shot (and to some degree velocity of the load), most saboted bullets will turn in best accuracy from a bore with a complete turn of the rifling in twenty-four to thirty-two inches. A good rule of thumb to follow is that the longer the bullet, the faster the rate of twist needed for optimum stabilization of the projectile. These are still cylindrical bullets, requiring more spin than a round ball for good accuracy.

I made the switch to a modern in-line muzzleloader early on. In fact, I got my first Knight MK-85 back in 1986, just the second year these rifles were offered, and I've shot mostly saboted bullets ever since. During the late 1980s and early 1990s, I tended to favor the .451-inch Speer 260-grain jacketed hollow-point bullets for deer-sized game. With a 100-grain charge of Pyrodex "RS/Select," the twenty-four inch barreled .50 caliber Knight MK-85 would get the bullet out of the muzzle at around 1,640 f.p.s., generating right at 1,500 f.p.e. The one-turn-in twenty-eight inches rate of twist Green Mountain barrels found on these rifles built since 1988 have always given me one inch three-shot groups at one hundred yards. This load has more than likely accounted for close to one hundred whitetails, mule deer, pronghorn and wild hogs during the six or seven years that I used it. And not one of those animals ever required a second shot.

Only a couple of companies currently produce sabots for the muzzleloading industry. Muzzleload Magnum Products presently sells sabots under its own brand label, and produces slightly different versions to a growing number of muzzleloading gunmakers and suppliers of saboted bullets, including Knight Rifles, Thompson/Center Arms, Hornady, Barnes Bullets, Winchester and a few others. C&D Specialty Products, maker of the Claybuster shotgun wads, also molds sabots of very similar design, marketing these under the Harvester brand name, plus provides sabots for several other companies as well, including Nosler.

Sabots have continually been improved and slightly redesigned since coming to market more than twenty years ago. The sabots muzzleloading hunters use today are definitely stronger and tougher than the sabots we were loading with just four or five years ago. Still, shooters tend to continue "blowing"

Introduced back in 1984, the Muzzleload Magnum Products sabots allowed shooters and hunters to use a wide range of modern jacketed handgun bullets in their larger-bore muzzleloading rifles. The 250-grain Hornady .452-inch "XTP" shown here has been one of the more popular whitetail bullets.

sabots for one main reason: because we're a never-satisfied bunch who keep trying to get our modern in-line muzzleloaded rifles to shoot faster . . . harder . . . and farther than any muzzleloaded big-game rifles and loads of the past.

The modern-day loads that most hunters rely on sure ask an awful lot of the tiny plastic cup that carries the bullet down and out of the bore. More and more are now loading the newer No. 209 primer-ignited rifles with *magnum* 150-grain compressed pellet charges of either Pyrodex or Triple Seven, to get 240- to 260-grain saboted bullets out of the muzzle at more than 2,000 f.p.s. (with 2,400 to 2,600 f.p.e.). Some of these loads are producing internal barrel pressures from around 25,000 to almost 30,000 p.s.i. It takes a tough polymer material to stand up to this kind of beating and still deliver a bullet with accuracy.

Muzzleloader Hunting

The Savage Model 10ML II is one of several *smokeless powder muzzleloaders* now available. The loads of modern nitrocellulose based powders, like VihtaVuori N110 and Accurate Arms 5744, which produce velocities of 2,300 to 2,400 f.p.s. with a saboted two hundred and fifty-grain bullet, also produce noticeably higher pressures and greater heat. And they can prove to be extremely temperamental. To better harness the power and efficiency of these loads, and to protect the sabot from pressures that can top 40,000 p.s.i., many of the shooters who have gone to the smokeless rifles are loading a *sub-base* between the powder charge and sabot/bullet combination. (This will be covered in more detail in the chapter detailing loading techniques.)

These days, no one seems to want a muzzleloaded load than cannot break 2,000 f.p.s.. At these speeds, the old jacketed hollow-point handgun bullets that were designed for velocities of about 1,000 to 1,400 f.p.s. just might not hold together well enough to get the job done. Fortunately, muzzleloader hunting has progressed to the point that a growing number of bullet manufacturers are now offering honest muzzleloaded hunting-bullet designs built for the higher velocities.

Barnes Bullets was the first to break from simply packaging an appropriate sabot with an existing handgun bullet, and back in the mid 1990s began offering their all-copper Expander MZ hollow-point bullet. The all-copper construction results in a considerably longer projectile than a jacketed lead-core bullet of the same weight. For the .50 caliber rifles,

The Barnes all-copper "Expander MZ" bullets were among the very first saboted bullets designed expressly for use in a muzzleloaded big-game rifle.

Barnes markets saboted 250- and 300-grain .451-inch Expander MZ bullets, the lighter of which is just as long as a 300-grain jacketed lead-core bullet. For the .45 caliber rifles, the company offers a saboted 195-grain .400-inch bullet, and for the .54 caliber bores Barnes has two saboted .500-inch bullets, in 275- and 325-grains.

The Expander MZ has been designed with a huge volcanic hollow-point nose that opens into four separate petals upon impact. A great deal of research and development went into this bullet to insure that it would properly expand at velocities as slow as 800 to 900 f.p.s., or at speeds the bullet would still be flying out at one hundred and seventy-five to two hundred yards. Once the bullet does open, the

The Hornady polymer tipped "SST" has quickly become one of the top-selling saboted bullets on the market. This recovered bullet came from a sizeable whitetail buck taken at about one hundred and fifty yards.

solid copper base that's behind the rolled-back petals continues to keep on pushing this bullet for unbelievable penetration. I once shot a huge 900-pound bull elk at almost one hundred yards with the 300-grain .50 caliber Expander MZ (and 110-grain charge of Pyrodex "RS/Select"), and that bullet was found perfectly expanded just under the hide on the opposite side. That bull went just sixty yards before going down.

Since the introduction of the Barnes Expander MZ, a lot of game has been harvested with the all-copper bullets. About the only complaint hunters have had has been the huge hollow-point that gives this bullet a very blunt frontal shape. Now that muzzle velocities of 2,000 f.p.s. have become more the norm rather than the exception, the modern-day muzzleloading big-game hunter is demanding bullet designs with much better aerodynamics and improved flight characteristics.

Hornady Manufacturing has been a major supplier of saboted muzzleloader bullets for nearly two decades, or almost since the projectile system became popular. For most of that time, Hornady simply offered saboted versions of their XTP jacketed hollow-point bullets, which have been excellent performers on big game. More recently, the company has added a sleek, very aerodynamic spire-point saboted bullet dubbed the SST (Super Shock Tip). Actually, the bullet is nothing more than the muzzleloader version of a design that Hornady offers handloaders of center-fire rifle cartridges. And like the center-fire SST bullets, the muzzleloader bullet is built with a sharp, polymer-tip jacket that tapers in thickness and the company's *"Inter-Lock"* ring. Here is a serious hunting bullet designed for better retention of velocity and energy out at two hundred yards (and farther), plus positive expansion at velocities of 900 to 1,000 f.p.s., and internal construction that contributes to preventing jacket and core separation.

With some of the hotter loads of smokeless powder in the Savage Model 10ML II, I've been able to get the 250-grain .452-inch diameter saboted SST out of the muzzle at around 2,350 to 2,400 f.p.s. These loads generate right at 3,200 foot-pounds of muzzle energy. The muzzle ballistics would be the same with the 250-grain XTP hollow-point when shot with the same powder charges. However, due to the vastly improved aerodynamics (and higher *ballistic coefficient*) of the spire-point, a 250-grain SST that left the muzzle at 2,400 f.p.s. would hit a whitetail at two hundred yards with around 1,700 foot-pounds of retained energy, while the blunt-nosed hollow-point XTP of the same weight would retain just

The expanded 250-grain Hornady "XTP" shown in the center was recovered from a whitetail buck that was dropped cleanly at one hundred and sixty yards.

1,300 f.p.e.. The four hundred added foot-pounds of knockdown power of this load at two hundred yards is the result of better-retained velocity with the sleek spire-point design, which in turn also means a flatter trajectory.

Hornady currently offers both 250- and 300-grain .452-inch diameter SST bullets for the .50 caliber, and a 200-grain saboted .400-inch SST for the .45 caliber bores. With hot loads of Pyrodex or Triple Seven, loose grain or pellet, the light bullet for the .45 should be able to reach muzzle velocities of 2,100 to 2,200 f.p.s. At two hundred yards, such loads would still take big game with more than 1,200 foot-pounds of retained energy.

Barnes Bullets has also stepped up to the plate with a new saboted high-performance muzzleloader bullet known as the Spit-Fire. It is another all-copper hollow-point. However, instead of the huge hollow-point nose found on the earlier Expander MZ designs, this bullet features a much smaller hollow-point opening and a sharp spire-point front. Adding to the aerodynamics of this bullet is a slight boat-tail at the base. As this book was being written, Barnes offered the new Spit-Fire for just the .50 caliber rifles, in 245- and 285-grain weights.

With a hefty 130-grain charge of FFFg Triple Seven, I have been able to get the 245-grain Spit-Fire out of the muzzle of a twenty-six inch White Rifles ThunderBolt barrel at around 2,075 f.p.s., which generates close to 2,600 f.p.e. at

New, extremely aerodynamic bullet designs, like the polymer-tipper Precision Rifle Bullet "Dead Center" shown here, maintain both velocity and energy better down range than the big, blunt-faced hollow-point handgun bullets.

the muzzle. At that muzzle velocity, the bullet would cleanly take a whitetail at two hundred yards with around 1,050 foot-pounds of retained energy. When the lighter Spit-Fire was loaded into the smokeless Savage Model 10ML II, a forty-five grain charge of VihtaVuori N110 got the 245-grain all-copper bullet out of the muzzle at 2,420 f.p.s. That translates into 3,175 f.p.e. at the muzzle, which in turn results in more than 1,500 foot-pounds of knockdown power at two hundred yards.

Easily some of the more aerodynamic bullets currently available are produced by Precision Rifle Custom Muzzleloader Bullets, of Manitoba, Canada. This maker's "Dead Center"and "QT" bullets come in a wide range of weights, from a light 175-grain saboted bullet for the .45 caliber bores to a huge 500-grain saboted slug for .54 caliber rifles. These are precision cold-swaged soft-lead bullets that feature a sharp polymer tip that pushes ballistic coefficients right to the very top of current muzzleloader projectile offerings. Most of the poly-tipped spire-point bullets offered by this maker top .300 b.c.

Cecil Epp, owner of PR Custom Muzzleloader Bullets, often loads a .50 caliber Thompson/Center Encore 209x50 Magnum with a 110-grain charge of FFg Triple Seven behind his 340-grain "Dead Center" saboted .451-inch diameter bullet. The load is good for 1,795 f.p.s. at the muzzle, developing 2,432 f.p.e. Now, this bullet has a b.c. of .376, making it one of the most streamlined and aerodynamic muzzleloaded projectiles currently available. At one hundred yards, the big soft-lead bullet is still moving along at 1,616 f.p.s., with 1,971 foot-pounds of wallop. At two hundred yards, this bullet is still flying at 1,455 f.p.s. and would hit a bull elk with 1,598 f.p.e. All the way out at three hundred yards, the 340-grain "Dead Center" would retain 1,311 f.p.s. with 1,298 foot-pounds of game-taking energy.

Muzzleloader Hunting

Now, that's some kind of down-range performance from a non-smokeless muzzleloader.

One of the more unique saboted bullets currently available is produced by a small operation known as JADA Enterprise, of Maranza, Arizona. They simply refer to their product as "The Bullet," and what makes this saboted muzzleloader projectile so different from anything else is that it has a hole running clear through the center of the bullet . . . from nose to base. The thinking here is to reduce air drag on the bullet and have a projectile that literally *cuts through the air!* "The Bullet" is a copper-jacketed lead tube, and it is offered in several different diameters and weights, from 180 to 240 grains.

Without center mass, it takes a rather long .430-inch or .451-inch bullet to push weight to 240 grains. To keep the plastic of the sabot from being blown into the hollow base of "The Bullet," the maker inserts a thin Lexan disc directly under the projectile. I've shot most variations of this saboted bullet with exceptional accuracy. And with the smokeless loads in the Savage Model 10ML II, I've gotten a 200-grain "The Bullet" up over 2,500 f.p.s. Bullet drop between one hundred and two hundred yards was practically nil, allowing pretty much a "dead-on" hold all the way to two hundred yards. I've only shot a couple of whitetails with this bullet, but both went down on the spot and the recovered bullets were very, very flattened.

More than just muzzleloading rifles have changed. So has what we're shooting out of them. Today's modern saboted muzzleloading projectiles not only maintain velocity and energy better with flatter trajectory at the longer ranges, but also, thanks to their streamlined and sleek configurations, these bullets are often very capable of printing sub one-inch groups at one hundred yards. In fact, a growing number of today's performance-minded shooters actually expect and demand that degree of accuracy. And they're getting it with unbelievable regularity. ▪

4

A Look at Muzzleloader Propellants

Then ...

That concoction of charcoal, potassium nitrate (saltpeter) and sulfur which becomes *black powder* when properly mixed, and which became the one and only muzzleloaded propellant for almost six hundred years, has actually been around for more than twice as long as the firearm. No one really knows where it was first used, or who first discovered the explosive nature of these ingredients. All we know is that early forms of the powder were regularly used for pyrotechnical displays (fireworks) in China, Turkey, and all across Europe for nearly one thousand years before the birth of the muzzleloaded firearm.

Historians often credit one name with being the first to harness the power of black powder—a German monk known as Berthold Schwarz. Other than a monument erected in honor of Schwarz, crediting him with the discovery of gunpowder, there is no known documentation of him ever really existing. Legend has it that he made his discovery in 1259. The use of black powder had most definitely been documented as much as seven hundred to eight hundred years earlier. However, it is very possible that this one individual stumbled upon black powder's potential as a propellant. And that discovery may have led to the development of the first firearms by the end of the 13th century.

The basic make-up of this ancient powder has pretty well remained the same since its first use in firearms: potassium nitrate (saltpeter), sulfur and charcoal. Makers of this explosive mixture have occasionally used varying amounts of these ingredients, resulting in varying degrees of effectiveness. Likewise, through the years, they incorporated various methods of mixing, milling and grinding the powder into a usable form.

The improved black powders that were produced from about 1840 on through to the end of the original muzzleloading period contained about 75 percent saltpeter, 10 percent sulfur and 15 percent charcoal. An old saying dating from the mid 1800s proclaimed, *"The saltpeter is the soul . . . the sulfur is the life . . . and the charcoal the body"* of black powder. In other words, the potassium nitrate supplies oxygen for combustion, the sulfur makes the concoction fire-sensitive and gives the mixture its explosive nature, while the charcoal provides the base.

Muzzleloader Hunting

Generally speaking, the following steps are used to turn these ingredients into black powder. First, the ingredients are *mixed,* usually with a wetting agent to keep an explosive dust out of the air. Then the wet components are *milled* for several hours to insure a uniform mix and combination of the various elements. After that, the still very-damp compound is *pressed* into a flat cake and dried, then *"corned"* or granulated. This last step is accomplished by rolling a huge stone wheel over the mixture until it is sufficiently broken up. The rough granules are then *finished,* often by tumbling in a huge wooden barrel to round sharp edges and further break up fractured granules into separate pieces. Finally, the powder is *graded* by sifting it through various-size screens to separate the different-size granules.

The first powder mill established in the American colonies was built in 1675 near Milton, Massachusetts. At that time, there were no known deposits of saltpeter in North America. To produce the much-needed element, vegetable and animal refuse was mixed with lime and water, then stored in saltpeter sheds, known as *"nitriaries."* When these piles became completely decomposed, they were leached with clean water, which carried away soluble components. Left behind was crystalline potassium nitrate.

By 1800, there were more than two hundred black-powder plants operating in the newly established United States. Powder production at most of these sites was relatively limited. In fact, the largest producer of black powder of the period was the Laflin & Rand Company, located near Baltimore, Maryland, and the plant produced only slightly more than one hundred and twenty-five tons of black powder a year.

By 1804, the powder-making operation of E. Irene du Pont, near Wilmington, Delaware, had risen to the number-one spot. Prior to the building of the du Pont plant, the finest black powder had come from France, with British-made powder not far behind. But in that year, du Pont invented and patented a machine that separated the different sizes of granules. His *"Eagle"*-grade powder quickly became world renowned for its consistent grain size.

Du Pont had purposely selected his plant site next to Brandywine Creek, and the abundance of willow trees that provided the charcoal for his powder. The sulfur used was imported from France and Sicily, the saltpeter from India. Thanks to du Pont's foresight to store large quantities of these ingredients, production at the plant was slowed little by British blockades during the War of 1812.

The company's Eagle powder was sold in seven different grades. The American powder-making operation had adopted the *"F"* system devised by the French to distinguish the different granulations; the more *"Fs"* in the grade designation, the finer the powder. Black-powder makers today still use the system for grading this ancient propellant.

As far as the use of black powder in all hunting muzzleloaders is concerned, shooters need to only concentrate on Fg, FFg, FFFg and FFFFg granulations. Powder of Fg granulation is likely the least used these days. It was once commonly loaded in really large-bore rifles and smooth-bore muskets of .75 caliber and larger. Often, the extremely coarse grade of black powder produces the best patterns from really big-bored muzzleloaded scatterguns. Just keep in mind that today, anything larger than a ten-gauge cannot be used for hunting waterfowl, and in some states it is even illegal to use on certain other game.

The most commonly used granulations of black powder still loaded by muzzleloading rifle shooters are FFg and FFFg. Rifles

When a shooter goes to the extent of building or having built a nice custom copy of an original gun, like this later-period percussion "Kentucky" rifle, chances are he or she will want to use the traditional muzzleloader propellant: black powder.

of .50 caliber and larger tend to perform best when loaded with FFg black powder, especially when stuffed with one of the heavy bore-sized conical bullets. Still, some rifle makers recommend the use of FFFg black powder in a .50-caliber round-ball rifle. The finer grain FFFg does burn cleaner, and many competition shooters prefer the finer grade in just about any muzzleloaded rifle, but load with light target charges that may be half that of a big-game hunting charge. The finer FFFg black powder also burns faster and produces higher velocities than an equal amount of FFg black powder. Small-bore muzzleloading rifle shooters (.32 through .45) favor finer FFFg, since small bores do tend to foul more easily. (More on choosing the right grade of black powder in Chapter 6, "Load Data.")

Really fine FFFFg black powder is used for priming the pan of a flintlock-ignition system. Rarely will it (or should it) be used as the primary powder charge in the barrel. It produces significantly higher pressures than FFFg black powder, and if loaded in sufficient quantity, the excessive pressures could severely damage a top-quality muzzleloader. Often, knowledgeable small-bore rifle shooters will load light, fifteen to twenty grain charges of FFFFg into a .32 or .36 "squirrel rifle" to better tap the head-shot accuracy and knockdown power of these small-game frontloaders.

Today, black powder is imported to the U.S. from several countries, for both sporting and commercial uses. Still, one American powder producer provides the majority of the black powder loaded and shot by muzzleloading shooters and hunters who continue to favor this propellant, usually in muzzleloaded guns of very traditional design. That company is simply known as GOEX (Gearhart-Owen Explosives).

In April of 1973, E. I. Du Pont de Nemours & Company decided to cease all production of black powder at their Pennsylvania plant due to the drastic decline in its commercial and military use. The plant, which opened in 1912 and produced its first batch of black powder that year, had become the world's second largest producer of black powder in just three years. During the sixty-two years that Du Pont made black powder on the site, millions of pounds were produced for military use in World War I and World War II, as well as in the Korean and Vietnam conflicts. At the time of its closing, the plant was the last American manufacturer of black powder for muzzleloading shooters.

None of the black-powder substitutes can match FFFFg black powder for priming the pan of a flintlock.

Fortunately, the Gearhart-Owens Company stepped in and purchased the powder-making operation. In fact, they did it so quickly that the majority of the skilled black-powder making employees working there continued to remain with the newly named operation. In 1997, GOEX moved the entire enterprise into an updated facility at the old Louisiana Army Ammunition Plant located in Doyline, Louisiana. The company still produces black powder there today—the sole manufacturer in North America.

Today, only about ten percent of all muzzleloading shooters still load with charges of black powder. The age-old mixture is extremely heat- and impact-sensitive, and has

Many of the big bore-sized conical bullets tend to perform best when loaded with black powder.

been classified as a "Class-A Explosive," which means it is closely regulated and there are numerous restrictions on how it may be stored, transported and purchased. Federal, state, and local laws continue to make it more and more difficult to find retailers willing to cope with all the red tape involved with selling an "explosive." Most shooters have made the switch to easier-to-find *black-powder substitutes,* which are classified as *"Flammable Solids,"* the same as modern smokeless powders.

Still, for some guns and some loads, black powder is hard to beat. As mentioned earlier in this chapter, some of the big bore-sized conical bullets shoot their

Fire and smoke are a part of muzzleloading that appeals to many shooters—both young and old.

absolute best when loaded with a hefty charge of FFg black powder. Also, many of the pipsqueak-bored small-game rifles just don't shoot as well unless loaded with fine FFFg black powder behind a tight-fitting patched round ball. Even so, the use of this powder has declined drastically since the mid 1970s. In the next part of this chapter, we'll take a look at a few other reasons why, and the modern powders that have all but replaced the use of black powder.

Now...

Now... ▪▪▪ Not only have the more popular muzzleloaded big game rifle models gone ultra-modern, but so have the components now being loaded into these rifles. Plastic saboted bullets have gotten noticeably sleeker and more aerodynamic for better retention of velocity and energy down range. Old No. 11 percussion-cap ignition has practically become a thing of the past, and most serious muzzleloading hunters have now gone to much hotter and more sure-fire No. 209 shotshell-primer ignition. And black powder has definitely been replaced by hotter and more efficient modern substitutes.

The new black-powder substitutes can prove a little more difficult to ignite than black powder, and many of the latest rifle models now incorporate much hotter No. 209 primer ignition to guarantee the rifle will fire.

There is an extremely good chance that the majority of you reading this book have never actually fired a load of *real* black powder, even though you may have been muzzleloader hunting for the past ten or fifteen years, or perhaps longer. The heyday of modern *"black powder-shooting"* was likely during the early 1970s. Oh, there are a lot more *muzzleloader shooters* today than there were back then, but not many still load and shoot black powder. So it's kind of ironic that many muzzleloading hunters still refer to the special muzzleloader hunts as *black-powder seasons.*

Over the course of the past three decades, the mixture of potassium nitrate, sulfur and charcoal that had been loaded into firearms of muzzleloaded design since about 1300 has lost ground to several modern *black-powder substitutes.* The one thing early modern black-powder shooters had to accept was that the old powder was extremely dirty, leaving behind a high percentage of each and every load as fouling. That fouling tended to build with each succeeding shot, making every shot harder to load than the one before it. Such fouling also greatly affected accuracy and had to be wiped from the bore after each shot in order to maintain pin-point placement of the next one. Plus, if the shooter failed to give a dirty muzzleloader a good, thorough cleaning after it had been shot, that rifle could be ruined in as little as a day or overnight. It didn't matter if the shooter had fired one shot or a dozen.

Manufacturing black powder has always been a risky business. Domestic production of the old muzzleloader propellant has often been shut down for months at a time due to a mishap that may have destroyed or severely damaged production facilities. Likewise, imported black powder has often been unavailable for one reason or another, and muzzleloading shooters of the 1960s and early 1970s often found themselves faced with a shortage of the necessary propellant.

Pyrodex

Securing a supply of muzzleloader propellant became less troublesome with the development of a brand-new substitute known as Pyrodex during the early 1970s. The powder, invented by Dan Pawlak of Washington state, utilized all the ingredients found in black powder, plus a few other additives that tended to make Pyrodex slightly cleaner burning and more stable. Most importantly, the revamped chemical make-up of the new powder earned it a "Flammable Solid" classification, freeing it from many of the regulations that haunted its explosive predecessor.

Unfortunately, Dan Pawlak never saw the fruition of all the hard work and research he had put into the new powder. An explosion at the original Pyrodex plant in Issaquah, Washington, in January 1977 claimed his life. Fortunately for future muzzleloading shooters and hunters, Hodgdon Powder Company picked up the pieces, built a new facility and put the black-powder substitute into production.

Introduced in the late 1970s, Pyrodex had pretty well replaced black powder by the early 1990s.

Muzzleloader Hunting

I can remember getting a phone call from Bob Hodgdon several months before Pyrodex went on the market. He asked if I would mind doing some shooting with the new propellant, comparing it to black powder. Of course, I jumped at the opportunity. I can also remember receiving two unmarked one-pound white-cardboard containers of the new powder, which sort of looked like coarse Fg black powder, only light gray in color. The only "loading recommendation" that came with the powder was to use about twenty-five percent less if I measured by actual weight.

My first shooting with the pre-production Pyrodex (what I feel became the "RS" grade) indicated that volume-to-volume charges produced about the same velocity and point of impact as the same amount of FFg black powder. Early on, I discovered that the new propellant tended to shoot more consistently, with best ignition when the projectile was seated with about thirty to forty pounds of pressure, somewhat compressing the loose-grain powder charge. Also, when loading with a well-lubed patched round ball or lubed Thompson/Center "Maxi-Ball," I found that I could load three or four shots without *having* to wipe fouling from the bore. While the powder was not as uniform as later production-run Pyrodex, I was very impressed with it from the very beginning. I only wish I had kept one of those unmarked-paper powder containers as a keepsake!

A charge of Pyrodex "RS/Select" and a saboted bullet ready to be loaded for the hunt. The availability of the black-powder substitutes has been a contributing factor in the growth of muzzleloading and muzzleloader hunting.

By 1980, Hodgdon Powder Company offered loose-grain Pyrodex in a variety of grades—"P" grade for pistols; "RS" grade for rifles and shotguns; "C" grade for small cannon; and "Ctg" grade for loading black-powder cartridges. Over the course of the following ten years, Pyrodex quickly replaced black powder as the number-one muzzleloading propellant. During the mid 1990s, Hodgdon began offering compressed Pyrodex Pellets, making it easier than ever to precisely load a muzzleloaded big-game rifle. Loose-grain Pyrodex is approximately twenty-five percent bulkier than black powder, and should be loaded on a volume-to-volume basis to black-powder loads. In other words, a so-called 100-grain charge of Pyrodex "RS," by actual weight, weighs just seventy-five or so grains. Being bulkier, a pound of Pyrodex will give a shooter approximately twenty-five more shots per pound than black powder as well.

Pyrodex Pellets were initially offered only for the .50 caliber in-line rifles, which at that time already represented close to seventy percent of all muzzleloader sales. At first, Hodgdon only offered pellets that were equivalent to a 50-grain charge of FFg black powder. By actual weight, those pellets only weighed around 40 grains, but gave the performance of a 50-grain black-powder charge. To insure consistent ignition of the pellets, one end was coated with a more sensitive *igniter,* which many knowledgeable muzzleloading shooters claim is nothing more than a light coat of black powder. When the pellets are dropped into the bore, the darker igniter end is loaded toward the source of fire for ignition. To enhance a complete burn of the compressed-powder charge, each pellet features a small diameter hole running lengthwise through the pellet, allowing it to burn both from the inside and outside.

Today, Pyrodex Pellets are offered in still more variations, in a variety of weights and for .45 and .54 caliber rifles as well. Quite a few in-line rifle manufacturers now heavily promote the use of a "three-pellet charge"—or loading the equivalent of 150-grains of FFg black powder behind a saboted bullet. With light 150-grain bullets, some of the so-called "Super .45" in-line rifle makers are now boasting of muzzle velocities exceeding 2,500 f.p.s. However, out of a more popular .50 caliber in-line rifle, such a charge will produce around 2,000 to 2,100 f.p.s. with a saboted 250-grain bullet.

When shooting saboted bullets, which are loaded without any lube whatsoever, any shooter looking to produce tight one hundred-yard groups with either loose-grain or pelletized Pyrodex charges will find it absolutely necessary to run a damp cleaning patch down the bore between shots to remove fouling. While Pyrodex fouling may not build as quickly as black powder fouling, after just a couple of shots, pushing another saboted bullet down the bore with the ramrod can become next to impossible. Since this powder is made with the same basic ingredients as black powder, the fouling left behind is just as corrosive—meaning that any rifle that's shot just once will have to be cleaned that same day.

Triple Seven

In 2002, Hodgdon Powder Company brought a totally new black-powder substitute onto the market—Triple Seven. Two qualities separate this powder from the company's earlier (and still widely used) Pyrodex propellant. First, *Triple Seven* does not contain any sulfur in its chemical make-up, resulting in less bore fouling when a charge is burnt. Secondly, this powder is hotter. Significantly hotter. And it produces significantly higher velocities than Pyrodex charges of equal volume.

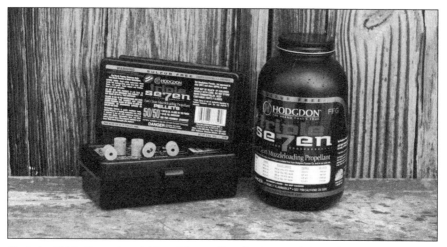

Hodgdon Triple Seven is quickly gaining on Pyrodex in popularity. This new black-powder substitute is "sulfur free" and produces higher velocities than an equal amount of Pyrodex.

Now, Triple Seven is not the first so-called black-powder substitute to be formulated without sulfur. In fact, several such powders existed back in the late 1800s. A propellant known as *ammonpulver* powder was patented in Germany in 1885. The basic ingredients included good ol' saltpeter and charcoal. However, instead of sulfur, this early substitute was made with ammonium nitrate. The resulting powder, depending on the percentages of the ingredients used, often proved nearly as powerful as nitrocellulose-based smokeless powders, and produced very little smoke. Considering that there were still quite a few older muzzleloading guns in use, plus many early breechloaded cartridge guns with weak actions, quite a few were likely lost to the higher pressure produced by such powders.

Instead of wood charcoal, Hodgdon Powder Company utilizes a sugar-based carbon in the production of their all-new Triple Seven. Whether or not the mixture contains ammonium nitrate, the company isn't saying. However, charges of Triple Seven definitely produce higher internal barrel pressures, resulting in faster muzzle velocities. But again, Hodgdon Powder Company has not openly shared the pressures produced by the hot "magnum" hunting charges now favored by the performance-minded muzzleloading hunter.

Since Pyrodex first hit the market in the mid to late 1970s, and especially after the introduction of the compressed Pyrodex Pellet charges, quite a few muzzleloading rifle and loading component makers have conducted their own pressure testing. Out of most .50 caliber modern in-line rifles, a 100-grain charge of Pyrodex "RS/Select" behind a saboted 250-grain bullet will generate around 14,000 p.s.i. inside the barrel. When the rifle is loaded with one of the hot 150-grain charges now promoted by modern in-line rifle makers, the internal barrel pressure jumps to around 20,000 p.s.i. When a 150-grain equivalent load of Triple Seven Pellets is loaded behind a saboted bullet of 250-grains, bore pressure is pushed to 25,000+ p.s.i.

Such higher pressures result in noticeably higher velocities, with either Triple Seven Pellets of loose-grain Triple Seven, which is offered in FFg and FFFg granulations. My favored load for an early Knight stainless steel .50 caliber MK-85 in-line rifle has long been one hundred grains of Pyrodex "Select" (the premium grade of "RS") behind a saboted 260 grain, .451-inch Speer jacketed hollowpoint bullet. The load is good for right at 1,640 f.p.s. at the muzzle. Even when I go to much finer "P" grade Pyrodex in the same dose, the hotter powder only ups velocity to just under 1,700 f.p.s. In comparison, a 100-grain charge of FFFg Triple Seven behind the same saboted bullet out of the same rifle gives 1,865 f.p.s.

(In Chapter 6, "Load Data," we'll get into specific loads in considerably greater detail. Here, we're just detailing the powder choices available to today's muzzleloading hunter.)

For the performance-minded muzzleloading hunter, Triple Seven has to be the best of the current lot of black-powder substitutes. Hodgdon Powder Company will surely offer the powder in a greater variety of granulations and pellet sizes as more and more shooters begin to enjoy the higher velocities, flatter trajectory and harder hitting knockdown power possible with this modern substitute. A few modern in-line rifle manufacturers are already pushing the use of massive 150-grain Triple Seven Pellet loads. Just keep in mind the high pressures produced by such loads—and that many of the older "plunger"-style in-line rifles are not built to handle such pressures.

When time is taken to work up a good load, the combination of Pyrodex or Triple Seven and a saboted bullet, whether all lead or jacketed, can prove deadly accurate.

Muzzleloader Hunting

The powder maker states on its website (www.hodgdon.com): *"Hodgdon Powder Company does not set maximum charges of Triple Seven nor does it provide recommended loads for specific guns. Persons using Triple Seven should not exceed the maximum loads specified by the gun or bullet manufacturer. Exceeding these maximum loads can result in injury or death to the user and/or bystanders."*

Actually, the only complaint I have heard (and personally experienced) with Triple Seven has been the crusty fouling ring it tends to leave in the bore, at approximately the point where the seated projectile sits over the powder charge. After three or four shots, especially with non-lubed saboted bullets, the ring builds to the point where it become difficult to get the next projectile seated in exactly the same spot, which can and usually will affect accuracy. Fouling in the remainder of the barrel is usually very light, and does not hamper loading at all. Fortunately, Triple Seven is completely water (and saliva) soluble, and a lightly dampened patch run down the bore between shots is generally enough to keep the ring buildup from hampering projectile seating.

Like Pyrodex, Triple Seven is bulkier than black powder, and the loose-grain powder should be loaded on a volume-to-volume basis with the propellants' black powder equivalent. The 50-grain Triple Seven Pellets duplicate the performance of a 50-grain charge of black powder. By actual weight, the pellets weigh right at only thirty grains.

Modern Smokeless Powders

Until the past few years, just the thought of loading and shooting modern nitrocellulose-based *smokeless powder* in any muzzleloader was considered strictly taboo. Well, all of that changed with the introduction of the .50 caliber Savage Model 10ML during the summer of 2000.

The "idea man" behind this innovative muzzleloader is a custom gunsmith from Greensboro, North Carolina, by the name of Henry Ball. Back in the mid 1990s, Ball designed a breech plug that incorporated a tiny removable (and replaceable) vent liner that tended to throttle-down the flame from a hot No. 209 primer, making the fire even hotter to insure

Both of these charges are one hundred grains. Granular Pyrodex "RS/Select" is shown at left, two 50-grain Pyrodex pellets at right.

the ignition of hard-to-ignite nitrocellulose-based powders. Although the smallest component in the four patents Ball acquired on the system, that vent liner could also be replaced for just a few dollars once the orifice running through it had become eroded from the hot flash of the shot-shell primer and the heat of the burning powder charge. This was usually after seventy-five to one hundred shots.

Ball's original design utilized reusable stainless steel *ignition modules,* which were chambered into the breech plug. When Savage Arms, of Westfield, Massachusetts, first put his concept into production in 2000, the first model (the Model 10ML) also relied on these modules for carrying the primer into the breech plug. However, during the second year of production, Savage engineers went to work and designed the Model 10ML II, which eliminated the separate ignition module. The new design allowed the primer to fit right into a much smaller chamber in the breech plug. The front of the bolt then became the primer carrier, and extractor.

Thanks to the ingenious design of the breech plug and vent liner, plus the strong modern rifle-grade steel Savage uses in the barrel and receiver of these muzzleloaders, not only are the guns extremely smokeless compatible, the manufacturer actually recommends the use of smokeless powders in this model. With the right combinations of powders, sabots and bullets, these rifles are extremely fast, accurate and hard-hitting. And thanks to the non-fouling, non-corrosive nature of the modern smokeless powders, this futuristic muzzleloading concept is much more user-friendly than any other design that has ever been available.

I first shot Henry Ball's original concept several years before Savage put it into production. Ball had built a number of custom rifles on Mauser, Howa, Sako and other bolt-action center-fire rifle receivers, plus a variety of single-shot actions, including a Ruger No. 1, a Remington rolling-block and even an old BSA Martini action. In 1997, I had him build one in .50 caliber on a Howa Model 1500 bolt-action. That summer, I shot *smokeless muzzleloading* for the very first time— and have ever since.

The designer of this system originally loaded with Winchester 571 ball powder and Alliant 2400 rolled powder. Both are relatively hot, and while the center-fire rifle actions and custom McGowan rifle barrels easily contained the pressures created, the frail plastic sabots of the time simply could not once charges heavier than thirty-three or thirty-four grains were loaded and shot. Still, my initial loads of 33 grains of 2400 produced muzzle velocities of about 2,200 f.p.s. with a saboted 250-grain Hornady XTP. Recoil was extremely light and accuracy exceptional. I quickly discovered I could get this kind of performance with an extremely light charge of powder that burned clean and did not foul the barrel. Plus, if

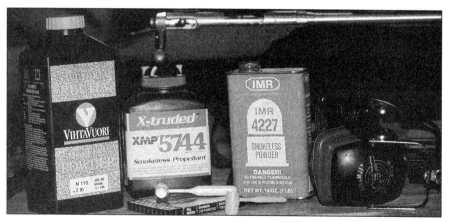

The still-controversial Savage Model 10ML II "smokeless powder" muzzleloader shown with three of the powders the manufacturer recommends for the rifle—from left to right, VihtaVuori N110, Accurate Arms 5744 and IMR-4227.

I shot right 'til dark, I didn't have to worry about cleaning the rifle until the next day . . . the next week . . . or the next month, if I didn't want to.

The first buck I ever shot with the custom Ball smokeless muzzleloader was a nice Iowa eight-pointer that I took on Christmas morning that same year. The deer was with four other good bucks. As the deer filed past my stand, nearly one hundred and seventy-five yards away, I chose the buck I wanted, put the crosshairs right on him and squeezed off the shot. At the crack of the muzzleloader, the deer literally collapsed where it stood.

When Savage put the design into production in early 2000, they asked me to wring out one of the first prototypes, and help them identify those powders that were most compatible. Winchester was phasing out 571 ball powder, which I felt was a little too hot anyway. So, I started with Alliant 2400 and began playing with powders of about the same burn rate. Anything faster proved too hot for the plastic sabot, so I went the other direction. Over the course of the first year, I had found IMR-4227 (or H-4227), VihtaVuori N110 and Accurate Arms XMP5744 to all be outstanding performers in the new .50 caliber Savage Model 10ML.

Thanks to continued load development and the improvement of the polymers used in the sabots today, plus the development of special sub-bases, the Savage Model 10ML II can now be loaded with close to a dozen different smokeless powders. Since that first year of working with the loads for the Model 10ML, the list of compatible powders has grown to include IMR-SR4759, VihtaVuori N120, Accurate Arms XMR2015, VihtaVuori N130 and N133, Alliant Reloder 7, IMR- or H-4198, and a few other "medium burn rate" smokeless powders.

Easily, the author's favorite powder for the Savage muzzleloader is VihtaVuori

N110. With a 45-grain charge of the powder, I've found that I can get a saboted aerodynamic bullet, like the 250-grain Hornady SST, out of the twenty-four-inch Savage barrel right at 2,400 f.p.s., generating an astounding 3,200 foot-pounds of muzzle energy. Out at two hundred yards, this load will punch a big ol' whitetail buck with more than 1,600 foot-pounds of retained energy. That's more energy at that range than my old Knight MK-85 developed at the muzzle with the load I shot back in the early 1990s!

> ## Note:
> There have been a number of Savage 10ML II muzzleloaders seriously damaged by the extremely high pressures of the smokeless loads. Use caution when working with the hotter recommended loads.

Other muzzleloading rifle manufacturers have fought the legalization of the Savage muzzleloader, primarily since their rifles and loads just can't compare. A number of states initially listened to the claims those manufacturers were making about the dangers of smokeless powder in a muzzleloader and banned the use of such powders in any muzzleloaded gun. A few unfortunate incidents with the 10ML II have given the smokeless muzzleloader a bit of a black eye, but the company still claims it is safe. However, technically and legally, both Pyrodex and Triple Seven are classified as "smokeless powders" (early canisters of Pyrodex were even marked "Smokeless Propellant"). Some shooters have challenged game departments, accusing them of discrimination. Even so, Savage has its work cut out for them—to convince game-management officials that the concept is safe.

Today, Savage is no longer alone in the smokeless muzzleloading business. A small company located in north-central Indiana, calling itself Smokeless Muzzleloading, Inc., now offers a drop-in smokeless muzzleloader barrel for the break-open H&R single-shot shotgun actions, and offers the same for the Thompson/Center Arms "Encore 209x50 Magnum." The New Ultra Light Arms, of Granville, West Virginia, is also now marketing another bolt-action smokeless-compatible muzzleloaded big-game rifle. Many of the same powders that shoot so well out of the Savage Model 10ML II also perform nicely out of these rifles as well.

Smokeless muzzleloading very well may be the future of this age-old sport. However, as this was written, in the eyes of some very knowledgeable muzzleloading shooters, the concept still needs far more study and improvement before its ready to be unleashed on the average shooter. Those I know who have made the switch to the Model 10ML II claim they would never go back to shooting "dirty" traditional muzzleloading powders, including Pyrodex or Triple Seven. As one older shooter proclaimed, *"I always thought there was something wrong with a sport when it took longer to clean the rifle than the deer you just shot with it!"* After shooting one of the Savage Model 10ML II rifles for the first time, he bought one. ■

Caution:

If the manufacturer of your muzzleloading rifle does not recommend loading and shooting modern smokeless powders, then it is still muzzleloading as usual—Black Powder, Pyrodex or Triple Seven ONLY!

Smokeless Muzzleloader Velocities Without the Smokeless

Muzzleloader marketing has become a game of *"one upmanship."* No muzzleloading rifle manufacturer wants to market anything but the fastest, flattest, and hardest shooting muzzleloaded big game rifle. And some of the ballistics now being  thrown around by some modern in-line rifle makers are bordering on the impossible.

The need for speed has become one of the major driving factors in muzzleloading rifle and loading component development. More than at any time in history, the muzzleloading hunter is now trying harder and harder to get his front-loaded big game rifle to shoot more and more like a modern center-fire hunting rifle. And some of the more recent models have accomplished that goal.

Perhaps the most controversial muzzleloading rifle available today has been the Savage Model 10ML II. While the majority of shooters have tended to stand back and watch to see if the company has indeed harnessed the efficiency (and dangerously high pressures) of smokeless powders in this rifle, the few who have jumped on the smokeless muzzleloading bandwagon are reporting some extremely top-end velocities. Most of the loads being shot are getting a saboted 250-grain bullet out of the muzzle at around 2,300 f.p.s. But, do you really have to shoot a rifle built to handle smokeless powder to get these kinds of bullet speeds?

One of the top selling and top performing non-smokeless powder frontloaders now available is the Thompson/Center Arms "Omega." And when combined with top-end loads of Hodgdon Powder Company's new Triple Seven black powder substitute, T/C's twenty-eight-inch barreled muzzleloader is giving the Savage muzzleloader a run for its money.

A 100-grain charge of FFFg Triple Seven behind a modern saboted 250-grain bullet, such as T/C's own polymer tipped "Shock Wave," produces a muzzle velocity of right at 2,000 f.p.s. from a .50 caliber Omega. Some shooters have upped charges of FFFg Triple Seven to 130 grains, which brings the velocity up to around 2,275 f.p.s.

So, as you can see, it is possible to load some of the current more advanced in-line rifle models with today's improved black powder substitutes and improved sabot/bullet combinations and take performance into the realm of smokeless ballistics. However, if you are still drawn to the cleaner shooting aspect of smokeless powder loads in the Savage rifle, and others of similar capability that are likely to follow, just be sure that the rifle is legal where you plan to hunt. A very large percentage of states still do not embrace the use of smokeless powders in a muzzleloaded big game rifle.

5

Working Up Loads for Top Performance

Then... Since the first muzzleloading shooter ever decided to actually try to hit a distant target, all muzzleloading shooters with the same intentions have pretty much been faced with the same challenge—determining the top-performing load for the muzzleloader being shot. If a shooter is attempting to use the same muzzleloaded rifle for both competitive shooting and for hunting big game, he or she just may be attempting to bite off more than their frontloader can chew!

Very often, the load that tends to produce the very best accuracy for serious target shooting just can't produce enough energy for effectively bringing down game as large as a whitetail deer. Likewise, the load that generates adequate knockdown power for cleanly harvesting larger game is often built around a type of projectile that may not be allowed during sanctioned matches. Or the projectile may shoot well enough for hunting, but not consistently enough to produce winning scores in competition. And this seems to be more a problem with rifles of traditional styling than with more modern designs. But then, not many matches allow the use of modern in-line rifles anyway, which were designed for the muzzleloading big-game hunter.

Throughout this book, we've discussed the types of rifling required to get the best accuracy from either a patched round ball or a harder-hitting conical bullet. To keep you from having to thumb back or turn ahead to ferret out this information, I'll give you the short interpretation here.

Generally speaking, the patched *round ball* shoots most accurately from a bore that's rifled with .008- to .010-inch-deep grooves that spiral with a relatively slow *one turn-in-sixty to sevety-two inches* (for .50 caliber and larger bores). On the other hand, the bore which tends to turn in the best accuracy with a heavier, longer and much harder-hitting *conical hunting bullet* will commonly feature shallow grooves of around .005-inch depth which spin with a much faster *one-turn-in-twenty to forty-eight inches* rate of rifling twist (again for .50 caliber and larger bores).

All the experimenting in the world with different conical bullets and with varying powder charges most often will not make a slow-twist round ball barrel shoot an elongated bullet accurately enough for either hunting or target use. Nor will a faster twist "bullet-shooting" bore ever match slow-pitch rifling for accuracy with a patched round ball.

The most successful traditionally styled reproduction muzzleloaded rifle ever sold in this country, or in the world for that matter, has been the Thompson/Center Arms "Hawken" rifle. It was introduced during the early 1970s, and is still available today. If the serial numbers that appear on these guns are any indication—both the factory-finished and the kit guns that have been offered in the past—more than 500,000 of them have been sold to modern-day muzzleloading shooters.

When the late Warren Center designed this rifle, his intentions were to offer a rifle that could be loaded with either the patched round ball or an elongated conical bullet he designed in conjunction with the "Hawken." That bullet was the T/C "Maxi-Ball." To accomplish this difficult task, he chose to rifle the bore of the attractive brass-mounted half-stock muzzleloader with a *one-turn-in-forty-eight inches* rate of rifling twist. At best, this rate of twist has proven to be something of a compromise.

Over the years, I have owned and hunted with a half-dozen different T/C "Hawken" rifles. Most of these guns were in .50 caliber, a few in the smaller .45 caliber. All shot the elongated "Maxi" conical bullet relatively well, but only one or two shot a patched round ball well enough to consider them "accurate."

Although the rate of the rifling twist found in the "Hawken" bore could be considered slow enough for good accuracy with the patched round ball and light powder charges, the .005-inch depth of the grooves is simply too shallow. Typically, match-winning round-ball shooters load with a ball diameter that's just .005-inch smaller than actual bore-size. And that ball is patched with material that's .010- to .020-inch in thickness. The shallow grooves in the "Hawken" factory barrel just aren't deep enough to allow loading such a combination. In fact, a ball that's a full .010 inch under bore-size can still prove exceptionally hard to load when patched with .015-inch thick patching material.

The shallow .005-inch grooves of the T/C barrel, however, are perfect for a bore-sized conical bullet like the "Maxi-Ball." Most bullets of this type require some *interference fit* between the soft-lead bullet and the lands of the rifling. In other words, the bullet must be lightly engraved by the rifling. That's how Warren Center designed the "Maxi-Ball"—with a base and middle *bearing band* that ride right on top of the rifling lands when inserted into the muzzle, then a slightly oversized bearing band at the nose. To get this on into the bore generally required the use of a *short starter* to force the bullet into the bore. When it does slip in, the lands of the rifling lightly engrave the soft lead of the band at the nose of the bullet.

Once the bullet has been forced into the bore, most resistance is lost. The bullet can then be seated over the powder charge using only moderate pressure on the ram-rod. However, the fit of the bullet with the bore is sufficient to keep it in place over the powder charge. Then, when the rifle is fired, the force of the expanding gases at the rear of the bullet, plus the momentary obturation (flattening of the bullet in the bore) at the instant of ignition allows the soft lead to be compressed right into the bottoms of the shallow grooves. The result is perfect *bullet-to-bore fit*.

Custom riflemaker Hershel House loads his long-barreled muzzleloader with the same care while hunting as he does during competition shooting.

The .50 caliber T/C "Hawken" rifles I've owned and hunted with have all shot very well with a ninety- or one hundred-grain charge of FFg black powder behind a 370-grain "Maxi-Ball." While the two .45s I've owned also tended to turn in very acceptable hunting accuracy with a 240-grain T/C bullet and seventy to eighty grains of FFFg black powder.

If I were purposely looking for a .45 or .50 caliber rifle designed expressly for shooting a bullet that could be twice (or more) in length as the caliber of the rifle, I'd look for something with a faster *one turn-in-twenty-four to thirty-eight inches* rate of rifling twist. However, the standard factory twist of the "Hawken" barrels does seem to shoot well enough with a conical bullet for most shots on deer-size and larger game out to around one hundred and twenty-five to one hundred and fifty yards.

Quite a few T/C "Hawken" owners have managed to turn their rifles into both a "conical" and a "round ball" rifle by purchasing a second barrel. Green Mountain Rifle Barrel Company offers some exceptionally high-quality barrels that are made to literally *"drop in"* the stock assembly of this rifle. The company offers these in

This is the custom fast-twist-bore bullet rifle the author had built before meeting Tony Knight and experiencing his modern in-line rifle design. Bridges built his rifle with a turn-in-twenty-four inches rate of twist, which shot both heavy conical and early saboted bullets well.

two types—one with a very fast *turn-in-twenty-eight inches* rate of rifling twist for best accuracy with an elongated bullet (bore-sized or saboted), and another .50 or .54 caliber barrel that comes with a slow *turn-in-seventy inches* twist for optimum accuracy with a round ball. So, if the factory barrel shoots a "Maxi"-style bullet just fine, which is usually the case, the purchase of a Green Mountain round ball barrel turns this muzzleloader into a true competition rifle.

Serious Hunting Loads

Since this book is actually devoted to "Muzzleloader Hunting," that's what we'll focus on here. Now, the loads used for hunting big game must deliver a projectile with enough energy to insure a clean kill while still maintaining a relatively high degree of accuracy. In order for that energy to be effective, you first have to put the projectile where it will do the most damage to vital organs.

Very likely seventy to seventy-five percent of today's muzzleloading hunters now rely on modern saboted bullets for the big game they hunt. Of the twenty-five to thirty percent who still use the patched round ball or conical bullet, it's the harder-hitting elongated bullet that easily fills that number-two spot. Quite honestly, fewer than ten percent of all muzzleloading hunters continue to load and shoot with the patched round ball. And that's because of the different muzzleloaded projectiles, the old, simple round ball is the least effective.

Now, quite a few round ball-shooting hunters may want to argue that statement, but knowledgeable muzzleloading hunters who use a patched ball have come to accept the limited effectiveness of the projectile and hunt accordingly. You see,

being a perfect sphere (when loaded, anyway), the lead ball sheds velocity and energy quickly as it heads down range. At the muzzle, a hefty round ball load can produce some pretty impressive energy levels, but once it gets past fifty yards, these levels really take a nose dive. In fact, a .50 caliber Thompson/Center "Hawken" rifle loaded with an 80-grain charge of FFg black powder and a tightly patched .490-inch round ball is good for 1,838 f.p.s. at the muzzle, with just over 1,300 f.p.e. However, by the time the 178-grain sphere of lead reaches one hundred yards, the amount of remaining energy has dropped to only a little more than four hundred foot-pounds.

Success in the deer woods does not begin in the deer woods, but rather at the range.

It is hardly a potent load for taking even game the size of a whitetail.

Most .50 caliber bores, and .54 caliber for that matter, can be stoked to get a patched round ball out of the muzzle at velocities exceeding 2,000 f.p.s., creating energy levels topping 2,000 f.p.e. But even these round ball loads are, at best, fifty to sixty yard effective loads. For example, a round ball that left the muzzle of a .50 caliber rifle at 2,000 f.p.s. will generate 1,580 f.p.e. But even this "magnum" round ball load will hit a whitetail with only about 500 f.p.e. at one hundred yards.

As bores get bigger, the more powder it takes to tap into the energy potential of the larger diameter and heavier ball. Back in the 1970s, Lyman Products

Muzzleloading hunter Glenn Thompson with a respectable record-book central-barren-ground caribou taken at almost two hundred yards, shooting a load he spent much of the previous summer building and shooting for repeatable performance.

conducted extensive testing of different powder charges and projectiles in every caliber muzzleloading rifle available. The highest velocity they could get out of a 32-inch .58 caliber barrel with a patched 279-grain .570-inch diameter round ball was about 1,730 f.p.s. To do that required loading with 180 grains of FFg black powder! The load was good for about 1,850 f.p.e., which dwindled to only about 675 f.p.e. out at one hundred yards.

Unfortunately, too many self-proclaimed black-powder authorities are overly romantic about the past and will readily tout the effectiveness of the ancient patched round ball as a big-game hunting projectile. Every time I hear an argument for how these simple projectiles somehow "magically" deliver that lethal blow to such game, just one question comes to mind: *"If the spheres of lead were so effective, why then were shooters during the early 1800s so quick to abandon the round ball in favor of conical bullets?"*

The answer is simple. The patched round ball just does not maintain energy well enough to be considered a truly effective big-game hunting projectile, even when fired with heavy hunting powder charges. *If you enjoy a nostalgic link to the past and feel compelled to hunt deer and other big game with a muzzleloader loaded with a patched ball, use something big and think twice about taking shots that approach one hundred yards . . . or farther.*

As already discussed in Chapter 3, "Muzzleloader Projectiles," bore-sized conical bullets have been with us in one form or another since the 1830s, and when loaded into any copy of an original percussion-rifle design, the bullets are just as traditional as the round ball. Percussion-rifle production didn't really begin until the mid to late 1820s, and within a few years of their introduction, shooters were playing around with improved elongated projectiles for greater game-taking effectiveness out past one hundred yards. And once riflemakers of the period learned the relationship between the size of the bore, bullet length and rate of rifling twist, the longer bullets generally also proved far more accurate at extended ranges. Today's muzzleloading hunter has a tremendous variety of bore-sized conical bullets from which to choose.

Thompson/Center Arms still offers the original "Maxi-Ball," plus a newer design known as the "Maxi-Hunter." Buffalo Bullet Company markets a line of cold-swaged conical bullets that feature a knurled surface running practically the length of the bullet. Hornady Manufacturing offers a very similar design known as the "Great Plains Bullet." Lee Precision of Hartford, Wisconsin, offers a line of REAL (Rifling Engraved At Loading) bullets in several lengths and weights for the .45, .50 and .54 caliber rifles.

Other great conical bullets available include the Parker Productions "Hydra-Con" and the White Rifles "Power Punch." Except for the White "Power Punch" in the same company's over-size bored in-line rifles, all of these bullets require engraving with the rifling when loaded. In rifles with normal bore-sizes, the White conical will also require that the bullet be engraved—just to get it into the bore!

One of the most popular bore-sized conical bullets available today combines a bit of the past with a bit of the present and future. Originally introduced as the "Black Belt" bullet, and currently sold as the "Power Belt," this design has won a strong following thanks to how easily it loads, plus the exceptional accuracy it delivers out of some rifles.

The bullet itself is .001 or .002 of an inch under bore-

This shooter has his Austin & Halleck in-line rifle grouping well; now it's time to make his final scope adjustment.

size. However, snapped onto a small post protruding from the rear of the bullet is a plastic skirt or base. This piece is .001 or .002 larger than the land-to-land measurement of the bore, so the design can be easily inserted into the bore and seated with very, very little exertion on the ramrod. The slightly oversized plastic skirt fits

Muzzleloader Hunting

just snug enough to keep the bullet in place over the powder.
Then, when the rifle is fired, the
hollow base of the skirt expands
into the rifling. But that alone
does not provide the bullet-to-bore
fit. "Power-Belt" bullets are
swaged from a very soft lead, and
when the powder charge ignites,
the obturation of the bullet is
enough to cause the slightly undersized projectile to flatten into the
grooves of the rifling.

Whether a shooter chooses
an original conical bullet design,
one of the popular conical bullets
from the 1970s and '80s, or a
more recent design, if it can be

Both the load and a shooter's ability can determine
the maximum effective range of a muzzleloading
rifle. In some states, regulations that prohibit
scopes can also determine just how far a
shooter should attempt a shot.

shot accurately ahead of a hunting charge of powder, it will deliver considerably
more knockdown power than the patched round ball. For comparison, let's go back
to the 370-grain Thompson/Center "Maxi-Ball," the first conical muzzleloding bullet I ever hunted with. When I load that big hunk of lead with a 100-grain charge
of Pyrodex "RS/Select," it is pushed from the muzzle of a twenty-eight-inch T/C
"Hawken" .50 caliber barrel at about 1,500 f.p.s., and develops right at 1,850 foot-
pounds of knockdown power. Being more aerodynamic than the patched round ball,
the bullet maintains velocity and energy better down range. At one hundred yards,
the big bullet would hit with just over 1,100 f.p.e., and close to 800 f.p.e. at one
hundred and fifty yards.

Through the 1970s, the T/C "Hawken" rifle and "Maxi-Ball" conical bullet
was the most widely used muzzleloader hunting combination.

Loading Tips

It should go without saying: Any hunter serious enough to hunt big game with a
muzzleloaded rifle should purchase the very best quality rifle he or she can afford.
When it comes to muzzleloading guns, there actually is something to the old saying,
"You get what you pay for!"

A $150 to $200 bargain-basement special muzzleloading rifle simply is not going to be equipped with as good a quality barrel as a top-of-the-line muzzleloader that can cost $500 or more. And while experienced shooters may be able to overcome less-than-great features, such as a tough five-pound plus trigger or slow lock time, a rifle that comes fitted with a barrel of shoddy quality can only be expected to deliver accuracy of the same quality. Sure, a bore that has a few rough spots can often be lapped and made to shoot better. But the time and frustration involved may prove more costly than the extra $$$ it takes to simply buy better quality in the first place.

The spontaneity of ignition will surely affect how well the vast majority of us shoot a particular muzzleloaded rifle. For that reason, the first-time or inexperienced muzzleloading shooter is advised to stick with a good percussion-ignition system. Leave the flintlocks for those with the nerves of steel or the solid hold of a bench-mounted vise. Any ignition system, flint or percussion, that has even a millisecond delay or lag in the time it takes for the hammer to drop, the priming

powder or cap to fire, and the resulting fire to reach the powder charge in the barrel, offers time for the shooter to move or flinch. The more spontaneous the ignition, the more likely most of us will hit the target.

Black powder, Pyrodex and even Hodgdon's new Triple Seven all leave considerable powder fouling behind when a muzzleloaded gun is fired. While the fouling left by the newer black-powder substitutes may not build as quickly as the fouling left

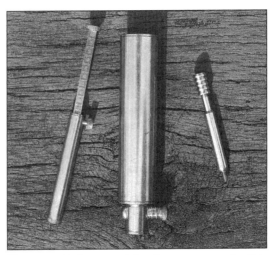

The secret to muzzleloader accuracy is the consistency of the loads, meaning the muzzleloading shooter will need an accurate means of measuring powder. When loading and shooting, a good cleaning jag will also be needed to wipe fouling between shots.

behind by a burning charge of real black powder, it can still affect accuracy.

Always take time to run a damp patch down the bore between shots to keep fouling to a minimum. This isn't to say that a bore must be spotless to turn in its best accuracy, but the fouling that accumulates from two or three shots can severely affect where the next shot goes. When shooting at the range, I have gotten into the habit of dampening a cleaning patch with saliva, running it down the bore with the cleaning jag on my ramrod (or auxiliary loading/cleaning rid), and pulling it back

If a muzzleloading big-game hunter has never shot his rifle and load at two hundred yards, or farther, then he or she has absolutely no business shooting at game at that distance.

out. Then, I turn the patch over and repeat the same process. This takes only a minute or so to do, and will keep fouling from affecting loading or accuracy. When hunting, if my first shot is where it is supposed to be, most times I do not even have to worry about cramming down a second shot. But I usually do, and for that reason, I rarely hunt with a load that utilizes black powder any longer. The lighter fouling left behind by Pyrodex or Triple Seven charges will easily permit a second shot with little effect on accuracy. However, if a third shot is needed, I will wipe the bore in the same manner as at the range before loading it.

Most muzzleloaded rifles will tend to shoot the first shot out of a perfectly clean bore an inch or two away from where the same load will print following shots—even if the bore has been wiped with a damp patch between shots. White Rifles has long been an advocate of firing a "fouling shot" before going for accuracy with any of their rifles, and few (if any) top-ranked competition muzzle-loading shooters will ever take a scoring shot with a rifle that has not already been fired at least once. When hunting game the size of a whitetail or larger, a shot that hits an inch, one way or the other, from where the shooter was holding at the moment of the shot really won't change whether or not the game is harvested. However, during a match where it takes five straight "bull's-eyes" just to be in the running, a first shot that is an inch off usually means someone else will take home top honors.

Conical bullet shooters have long known that best accuracy with these heavy hunks of soft lead is very often achieved when additional loading components are loaded between the powder charge and base of the bullet. Since the introduction of the elongated bullet in the early 1800s, some shooters have loaded either wool-felt or heavy card wads under the bullet to somewhat protect it from the burning powder charge. Without this added protection, the hot gases can cut the edges of the base, resulting in slight differences in every bullet that exits the muzzle. And it doesn't take much to severely change point of impact at one hundred yards.

A more modern approach for shooters of .50 caliber bullet rifles is to use the gas seal cut from the base of some one-piece plastic 28-gauge wads. I've found that the gas seal, or obturator cup, clipped from the rear of a Winchester 28-gauge "AA" wad is a perfect fit for most .50 caliber bores. This cup seems to do a much better job at sealing off the powder charge than felt or card wads.

Getting good accuracy and plenty of knockdown power for hunting larger game with a traditionally styled muzzleloading rifle or projectile simply takes making the effort to find the combination that works best out of a given rifle. Often it is the little things that make the biggest differences, such as the seating pressure used when ramrodding the projectile home over the powder charge. Always pay close attention to how each and every load is stuffed in. When you find one that lives up to your expectations, remember to load that rifle with the same components and in the same exact manner each and every time. Consistency has its rewards, and with a muzzleloaded rifle it's better accuracy and dependable performance.

Now...

Greater versatility . . . better accuracy . . . more range . . . less recoil . . . harder-hitting knockdown power. These are some of the reasons why modern-day muzzleloading shooters and hunters have abandoned the patched round ball or heavy bore-sized conical bullets and made the switch to plastic-saboted bullets. With each new hunting season, the number of muzzleloading shooters who forsake traditionally loaded guns and pick up a modern sabot-loaded in-line rifle for the first time continues to grow. And most are not looking back.

In almost the span of a single decade, plastic-saboted bullets overcame the criticism of most veteran black-powder shooters (and the muzzleloading industry as well) to become the most widely shot muzzleloaded hunting projectile. First introduced in the mid 1980s, the use of plastic sabots and jacketed handgun bullets were initially outlawed in more than a dozen states, and shunned by traditional muzzleloading hunters who felt that the projectile system made this old sport too modern. More than one manufacturer of muzzleloading guns even stated in their owners' manuals that the use of a plastic sabot would void the warranty on the rifle. They claimed that the small plastic sleeves left a buildup of dangerous residue in the bore that would hamper loading and prevent the shooter from properly seating the projectile

over the powder. But hunters liked the way saboted bullets shot and, equally important, how well they performed on game.

The role of the sabot is much like the role of the cloth patch used for loading and shooting a round ball. The cup-shaped sabot fills the void between the undersized projectile and the larger bore of the rifle. It also grips the rifling and transfers the spin of the bore to the bullet. When the sabot and bullet exit the bore,

Blunt-nosed hollow-point bullets like this 250-grain Nosler will slow quickly and lose energy fast, resulting in considerable drop once past one hundred or one hundred and fifty yards.

the thin plastic sleeves peel away from the bullet and a very well-designed modern projectile is on its way to the target.

One of the true benefits of hunting with saboted bullets is the opportunity to better tailor a load for the game being hunted. Today's shooter can decide whether to purchase the sabots alone, then match them with a bullet of their choice . . . or they can take a more convenient route and choose from an unbelievable selection of bullets and sabots that have already been matched and packaged. Knight Rifles, Thompson/Center Arms, Hornady Manufacturing, Nosler, Barnes Bullets and quite a few others now offer saboted bullets for the top-selling .50 caliber rifles, plus most have saboted offerings for both the .45 and .54 as well.

Since the introduction of the muzzleloaded sabot system by Muzzleload Magnum Products back in the mid 1980s, shooters have taken a lot of game with a variety of jacketed handgun bullets. These, especially some for the better-designed jacketed hollow-point bullets, offer a tremendous transfer of energy, and have proven to be great performers at moderate one hundred- to one hundred-fifty-yard ranges. However, today's top-end performance in-line rifles are fully capable of two hundred- to two hundred-fifty-yard performance, and more and more bullet makers are now leaning in the direction of more aerodynamic shapes that better retain velocity and energy out to and past the two hundred-yard mark.

One of the best-selling recent designs has been the Hornady "SST"—the designation standing for *Super Shock Tip.* This very modern bullet is purely a true *rifle bullet* that has been designed to be shot out of a muzzleloader with a sabot. The "SST" features a copper jacket that tapers in thickness, being heavier at the base and becoming thinner toward the sharp spire-point tip. The tip is made of a tough polymer material that pushes back into a slight hollow internal cavity upon impact. This insures that the bullet expands, while Hornady has incorporated the same InterLock ring round in its center-fire "SST" bullets to also guard against over expansion and fragmentation of the bullet. At this writing, Hornady offered the muzzleloader "SST" bullets in 250- and 300-grain for the popular .50 caliber rifles, plus a sleek 200-grain bullet for the .45 caliber bores.

Both Barnes Bullets and Precision Rifle Bullets also offer extremely aerodynamic designs for today's long-range performance-minded muzzleloading hunter. The Barnes "Spit-Fire" is an all-copper design that is basically an updated and improved version of the company's earlier "Expander MZ" saboted bullets. Barnes offers the "Spit-Fire" (at this writing) in two weights for the .50 caliber: 245- and 285-grain. Both feature a slight boat-tail base and sleek, sharp, hollow-point frontal design that cuts through the air with less effort than the huge hollow-point nose of the earlier "Expander MZ" design.

Precision Rifle offers a great selection of sleek poly-tipped spire-point cold-swaged lead bullets that bring a new level of aerodynamics into the muzzle-loading arena. The company's "Dead Center" line offers nearly a dozen choices for .45, .50 and .54 caliber rifles. Probably the bullet that offers the best retention of velocity and energy is the company's unique .40x.50 260-grain "Dead Center." This is a .400-inch diameter bullet, loaded into a special sabot for loading into and out of a .50 caliber rifle. The bullet offers what is likely the highest ballistic coefficient of any current saboted muzzleloader bullet, a b.c. of .376! What this means is that at the same 2,000 f.p.s. muzzle velocity, this bullet will exhibit only about one third the drop from one hundred to two hundred yards as a big hollow-point saboted bullet, like the 260-grain Speer .451-inch "JHP," which incidentally has a b.c. of just .150.

Unique new designs like the .40x.50 "Dead Center" will surely carry saboted-bullet design on into the future. However, most of the best-performing saboted bullets currently tend to be those that are as close to bore diameter as possible, and still leave room for use of a sabot. Most .50 caliber rifles tend to turn in their best performance with .451- to .452-inch diameter bullets, and some of the better performing choices for the .45 caliber in-line rifles now utilize a .400-inch diameter bullet.

Muzzleloader Hunting

William "Tony" Knight checking out one of his in-line ignition rifle designs and hunting load before going on a hunt.

Back in the late 1980s, Knight Rifles pretty much popularized the one-turn-in-twenty-eight inches rate of rifling twist as the best choice for saboted bullets. However, until the mid 1990s, practically all saboted bullets shot were relatively short in length, like the 250-grain .452-inch Hornady "XTP" or the 260-grain .451-inch Speer "JHP." The new all-copper "Expander MZ" designs from Barnes Bullets were noticeably longer, and while they still shot well out of the one-turn-in-twenty-eight-inches twist bores, they likely would have shot better out of something with a little faster pitch. With still longer overall bullet designs, like the "SST," "Spit-Fire" and "Precision Rifle" bullets, a few companies have gravitated to a faster one-turn-in twenty-four inches rate of rifling twist, such as that found in the Savage Model 10ML II and White Rifles muzzleloaders.

Velocity and range have become the new rage among muzzleloading hunters. The makers of most recent in-line rifle models have been pushing hard the use of hot 150-grain charges of Pyrodex or Triple Seven—in granular or pellet form. Such loads will get saboted 250-grain bullets out of the muzzle at around 2,000 f.p.s. (Yeah, I know several rifle makers have been claiming 2,200 f.p.s., but take those velocities with a grain of salt!) At such speeds, we're talking muzzle energies in the 2,200 foot-pound range with a 250-grain bullet and 2,650 foot-pound range with a 300-grain bullet. With one of the sleeker bullet designs, like the Hornady "SST," the above load for the 300-grain bullet would retain more than 1,300 f.p.e. out at two hundred yards.

Sabots today are produced from a tougher, more resilient polymer material than they were just a few years back. Consequently, they will withstand a lot more pressure from such heavy charges. One major bullet maker discovered that 150-grain charges of Triple Seven Pellets behind a saboted 250-grain bullet would produce internal barrel pressures of around 29,000 p.s.i. Now, this is hot for a non-smokeless powder. That much pressure can still damage the plastic bullet carrier that separates the projectile from the powder charge, and which transfers the twist of the rifling to the bullet.

To counter such "magnum" pressures, veteran sabot shooters looking to tap the full potential of a modern in-line rifle design like the Thompson/Center Arms "Omega" or Knight Rifles "Revolution" are now loading a sub-base between the powder charge and sabot base. Well, as you may have already guessed, the sub-base many are using in .50 caliber rifles is again nothing more than the gas seal or obturator cup that has been cut from the rear of a 28-gauge plastic shotgun wad. It is loaded, cupped-base down, right over the powder charge, then the sabot and bullet are loaded squarely on top. The sub-base then becomes the primary gas seal, and the sabot simply becomes a bullet carrier.

Muzzleload Magnum Products, who brought us the muzzleloading sabot system, now also offers a more thought-out .50 caliber sub-base, which the company offers as a *Ballistic Bridge Sub-Base.* The design features a deeper-cupped base than either the base of the sabot or the cup at the rear of a 28-gauge wad gas seal. Then the top of the MMP sub-base is domed to fit right up into the cupped base of the sabot that's loaded over it. Personally, I do not think a shooter can blow this sub-base with loads of any black-powder substitute currently available. Even with the hottest loads of Triple Seven that I have shot (150 grains of FFFg Triple Seven), the cupped base is nicely flared and displays very positive rifling marks, while the base of the sabot loaded ahead of the sub-base almost looks as if it wasn't even shot.

The smokeless powder loads now being shot out of the bolt-action Savage Model 10ML II, Smokeless Muzzleloading, Inc. break-open rifles and the New Ultra Light Arms bolt-action muzzleloaded rifles are definitely hotter than even the hottest loads recommended for any other in-line muzzleloading rifle. And the higher pressures created by these loads make more demands on the integrity of the sabot, and bullet for that matter. Getting optimum performance from these rifles often requires taking an entirely new look at how the rifles are loaded.

I've been fortunate enough to have been shooting with the "Savage System" since several years before the company put it into production. The design is actually the brainchild of a North Carolina custom gunsmith by the name of Henry Ball. Back in the late 1990s, Ball asked that I wring out his patented new design, and help him find the powders that performed best out of his custom smokeless muzzleloaders. As this is written, I have now logged more than 35,000 rounds through his and Savage built .50 caliber Model 10ML and 10ML II rifles.

The powders and charges capable of producing 2,300+ f.p.s. velocities with a saboted 250-grain bullet in the Savage Model 10ML II generate internal barrel pressures that are in the 40,000+ p.s.i. range. Now, such pressures can totally destroy other in-line muzzleloaders, so don't try them in your rifle . . . unless it is a Savage Model 10ML II or any other newer rifle specifically built to be shot with such powders—and clearly condoned by the rifle's maker. If the barrel of your gun is marked "Black Powder Only" (or even "Pyrodex" or "Triple Seven Only"), then it is still muzzleloading as usual. If you want to shoot cleaner-burning, non-corrosive, better-performing, easier-to-find and more economical nitrocellulose-based smokeless powders in a muzzleloader, you'll first have to buy a rifle that's been designed, engineered and built to be shot with such powders.

The powders which perform best out of the .50 caliber Savage rifle can be found in the range of so-called *medium burn rate* smokeless powders. Accurate Arms 5744, VihtaVuroi N110 and N120, IMR4227 (or Hodgdon's H4227) plus Alliant 2400 and Reloder 7 have all proven to be excellent performers in this rifle. However, Model 10ML II shooters quickly discover that those powders on the hotter end of this spectrum tend to be more finicky, requiring extremely precise weighing on a powder scale to insure uniformity of the charges and the consistency of the groups shot. Slower powders, like Reloder 7 and VihtaVuori N120, tend to be more forgiving, allowing shooters to use simple dipper measures, like those available from Lee Precision, to quickly and easily find a useable powder charge. Medium-burn rate smokeless powders that are on the slower burning end of the range can be off as much as one-half grain and still deliver one-and-a-half-inch 100-yard accuracy.

Easily my favorite powder for the Savage Model 10ML II has been VihtaVuori N110. With as little as 42 grains, I can get a saboted 250-grain bullet out of the muzzle at more than 2,300 f.p.s., and generate just over 2,900 f.p.e. When things cool down in the fall and I don't have to worry about the barrel of the Savage muzzleloader heating up too quickly, I usually move on up to 44 or 45 grains of N110 behind one saboted 250-grain bullet or another, my favorite weight for use on whitetails. Such loads get the bullet moving out of the muzzle at an astounding 2,400 f.p.s. and produce a muzzle energy of right at 3,200 foot-pounds. With an aerodynamic bullet design like the 250-grain Hornady "SST" or 245-grain Barnes "Spit-Fire," the hotter loads of N110 result in just three to four inches of drop from

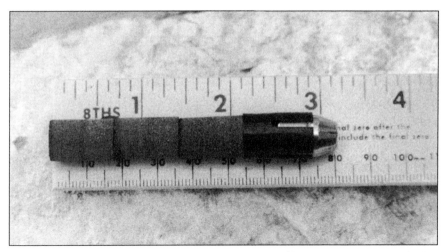

Did you know that a three-pellet 150-grain charge of Pyrodex and saboted bullet take up more than three inches of a rifle's bore?

one hundred to two hundred yards, allowing pretty much a dead-on hold when a deer walks out, whether at fifty yards or two hundred yards. And when that bullet reaches two hundred yards, it will hit with nearly 1,700 foot-pounds of knockdown power.

Whether today's performance-minded muzzleloading hunter goes with one of the newer non-smokeless designs, like the Knight Rifles "Revolution" or the popular Thompson/Center Arms "Encore 209x50 Magnum" and a stout charge of Triple Seven behind a light saboted bullet, or the new smokeless Savage Model 10ML II with its upper-end muzzleloader velocities and energy levels, muzzleloading has changed. Not only have performance levels been raised, but getting those performance levels has gotten easier than at any time in the past. Today's powders, especially the compressed Pryodex and Triple Seven charges, are more user-friendly than any powder from the past. They burn cleaner (especially the smokeless loads in the Savage) with less fouling of the bore, while delivering higher velocities and energy transfer to the target.

More than eighty percent of all muzzleloading hunters in the U.S. and Canada now hunt with a muzzleloader of modern in-line design, and the vast majority of those rifles are loaded with an equally modern saboted bullet. And it is all because today's rifles and loads are the best-performing hunting muzzleloaders of all time. Any shooter who will follow simple instructions and take the time to read a book such as this can take a brand-new in-line muzzleloading rifle and have it shooting saboted bullets with outstanding hunting accuracy in just a few hours. All the work . . . all the testing . . . and just about all the load development has already been done for you.

Sabot Loading Tips

It has never been easier to get great hunting performance from a muzzleloaded big-game rifle. The quality and consistency of today's in-line rifles and loading components is nothing short of amazing. About all a shooter has to do is find a load that has the velocity, energy and saboted bullet design he or she is looking for, then sight in for that load and go hunting. Well, almost!

Modern saboted bullets are loaded without any lubrication whatsoever on the sabot. Not only is the polymer used to make today's sabots exceptionally strong, it is also pretty darn slick. Even very tight-fitting sabot-and-bullet combinations can be pushed down with minimum exertion on the ramrod once they have been started into the bore.

A buildup of powder fouling in the bore likely affects the loading and accuracy of saboted bullets more than any other muzzleloader projectile. Without any lube on the sabot, black powder, Pyrodex, and even Triple Seven charges will quickly leave a layer of fouling in the bore. As few as two shots may make it impossible to ramrod the third sabot and bullet down to the exact same spot. Wiping the bore is critical to obtain good accuracy and reliable performance with these bullets.

As with loading and shooting a patched round ball or conical bullet, simply dampen a cleaning patch with a small amount of saliva, then run the patch down the

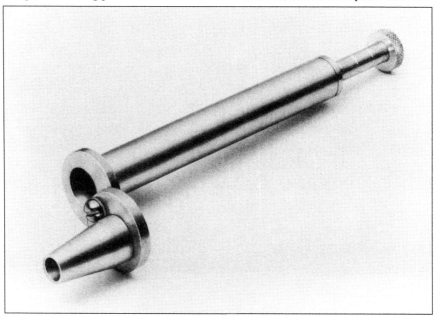

The shooter who loads with loose-grain (granular) powders will need a reliable powder measure to insure the same volume of powder each and every time a load is dumped through the muzzle.

bore. Pull it back to the muzzle, turn it over and run it down again. This will keep the bore easy to load, and those saboted bullets hitting right where you want them.

Pelletized powders, such as Pyrodex Pellets and Triple Seven Pellets, sure are handy when loading in the field, and they do eliminate the need for using a "volume type" powder measure. Most shooters simply drop in two or three of the so-called 50-grain pellets, push a sabot and bullet over these, place a cap on the nipple or primer in the chamber, and they're ready to go.

However, shooters who really take the time to compare usually find that careful-ly measured charges of granular Pyrodex "RS/Select" or FFg and FFFg Triple Seven will produce better groups. It's not that the powders in this form are actually better, it's just that when the shooter takes the time to measure out these charges, they do tend to be more consistent. By actual weight, a 50-grain (black powder equivalent) pellet of Triple Seven weighs only about thirty grains. Shooters have taken a 100-pellet box and weighed each and every

If you look very closely, you'll see that this hunter has marked his ramrod so that the mark is flush with the muzzle when his load is correctly seated.

pellet on an electronic scale, to find that from high to low there can be about a two-and-a-half-grain variation in pellet weight.

When loaded right out of the box, a hefty three-pellet charge of Triple Seven could be as much as seven-and-a-half grains off. With such a hot black substitute, that is enough to really open groups at one hundred yards. I ran into that problem with several rifles. However, when I took the time to weigh my pellets on an RCBS electronic powder scale, then separate them into lots that were within two-tenths or three-tenths of a grain, a rifle that would not punch a two-inch one-hundred-yard group with non-weighed pellets would consistently produce sub one-and-a-half-inch groups.

Saboted bullets can be very seating-pressure sensitive. Always try to use around thirty to forty pounds of pressure on the ramrod when loading over loose-grain Pyrodex or Triple Seven in any in-line rifle, and especially when loading saboted bullets over the smokeless loads in the Savage Model 10ML II. Surprisingly, a shooter can develop a feel for seating pressure after loading just a few rounds. Most mark their ramrods to indicate that their load of choice is seated all the way. When the mark on the rod is flush with the muzzle, the bullet is where it should be. If the mark disappears into the muzzle, it must mean that the shooter either didn't load a sufficient amount of powder . . . or forgot to dump in powder altogether.

Aerodynamic new bullet designs like the 220-grain all-copper Knight "Red Hot" bullet (by Barnes) generally exhibit a lot less drop out around two hundred yards than less aerodynamic flat-faced hollow-point bullets.

When loading with compressed-pellet charges, always take care not to crush or crumble those pellets. Any charge with a crushed pellet or two will definitely shoot differently than a charge that has been loaded properly, without crushing any of the pellets. Since these powder charges are already compressed, just make contact of the sabot with the powder charge, then let up on the ramrod pressure.

Heat is the number-one enemy of the saboted bullet. Never transport a package of saboted bullets laying on the dashboard of your car or pickup. Repeated exposure to high heat can quickly deteriorate the plastic, plus if you load a hot sabot into a hot barrel, you simply aren't going to hit what you're shooting at. Store sabots in a cool place.

When shooting at the range, always give your rifle some cool-down time between shots. During late summer, when many muzzleloading hunters rush to the range to check out their favorite muzzleloader hunting loads, temperatures can still top out in the 90s. It doesn't take too many shots before that barrel is hot, and a plastic sabot loaded into a hot barrel doesn't take long to become softer and less resilient. Even with moderately heavy charges of Pyrodex or Triple Seven, the sabot may not stand up to the pressures created. One thing is for certain, you won't get the same degree of accuracy with a hot barrel as you do with a barrel that has been placed in the shade and allowed to cool down for six or seven minutes.

Take your time and enjoy the time you spend working up the load you will be hunting with. It's that personal effort each of us puts into getting our rifles to shoot and shoot well that makes muzzleloader hunting so enjoyable.

Good shooting. ∎

6
Load Data

H unters today are more ballistics conscious than at any time in history, and this includes the current crowd of muzzleloading hunters. Back when I first started hunting deer with a .45 caliber Dixie Gun Works percussion "Kentucky" rifle, I had no idea of what kind of velocity and energy my load was producing. The thought simply never entered my mind. All I knew was that the 70-grain charge of FFFg black powder and light patched 128-grain .440-inch round ball shot accurately, and it brought down every whitetail I shot at with the rifle. Sure, some ran one hundred or more yards before going down, but the rifle and load did everything I could ask of the combination.

Back then, it probably wouldn't have mattered much to me to know that my

hunting load was good for right at 1,900 f.p.s. and 1,025 f.p.e. at the muzzle. There was little written about muzzleloading at that time, and even less about muzzleloader ballistics. Today, I wouldn't even consider going after deer-sized game with such a load. But in the early 1960s, I felt my long-barreled Dixie reproduction muzzleloader was far superior to the modern shotguns and slug loads the vast majority of other hunters used to hunt deer in my home state of Illinois.

In the following load data, you can get a good idea of the ballistics you can expect from any .45, .50 or .54 caliber muzzleloaded big-game rifle that's available today. Just remember, it is *energy* that brings the game down, not *velocity!*

The muzzleloading hunter of the past had to make every shot count. Often far from civilization, he found powder and lead were usually in short supply.

The exceptionally long 44-inch barrel found on this superb-condition original circa 1770 "Pennsylvania" flintlock was needed to fully tap every bit of performance that could be produced by the moderately light charges of black powder shot back then. It was not as refined as the black powder of today.

Then...

The main reason for the truly long forty- to forty-four-inch barrels found on original "Pennsylvania" and "Kentucky" rifles of the mid to late 1700s was to better utilize all the power a moderate sixty- to seventy-grain charge of black powder could produce. This was accomplished by providing enough bore to allow the charge to be completely burnt. If we could get our hands on some of the powders that were produced at that time, we would likely find that the quality is nowhere near that of a fresh can of today's GOEX black powder. Neither would the granules be of such consistent size. And because of all that, it is unlikely that the same amounts of those older black powders would produce the same velocities that are possible with today's black powder.

As discussed in Chapter 4, "A Look at Muzzleloader Propellants," the quality of black powder produced shortly after the turn of the 19th century improved dramatically, thanks to newly adopted screening techniques and powder grading. Likewise, the performance of the powder from maker to maker became more consistent. With the improved burning characteristics of the powder produced shortly before and on through the Civil War, the average length of a muzzleloaded rifle barrel was cut to around thirty-two or thirty-four inches. And these guns were fully capable of obtaining velocities equal to those produced by the longer barrels found on earlier American long rifles.

Shooters will experience slight differences in the velocities produced by some of the imported black powders, compared to the same grade of GOEX, but not enough to be of any real concern. All of the following traditional patched round ball and conical bullet ballistics were achieved shooting American-made GOEX black powder or appropriate Pyrodex powders out of modern-manufactured reproduction muzzleloading rifles.

Patched Round Ball Loads
(Black Powder)

Rifle/Cal.	Barrel	Powder	Ball Dia./Wt.	Velocity	Energy
T/C Hawken .45	28"	70 gr. FFg	.440"/128 gr.	1,675 f.ps.	850 f.p.e.
T/C Hawken .45	28"	70 gr. FFFg	.440"/128 gr.	1,860 f.p.s.	985 f.p.e.
Dixie Penn. Rifle .45	41½"	70 gr. FFFg	.440"/128 gr.	1,970 f.p.s.	1,105 f.p.e.
Lyman Trade Rifle .50	28"	80 gr. FFg	.490"/178 gr.	1,690 f.p.s.	1,130 f.p.e.
Lyman Gr. Plains .50	32"	90 gr. FFFg	.490"/178 gr.	1,890 f.p.s.	1,410 f.p.e.
Traditions Ky. .50	40"	90 gr. FFg	.490"/178 gr.	1,780 f.p.s.	1,250 f.p.e.
T/C Hawken .54	28"	100 gr. FFg	.530"/224 gr.	1,645 f.p.s.	1,345 f.p.e.
Lyman Gr. Plains .54	32"	100 gr. FFg	.530"/224 gr.	1,680 f.p.s.	1,405 f.p.e.
Zouave .58	32½"	70 gr. FFg	.570"/278 gr.	1,180 f.p.s.	860 f.p.e.

Note: Rifles of the same caliber with the same length barrel will produce very similar velocities to those listed here when loaded with same volume and granulation of black powder.

This traditional flintlock shooter practices from a sitting position on a slightly elevated platform. The elevation sort of duplicates shooting from a treestand.

Patched Round Ball Loads
(Pyrodex)

Rifle/Cal.	Barrel	Powder	Ball Dia./Wt.	Velocity	Energy
T/C Hawken .45	28"	70 gr. "P"	.440"/128 gr.	1,750 f.p.s.	870 f.p.e.
T/C Hawken .50	28"	90 gr. "RS"	.490"/178 gr.	1,835 f.p.s.	1,325 f.p.e.
T/C Hawken .54	28"	120 gr. "RS"	.530"/224 gr.	1,890 f.p.s.	1,775 f.p.e.
Lyman Gr. Plains .54	32"	120 gr. "RS"	.530"/224 gr.	1,920 f.p.s.	1,830 f.p.e.
Zouave .58	32½"	100 gr. "RS"	.570"/278 gr.	1,230 f.p.s.	935 f.p.e.

Note: Rifles of the same caliber with the same barrel length will produce very similar velocities to those listed here when loaded with the same volume and granulation of Pyrodex.

Conical Bullet Loads
(Black Powder)

Rifle/Cal.	Barrel	Powder	Bullet Dia./Wt.	Velocity	Energy
T/C Hawken .45	28"	90 gr. FFg	285 gr. Hornady Gr. Plains Bullet	1,485 f.p.s.	1,395 f.p.e.
T/C Hawken .45	28"	90 gr. FFFg	285 gr. Hornady Gr. Plains Bullet	1,570 f.p.s.	1,560 f.p.e.
T/C Hawken .50	28"	100 gr. FFg	370 gr. T/C Maxi-Ball	1,470 f.p.s.	1,770 f.p.e.
A&H Mtn. Rifle .50	32"	90 gr. FFFg	250 gr. Lee REAL Bullet	1,575 f.p.s.	1,375 f.p.e.
Lyman Deerstalker .50	24"	100 gr. FFg	410 gr. Hornady Gr. Plains Bullet	1,385 f.p.s.	1,740 f.p.e.
Lyman Trade Rifle .54	28"	110 gr. FFg	380 gr. Lee REAL Bullet	1,490 f.p.s.	1,875 f.p.e.
Dixie 1861 Spfd. .58	40"	60 gr. FFg	460 gr. .575" Minié Bullet	753 f.p.s.	578 f.p.e.

Note: Rifles of the same caliber with the same barrel length will produce very similar velocities to those listed here when loaded with the same volume and granulation of black powder.

Pronghorn aren't particularly tough game animals to put down. The author took this muzzleloading book-class buck at over two hundred yards, using a load he developed specifically for maintaining adequate energy at such range.

Conical Bullet Loads
(Pyrodex)

Rifle/Cal.	Barrel	Powder	Bullet Dia./Wt.	Velocity	Energy
T/C Hawken		100 gr.	285 gr. Buffalo		
.45	28"	"RS/Sel."	Bullet HPHB	1,495 f.p.s.	1,410 f.p.e.
T/C Hawken		100 gr.	325 gr. Buffalo		
.45 caliber	28"	"RS/Sel."	Bullet HPHB	1,455 f.p.s.	1,525 f.p.e.
T/C Hawken		110 gr.	370 gr. T/C		
.50 caliber	28"	"RS/Sel."	Maxi-Ball	1,495 f.p.s.	1,830 f.p.e.
Pedersoli Kodiak	110 gr.		385 gr. Buffalo		
.50	28½"	"RS/Sel."	Bullet HPHB	1,478 f.p.s.	1,865 f.p.e.
Dixie Per. Jaeger	110 gr.		425 gr. Hornady		
.54	27½"	"RS/Sel."	Gr. Plains Bullet	1,425 f.p.s.	1,910 f.p.e.
Navy Arms 1863 Spfd.		90 gr.	505 gr. .575"		
.58	40"	"RS/Sel."	Minié Bullet	865 f.p.s.	835 f.p.e.

Note: Rifles of the same caliber with the same barrel length will produce very similar velocities to those listed here when loaded with the same volume and granulations of Pyrodex.

Noted muzzleloading hunter Jim Shockey, shown here with a dandy Saskatchewan buck. Jim is a firm believer in shooting the same load for everything from prong-horn to grizzlies, and shoots that load enough to know how it hits at all the ranges he expects to encounter.

Now ▪ ▪ ▪

These days, it seems that the majority of those who hunt deer and other big game with a muzzleloaded rifle aren't satisfied unless they can get the frontloader to send a bullet of adequate weight out of the muzzle at around 2,000 f.p.s. I can well remember *muzzleloading experts* of the early to mid 1960s, such as the late Major George Nonte and the late Al Goerg, repeatedly stating that the muzzleloading big-game rifle was basically a one hundred-yard maximum effective hunting arm. Those who read the few muzzleloading articles of the time came to accept that fact.

Well, those days are long gone. While the rifles and loads that were popular forty years ago generally failed to deliver enough energy at one hundred and fifty and especially two hundred yards to effectively down game that weighed one hundred pounds or more, today's top-performing muzzleloaders and loads are a completely different story.

If you quickly thumbed through the first half of this chapter in order to get to the ballistics of today's loads, take a few minute to go back for another look at the velocities and energies produced by so-called *traditional rifle loads*. Why? Because in order to appreciate the ballistics capable with the modern in-line rifles, newer powders and improved projectiles, one must first realize the limitations of the loads once used by early muzzleloading hunters—whether they lived and hunted during the late 1700s/early 1800s . . . or during the 1960s and '70s, when the first muzzle-loader-hunting seasons were being established in this country.

Here and there in this book, I refer to the .45 caliber Dixie "Kentucky" rifle I first hunted with as a fourteen-year-old teenager. The 70-grain charge of FFFg I shot out of the forty-inch barreled muzzleloader pushed a 128-grain round ball out fast enough to generate 1,025 foot-pounds of energy (f.p.e.) at the muzzle. But, I never did shoot a deer *"at the muzzle."* In fact, the closest deer I ever shot with the rifle was about thirty-five yards away, the farthest almost one hundred yards. Most of the dozen or so deer harvested with the long rifle were taken at about fifty yards—where the rifle and load were still good for only a little over 500 f.p.e. The buck I shot at one hundred yards with that rifle was hit with little more than three hundred foot-pounds of remaining energy!

One rifle I've hunted a great deal with for the past five years is the innovative Savage Model 10ML II. It's an ultra-modern .50 caliber *bolt-action* in-line rifle that features hot No. 209 shotgun-primer ignition and has the distinction of being the first production muzzleloader ever manufactured capable of shooting modern nitrocellulose-based smokeless powders. My favorite load has been forty-five grains of VihtaVuori N110 loaded under a saboted 250-grain Hornady .452-inch diameter SST poly-tipped spire point. The load is good for an astounding 2,405 f.p.s. at the muzzle, with 3,200 f.p.e. And thanks to the very aerodynamic (and high ballistic coefficient) bullet, this load will wallop a big whitetail buck standing at two hundred yards with more than 1,600 foot-pounds of retained energy. That's fifty percent more than what my old .45 Dixie could muster at the muzzle.

Anyone who thinks that muzzleloading hasn't changed all that much during the past couple of decades simply hasn't been paying attention. When it comes to top end velocities and energy levels possible with a .50 caliber in-line rifle, the Savage Model 10ML II is now at the top of the heap, thanks to the hotter smokeless powders this rifle can be loaded and shot with. However, the performance of other non-smokeless in-line muzzleloaders isn't that far behind, thanks to Hodgdon Powder Company's new Triple Seven black powder substitute. With healthy charges of this powder, many of these rifles are now shooting saboted bullets at 2,200 to 2,500 f.p.s.

The following load data is broken down into "Pyrodex Loads" . . . "Triple Seven Loads" . . . and for Savage 10ML II "Smokeless Powder Loads." As just pointed out, the Savage 10ML II is currently (at the time of writing) the only production in-line rifle built to handle the significantly higher pressures of modern smokeless powders. Unless recommended by the manufacturer of the muzzleloader you own and shoot, DO NOT LOAD ANY SMOKELESS POWDER.

The muzzleloading hunter gets just one good shot; it takes patience to wait for that shot. And it takes a good load to insure that the animal will be laying there on the ground when the smoke clears.

Pyrodex Loads

Loose-Grain Powder & Saboted Bullets

Rifle/Cal.	Barrel	Powder	Bullet Dia./Wt.	Velocity	Energy
Knight DISC Extreme - .45	26"	90 gr. "RS/Sel."	150 gr. Knight .400" "Red Hot"	1,960 f.p.s.	1,290 f.p.e.
T/C Omega .45	28"	90 gr. "P"	158 gr. Hornady .357" XTP-JHP	2,070 f.p.s.	1,500 f.p.e.
Knight Wolverine - .50	22"	100 gr. "RS/Sel."	220 gr. Knight .451" "Red Hot"	1,715 f.p.s.	1,605 f.p.e.
A&H Model 420LR - .50	26"	100 gr. "RS/Sel."	250 gr. Hornady .452" SST	1,660 f.p.s.	1,530 f.p.e.
A&H Model 420LR - .50	26"	100 gr. "RS/Sel."	300 gr. Hornady .452" SST	1,540 f.p.s.	1,580 f.p.e.
Knight MK-85 - .54	24"	110 gr. "RS/Sel."	250 gr. Hornady .452" XTP-JHP	1,590 f.p.s.	1,405 f.p.e.
Knight MK-85 - .54	24"	120 gr. "RS/Sel."	300 gr. Hornady .452" XTP-JHP	1,505 f.p.s.	1,510 f.p.e.

Loose-Grain & Conical Bullets

Rifle/Cal.	Barrel	Powder	Bullet Dia./Wt.	Velocity	Energy
CVA Optima Pro - .45	29"	100 gr. "RS/Sel."	275 gr. Power Belt	1,610 f.p.s.	1,580 f.p.e.
Remington 700MLS - .45	26"	100 gr. "RS/Sel."	285 gr. Buffalo Bullet	1,495 f.p.s.	1,410 f.p.e.
White Rifles T-Bolt - .451	24"	120 gr. "P"	430 gr. White Power Punch	1,455 f.p.s.	1,881 f.p.e.
Knight DISC Extreme - .50	26"	100 gr. "RS/Sel."	295 gr. Power Belt	1,565 f.p.s.	1,600 f.p.e.
Remington 700ML - .50	24"	100 gr. "RS/Sel."	385 gr. Hornady Gr. Plains Bullet	1,485 f.p.s.	1,885 f.p.e.
White Rifles T-Bolt - .504	24"	120 gr. "P"	440 gr. White Power Punch	1,477 f.p.s.	2,135 f.p.e.
Knight MK-85 - .54	24"	110 gr. "RS/Sel."	390 gr. Buffalo Bullet	1,427 f.p.s.	1,755 f.p.e.
Knight MK-85 - .54	24"	110 gr. "RS/Sel."	425 gr. Hornady Gr. Plains Bullet	1,400 f.p.s.	1,845 f.p.e.

Pyrodex Pellet Loads

Pyrodex Pellets & Saboted Bullets

Rifle/Cal.	Barrel	Powder	Bullet Dia./Wt.	Velocity	Energy
Knight DISC Extreme - .45	26"	100 gr. (Two 50-gr. pel.)	150 gr. Knight .400" "Red Hot"	2,225 f.p.s.	1,650 f.p.e.
		150 gr. Equiv. (Three 50-gr. pel.)	150 gr. Knight .400" "Red Hot"	2,510 f.p.s.	2,115 f.p.e.
T/C Omega -.45	28"	100 gr. (Two 50-gr. pel)	195 gr. Barnes .400" Expander MZ	1,995 f.p.s.	1,725 f.p.e.
		150 gr. (Three 50-gr. pel)	195 gr. Barnes .400" Expander MZ	2,280 f.p.s.	2,250 f.p.e.
Savage 10ML II - .50	24"	150 gr. (Three 50-gr. pel.)	250 gr. Hornady .452" SST	1,955 f.p.s.	2,125 f.p.e.
Knight Revolution - .50	27"	150 gr. (Three 50-gr. pel.)	300 gr. Hornady .452" SST	1,920 f.p.s.	2,455 f.p.e.
Savage 10ML II - .50	24"	180 gr. (One 30, Three 50-gr. pel.)	300 gr. Hornady .452" SST	1,945 f.p.s.	2,520 f.p.e.
Knight MK-85 .54	24"	100 gr. (Two 50-gr. pel.)	250 gr. Hornady .452" XTP-JHP	1,670 f.p.s.	1,550 f.p.e.
Knight MK-85 .54	24"	100 gr. (Two 50-gr. pel.)	300 gr. Hornady .452" XTP-JHP	1,585 f.p.s.	1,665 f.p.e.

Pyrodex Pellets & Conical Bullets

Rifle/Cal.	Barrel	Powder	Bullet Dia./Wt.	Velocity	Energy
Winchester		100 gr.	225 gr.		
X-150 - .45	26"	(Two 50-gr. pel.)	Power Belt	1,750 f.p.s.	1,530 f.p.e.
		150 gr.	225 gr.		
		(Three 50-gr. pel.)	Power Belt	1,985 f.p.s.	1,970 f.p.e.
		100 gr.	275 gr.		
		(Two 50-gr. pel.)	Power Belt	1,660 f.p.s.	1,685 f.p.e.
		150 gr.	275 gr.		
		(Three 50-gr. pel.)	Power Belt	1,940 f.p.s.	2,295 f.p.e.
H&R		100 gr.	295 gr.		
Sidekick - .50	26"	(Two 50-gr. pel.)	Power Belt	1,610 f.p.s.	1,700 f.p.e.
		150 gr.	295 gr.		
		(Three 50-gr. pel.)	Power Belt	1,865 f.p.s.	2,270 f.p.e.
T/C Encore		100 gr.	385 gr. Hornady		
.50	26"	(Two 50-gr. pel.)	Gr. Plains	1,565 f.p.s.	2,100 f.p.e.
		150 gr.	385 gr. Hornady		
		(Three 50-gr. pel.)	Gr. Plains	1,740 f.p.s.	2,590 f.p.e.
Knight MK-85		100 gr.	430 gr. T/C		
.54	24"	(Two 50-gr. pel.)	Maxi-Ball	1,380 f.p.s.	1,815 f.p.e.

Triple Seven Loads

FFFg Triple Seven & Saboted Bullets

Rifle/Cal.	Barrel	Powder	Bullet Dia./Wt.	Velocity	Energy
Savage 10ML II		100 gr. FFFg	250 gr. .452"		
.50	24"	Triple Seven	Hornady SST	1,960 f.p.s.	2,130 f.p.e.
		100 gr. FFFg	300 gr. .452"		
		Triple Seven	Hornady SST	1,875 f.p.s.	2,340 f.p.e.
		120 gr. FFFg	250 gr. .452"		
		Triple Seven	Hornady SST	2,085 f.p.s.	2,410 f.p.e.
		120 gr. FFFg	300 gr. .452"		
		Triple Seven	Hornady SST	1,990 f.p.s.	2,637 f.p.e.
		140 gr. FFFg	250 gr. .452"		
		Triple Seven	Hornady SST	2,210 f.p.s.	2,700 f.p.e.
		140 gr. FFFg	300 gr. .452"		
		Triple Seven	Hornady SST	2,095 f.p.s.	2,925 f.p.e.
		150 gr. FFFg	250 gr. .452"		
		Triple Seven	Hornady SST	2,244 f.p.s.	2,800 f.p.e.
		150 gr. FFFg	300 gr. .452"		
		Triple Seven	Hornady SST	2,125 f.p.s.	3,000 f.p.e.

Note: Charges of FFg Triple Seven tend to produce muzzle velocities that are approximately five percent slower than those listed here for FFFg. All shooting for this data chart was done with the twenty-four-inch barreled .50 caliber Savage Model 10ML II to give shooters an opportunity to see how heavier charges of Triple Seven create higher velocities out of the same barrel. Before loading any of these loads, check with the manufacturer of your rifle to determine if they are recommended.

Triple Seven Pellets & Saboted Bullets

Rifle/Cal.	Barrel	Powder	Bullet Dia./Wt.	Velocity	Energy
Knight DISC Extreme - .45	26"	100 gr. Equiv. (Two 50-gr. pel.)	150 gr. Knight "Red Hot"	2,240 f.p.s.	1,670 f.p.e.
Savage 10ML II - .50	24"	100 gr. Equiv. (Two 50-gr. pel.)	250 gr. .452" Hornady SST	1,690 f.p.s.	1,585 f.p.e.
T/C Omega .50	28"	100 gr. Equiv. (Two 50-gr. pel.)	250 gr. .452" T/C Shock Wave*	1,730 f.p.s.	1,660 f.p.e.
Knight DISC Extreme - .45	26"	150 gr. Equiv. (Three 50-gr. pel.)	150 gr. Knight "Red Hot"	2,518 f.p.s.	2,115 f.p.e.
Savage 10ML II - .50	24"	150 gr. Equiv. (Three 50-gr. pel.)	250 gr. .452" Hornady SST	2,025 f.p.s.	2,275 f.p.e.
T/C Omega - .50	28"	150 gr. Equiv. (Three 50-gr. pel.)	250 gr. .452" T/C Shock Wave*	2,080 f.p.s.	2,400 f.p.e.
Savage 10ML II - .50	24"	150 gr. Equiv. (Three 50-gr. pel.)	300 gr. .452" Hornady SST	1,930 f.p.s.	2,480 f.p.e.
T/C Omega .50	28"	150 gr. Equiv. (Three 50-gr. pel.)	300 gr. .452" T/C Shock Wave*	1,975 f.p.e.	2,595 f.p.e.

*The Thompson/Center Arms "Shock Wave" is the same exact bullet as the Hornady "SST." The T/C bullet features a yellow polymner tip, while the Hornady bullet comes with a red tip.

Triple Seven & Conical Bullets
Granular

Rifle/Cal.	Barrel	Powder	Bullet Dia./Wt.	Velocity	Energy
Winchester Apex - .45	28"	100 gr. FFg	225 gr. Power Belt	1,905 f.p.s.	1,810 f.p.e.
		100 gr. FFFg	225 gr. Power Belt	2,025 f.p.s.	2,050 f.p.e.
T/C Omega .45	28"	100 gr. FFg	285 gr. Hornady Gr. Plains	1,675 f.p.s.	1,770 f.p.e.
Savage 10ML II - .50	24"	100 gr. FFg	348 gr. Power Belt	1,625 f.p.s.	2,035 f.p.e.
		100 gr. FFFg	348 gr. Power Belt	1,815 f.p.s.	2,540 f.p.e.
T/C Encore .50	26"	100 gr. FFg	385 gr. Hornady Gr. Plains	1,545 f.p.s.	2,040 f.p.e.

Pellets

Rifle/Cal.	Barrel	Powder	Bullet Dia./Wt.	Velocity	Energy
Winchester		100 gr. Equiv.	195 gr.		
Apex - .45	28"	(Two 50-gr. pel.) Power Belt		1,990 f.p.s.	1,715 f.p.e.
		150 gr. Equiv.	195 gr.		
		(Three 50-gr. pel.) Power Belt		2,160 f.p.s.	2,020 f.p.e.
		100 gr. Equiv.	225 gr.		
		(Two 50-gr. pel.) Power Belt		1,915 f.p.s.	1,835 f.p.e.
		150 gr. Equiv.	225 gr.		
		(Three 50-gr. pel.) Power Belt		2,090 f.p.s.	2,185 f.p.e.
Savage		100 gr. Equiv.	348 gr.		
10ML II - .50	24"	(Two 50-gr. pel.) Power Belt		1,670 f.p.s.	2,155 f.p.e.
		150 gr. Equiv.	348 gr.		
		(Three 50-gr. pel.) Power Belt		1,870 f.p.s.	2,715 f.p.e.

Note: Check with the manufacturer of your muzzleloading rifle in regard to "Maximum Recommended Triple Seven Pellet Charges" before loading with 150-grain charges.

Smokeless Power Loads for the Savage Model 10ML II
.50 Caliber Rifle With 24-inch Barrel

Powder Charge	Bullet	Velocity	Energy
VihtaVuori N110			
42 gr.	250 gr. Hornady SST	2,305 f.p.s.	2,950 f.p.e.
42 gr.	300 gr. Hornady SST	2,220 f.p.s.	3,280 f.p.e.
45 gr.	250 gr. Hornady SST	2,405 f.p.s.	3,200 f.p.e.
45 gr.	300 gr. Hornady SST	2,285 f.p.s.	3,480 f.p.e.
IMR-SR4759			
43 gr.	250 gr. Hornady SST	2,330 f.p.s.	3,015 f.p.e.
43 gr.	300 gr. Hornady SST	2,225 f.p.s.	3,300 f.p.e.
Accurate Arms 5744			
46 gr.	245 gr. Barnes "Spit-Fire"	2,115 f.p.s.	2,440 f.p.e.
46 gr.	285 gr. Barnes "Spit-Fire"	2,060 f.p.s.	2,685 f.p.e.
48 gr.	245 gr. Barnes "Spit-Fire"	2,245 f.p.s.	2,745 f.p.e.
48 gr.	285 gr. Barnes "Spit-Fire"	2,120 f.p.s.	2,845 f.p.e.
IMR-4227			
46 gr.	250 gr. Hornady SST	2,080 f.p.s.	2,400 f.p.e.
46 gr.	300 gr. Hornady SST	2,005 f.p.s.	2,670 f.p.e.
48 gr.	250 gr. Hornady SST	2,165 f.p.s.	2,600 f.p.e.
	300 gr. Hornady SST	2,090 f.p.s.	2,910 f.p.e.
VihtaVuori N120			
60 gr.	275 gr. Precision Rifle QT	2,085 f.p.s.	2,650 f.p.e.
60 gr.	300 gr. Precison Rifle DC	2,040 f.p.s.	2,770 f.p.e.
65 gr.	275 gr. Precision Rifle QT	2,235 f.p.s.	3,050 f.p.e.
65 gr.	300 gr. Precision Rifle DC	2,170 f.p.s.	3,135 f.p.e.

Note: Savage Arms Inc. does not recommend loading and shooting smokeless powder loads behind a bore-sized conical bullet. All of the company's recommended loads are with saboted .451" and .452" diameter bullets.

You've waited all season for the buck you've been hunting. When it shows up, the last thing you need to begin doubting is the effectiveness of your load.

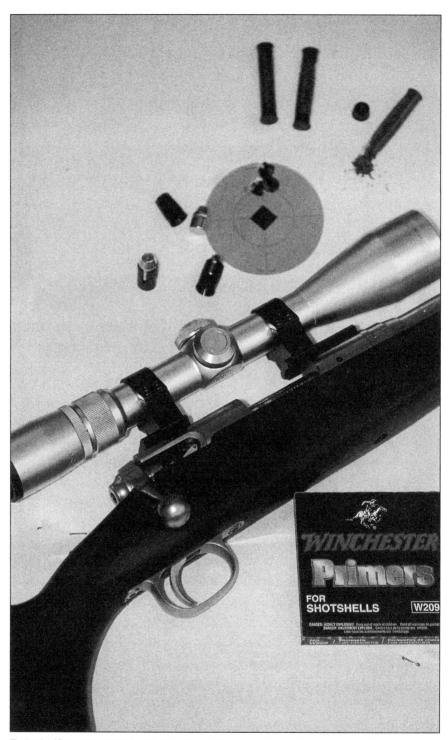

Today's rifles are capable of amazing accuracy when a shooter takes time to tweak a load for a specific rifle. Shown is the .50 caliber Savage Model 10ML II.

Many states in the midwest and east are either totally zoned "shotgun only" or have large areas that require the use of shotguns and slugs for hunting deer. In just about every such area, the hunter can use a muzzle-loaded rifle instead, and many are doing this to extend their range and effectiveness.

Hunter and guide with a great late-season muzzleloader buck.

Renowned game-call maker Will Primos with a dandy Idaho buck he dropped with a .50 caliber Remington Model 700 ML. Idaho is one of the few states that still does not allow the use of a scope during the muzzleloader seasons.

This hunter relied on one of the Italian-made 10-gauge percussion side-by-side shotguns. The proper load and combination of wads resulted in effective game-taking patterns.

Author Toby Bridges took this late muzzleloader season buck in a state that did not allow a scope, but which did permit the use of an electronic "Red Dot" sighting system. It's time for states to realize that the easier it is for the hunter to place the shot exactly where it needs to go, the better hunters and the game departments look in the eyes of the non-hunting public.

The $3,000 custom in-line muzzleloading rifle used by the author to take this buck not only looks and shoots much like a top quality center-fire rifle, it was even built with a modern center-fire rifle action.

As a rule, flintlock ignition rifles are not for the beginning muzzleloader shooter. Mastering one of these older style frontloaders is definitely harder than becoming proficient with a rifle of percussion ignition.

Young shooters who are familiar with modern firearms tend to be less intimidated by the operation of a modern in-line ignition muzzleloader. Here, the author coached a young first-time muzzleloader shooter to hit a 50-yard target. CREDIT: NATIONAL WILD TURKEY FEDERATION.

Hundreds of thousands of participants now relive our past through historical reenactments, such as the fur trader's rendezvous. Muzzleloading guns are a big part of this step back into time.

Muzzleloading hunters now seek an honest 200-yard hunting performance from the rifle, powder charge, and projectile. Many of today's rifles are fully capable of delivering the kind of accuracy and knockdown power now demanded.

Truly large game such as this can absorb a lot of energy. This 1,200-pound bull moose walked away after a solid heart shot, only to drop in its tracks several hundred yards away.

Variables in Muzzleloader Ballistics

There are a lot of factors that can and will affect the velocities a given powder charge and specific bullet weight produces from a muzzleloaded rifle. Simple seating pressure of some projectiles can result in a variation of 20 to 40 f.p.s.— out of the same rifle with the same load. Usually, the tighter the load is packed, or seated, the higher the velocity produced. This is especially true when shooting loads that comprise either granular Pyrodex or Triple Seven powders.

Hotter ignition, such as that produced by the No. 209 shot-shell ignition systems most in-line riflemakers have now gone to, results in a better initial burn of the powder charge, plus a more complete consumption of heavier "magnum" charges. The result can be fifty or more feet-per-second than with the same load set off by a simple ol' No. 11 percussion cap. This is especially true with loads made up of compressed-powder pellets.

As you can clearly see in the accompanying loading charts and loads, the longer the barrel (within reason), the more room a heavy charge has to fully burn, generally resulting in faster muzzle velocities than a noticeably shorter barrel of the same caliber loaded with an identical load. Again, this seems to be especially true with the compressed-pellet charges. With these, there is a point where an additional pellet added to the charge does not necessarily mean increased speed. You see, the other pellets must push this unburnt pellet down the bore, along with the bullet. It's like shooting a bullet that's thirty to fifty grains heavier, which generally means slower velocity. Likewise, just twenty or so grains of additional bullet weight can slow muzzle speeds considerably.

Powder fouling left in the bore tends to grip some projectiles more tightly than the same bullet stuffed into a spotless bore. This creates higher pressures, which will tend to continue building slightly with each additional shot until the bore is wiped clean. And even things like elevation and humidity levels will affect the velocities produced.

So, next time you are looking at the loading data provided by the muzzleloading rifle manufacturers or the loading component makers, and you see conflicting velocities published, keep all of these things in mind. Even out of a barrel of the same length, shooting the same amount of the same granulation/grade/pellet size of powder and a bullet of equal weight, velocities can easily vary as much as fifty or more f.p.s. from source to source. However, when you witness data with velocities that are two hundred or more f.p.s. faster than their competition's published data, simply accept it for what it most likely is—promotional sales copy! ■

Velocity Isn't Everything

Given that the following two loads deliver the same 1½ inch degree of accuracy at one hundred yards, which is the better choice for taking a great buck at two hundred yards: A modern in-line ignition .50 caliber rifle that can get a saboted 250-grain jacketed hollow-point out of the muzzle at 2,200 f.p.s . . . Or . . . The same model rifle in .45 caliber that pushes a spire-pointed 240-grain bullet out of the muzzle at 2,000 f.p.s.?

Didn't know there was going to be a test did you?

Well, the faster load doesn't always produce the best hunting load. With a 130-grain charge of FFFg Triple Seven behind a saboted 250-grain Hornady .452" XTP jacketed hollow point, a twenty-six-inch barreled Knight DISC Extreme is good for right at 2,200 f.p.s. And that load develops a whopping 2,680 f.p.e.—at the muzzle. However, this bullet has a

ballistic coefficient of just .147, meaning it is not very aerodynamic. And by the time that bullet reaches two hundred yards, the speed has dropped to about 1,300 f.p.s. The hollow-point bullet that had 2,680 f.p.e. at the muzzle will hit a whitetail at two hundred yards with just 940 foot-pounds of remaining energy. With just 110 grains of FFFg Triple Seven, a 26-inch barreled Knight DISC Extreme in .45 caliber will push a saboted 240-grain Precision Rifle "Dead Center" bullet from the muzzle at about 2,000 f.p.s., with around 2,130 f.p.e. Now, this is a very aerodynamic polymer-tipped .400"-diameter bullet with an extremely high .351 b.c. And when this one gets to two hundred yards, it is still moving along at 1,595 f.p.s., meaning this bullet will smack a big buck with more than 1,350 foot-pounds of knockdown power.

Sure, the 940 f.p.e. remaining at two hundred yards with the 250-grain jacketed hollow-point fired from the .50 caliber rifle is plenty for bringing down any whitetail with good shot placement. However, the 400 added foot-pounds of energy retained by the lighter and smaller diameter 240-grain bullet shot from the .45 caliber Knight DISC Extreme is still the better choice in this comparison. Plus, the higher retained velocities of the more aerodynamic bullet also mean far less bullet drop between one hundred and fifty and two hundred yards.

When choosing a bullet design for shooting out past one hundred and fifty yards, especially at two hundred yards, concentrate on those sleek designs that maintain ballistics better downrange. Faster is better, but only out on the receiving end.

7

Loading in the Field

At first, loading just about any muzzleloading rifle seems simple enough. A shooter pours a given amount of powder down the bore . . . seats a projectile over the powder charge with the ramrod . . . caps or primes the ignition system . . . then takes the shot. Right? Well, kind of, but it is how all of this is done that determines the degree of accuracy possible, or even what should be expected. Plus, different styles of muzzleloaded rifles that are loaded with different types of projectiles can require the use of different *loading accessories*.

In this chapter, we'll cover the basics of loading any muzzleloaded rifle, and the accessories that make loading easier. Now, it's a lot easier to pack all of the gadgets available to the range than it is to carry all of this gear into the field. So, what we will concentrate on here more than anything else will be the *necessities* and *loading techniques* that are most likely to reward a shooter with top game-taking performance and accuracy.

Then... When it comes to repeatable performance with a muzzle-

loaded big-game rifle, consistency has its rewards. It is usually a load that will shoot into the same spot time and time again. Whereas the early military use of muzzleloading firearms simply relied upon a line of shooters pelting an oncoming force with a constant barrage of lead balls or bullets, early firearm-toting hunters and adventurers quickly realized the need for careful, precise placement of each and every shot. As often as not, the prospects of an evening meal, or perhaps one's life, hung in the balance of whether or not a single shot hit its mark.

The long-ranging eastern frontier hunters of colonial America became known as *longhunters*. Many think they earned this name due to the exceptionally long-barreled muzzleloading rifles they carried. However, in reality the term referred to those adventurous individuals who often left home for months on end to traipse the wild, generally unmapped and unsettled lands that lay beyond the few civilized centers of the time. Far from any source of provisions, they carried everything needed for the long journey. This also meant an adequate supply of powder, balls, patching, flints, plus loading and rifle cleaning accessories. And most of these necessities were carried in a bag that hung along the hunter's side. That bag became known as a *possibles bag,* since it was possible to find just about anything in it!

Back home, this same hunter may have regularly joined in the fun of shooting matches that were often held at local taverns, and which were often referred to as *rifle frolics.* They gave shooters an opportunity to hone shooting skills, and often compete for a side of bacon or a whole pig. But when traveling the wilderness alone, or in small groups, these same shooters became extremely frugal with the powder and lead they packed with them. Far from towns and cities, one just didn't run down to the store and buy more

It often gets kind of cramped in a treestand twenty feet off of the ground. Most muzzleloading hunters don't want to be bothered with carrying anything that's not absolutely necessary.

loading components. During a *longhunt,* something usually died when a rifle fired.

I can remember my first possibles bag. Shortly after acquiring my first muzzleloader, a .45 Dixie Gun Works "Kentucky" rifle, I felt compelled to accessorize it with all of the loading gear and components of the past. Before I knew it, I was carrying an added seven or eight pounds of weight every time I went to shoot that rifle . . . or to hunt with it. In my bag, one would almost always find a bag of round balls, an adjustable powder measure, an ample supply of patching material, a patch knife, a tin or two of percussion caps, a capper, a ball starter, a few cleaning patches, an extra cleaning jag, a worm for pulling lost patches from the bore, a screw-like ball-puller attachment for my ramrod, a small screwdriver, and a few other odds and ends. To complete the look, I also packed along an authentically-styled powder horn that would hold more than a half-pound of black powder.

Did I need all of that stuff? At times yes, but after carrying it all afield for several seasons, I slowly began to carry less and less. I narrowed down the array of gear and components so much that by the start of my third season of hunting with the rifle, I headed for my stand every morning with just enough gear in my pockets to reload the rifle four or five times. I was packing just the *bare necessities!* I figured if I needed anything else, my pickup was usually parked less than a half-mile away.

When loading at the range, the basic accessories needed are: 1) An accurate powder measure; 2) A ball or bullet starter; 3) The ramrod on the rifle or an auxiliary loading rod; 4) A cleaning jag; 5) A supply of cleaning patches. As for loading components, basically they boil down to powder, projectile and source for ignition, which for a traditionally-styled muzzleloader means either a good, sharp flint for a flintlock, or a supply of percussion caps.

Powder measures come in all types, shapes and sizes. The most commonly used today are adjustable from zero to one hundred and twenty grains. This is usually accomplished by loosening a lock screw on the side, then pulling a graduated scale down from the bottom, which increases the capacity of the measure cavity and allows a larger volume of powder to be poured in. As a rule, the charge weight is marked in five-grain increments on the portion of the measure that slides out the bottom. The lock screw can be tightened to keep the measure set at the desired charge. Once filled, the charge is simply leveled off, either by the shooter or a swivel funnel head that comes on some of the better measures.

How tightly a patched ball fits into the bore of a rifle depends on the thickness of the patch and the actual diameter of the ball. Many target shooters load with a ball that's just .005-inch smaller in diameter than that of the bore, using a patch of

A hunter preparing a pocketful of speedloaders for the next day's hunt.

.010-inch to .015-inch thickness. Forcing such a combination through the muzzle can be tough, even with a good "ball starter." Without a ball starter, getting even a looser-fitting combination started into the bore can be nearly impossible, especially when loading with "bulk patching," which requires forcing the ball and material into the bore until it is nearly flush with the muzzle, then using a sharp knife to trim the material across the crown of the muzzle.

Hunters who still use the patched round ball very often work up a hunting load that permits the use of a ball that's .010-inch under bore-size, and which is loaded with a .010-inch patch. Such combinations load relatively easily. Using pre-cut, pre-lubed patches dramatically cuts loading time.

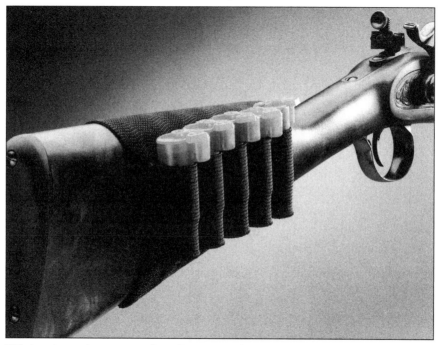

This handy stock accessory from Thompson/Center Arms keeps five "Quick Shot" charges easily accessible and ready for use.

When a bore-sized conical bullet is the projectile of choice, the "ball starter" then becomes a "bullet starter." Most of the more popular conical hunting bullets available today require that one or more slightly oversized surfaces be engraved by the rifling when the bullet is loaded through the muzzle. Again, without a good bullet starter to heartily shove or whack the bullet into the bore, loading these bullets can be a real pain. However, with a starter, they generally take very little effort to get into the bore.

Few hunters continue to carry powder in bulk into the field. Most have come to realize that during a full day of hunting whitetails or any other big game, it is extremely unlikely that they will take more than five or six shots. So why carry enough powder for twenty or thirty? Instead, hunters are now relying more and more on so-called *"speed loaders."* These are tube-like arrangements that permit the hunter to carry one pre-measured powder charge, sealed from the elements and ready for use. Then, when it's time to reload the rifle, the cap is removed and the powder dumped into the bore. No more fumbling for a powder measure and separate powder horn . . . flask . . . or container. To make loading even faster, many of the commercial speed loaders now available have a compartment for holding the projectile, and many of the loaders also have a "short starter" protruding from the side.

Reloading doesn't have to take forever, nor does today's "traditionally minded" muzzleloading hunter have to carry a bag full of gear and components into the field. All of that has now been replaced by four or five speed loaders (with projectiles included), a small flash pan primer for a flintlock or a capper filled with No. 11 caps for a traditional side-hammer percussion rifle. So equipped, even the average muzzleloading hunter can reload in the field in less than a minute.

Now . . . ■ ■ ■ Loading a rifle of frontloading design has never been easier.

Today's rifles and especially loading components not only deliver superior accuracy and better terminal game-taking performance than any muzzleloaded rifle and load from the past, many can now be loaded, and reloaded, with very little effort.

In Chapter 4, "A Look at Muzzleloader Propellants," we covered the convenience of loading and shooting with today's compressed Pyrodex and Triple Seven pellets.

No longer does the muzzleloading hunter have to take the time to measure or pre-measure charges with these powders. Hodgdon Powder Company has already done that for you. Now, it's just a matter of dropping in two . . . or three . . . of the pellets, seating the projectile, then slipping a percussion cap on the nipple or a primer into the chamber and going hunting. Well, almost!

With a load in the rifle, and three speedloaders plus a capper in a jacket pocket, most hunters are ready for the day.

The majority of today's modern performance-minded hunters have either come into muzzleloader hunting shooting a rifle of in-line ignition design, or they have gravitated to the newer guns after hunting with an older traditional design. Either way, the vast majority aren't looking back. When it's time to hunt with a muzzle-loader, it's hard not to realize just how much more effective the modern in-line rifles and loads are compared to older designs loaded with either the patched round ball or conical hunting bullet.

When loading with compressed-pellet charges, a hunter must be careful not to crush the pellets when seating the projectile. Both Pyrodex pellets and Triple Seven pellets feature a hole running full length through the center of each. Upon ignition, not only does the flame of a hot primer-ignition system engulf the rear and around

the rear edges of the bottom pellet, but also travels up through this hole. Pellets are combusting from the outside in and the inside out. If the pellets become crushed, the hole no longer exists, and the burning characteristics of the pellet charge changes considerably. The result is a shot that will likely not hit in the same spot as loads made up of non-crushed pellets.

So, in the hurried moment of reloading a modern muzzleloader with a pellet charge, at least make the effort to slow down enough to

The mobile hunter, stalking as quietly as possible through a calm woods, does not need the rustling and clinking of useless accessories.

feel when the bullet makes contact with the powder charge. At that point, simply let up on the pressure on the ramrod. Cap or prime the rifle and you're ready to get in that second or third follow-up shot . . . if needed.

On the other hand, when loading with loose-grain Pyrodex or Triple Seven, always compress the powder charge with thirty to forty pounds of seating pressure. These powders require some compression to insure positive ignition and repeatable point of impact. While a misfire or flier may not be such a big deal at the range, they can impact what may have otherwise been a successful hunt. Worst of all is a hang-fire that results in a very bad hit on an animal that you lose, but which you know will likely die. Never get in such a hurry that you fail to reload your muzzle-loader with basically the same care as when shooting for accuracy at the range.

While Pyrodex pellets and Triple Seven pellets may look very similar, they are also different and should not be arbitrarily substituted for one another. Don't sight-in with one, then switch to the other for the hunt . . . not without first doing some target work to determine if the loads impact the same, or adjusting the sights or scope for a new point of impact.

One difference between the two pellets is that the Pyrodex pellets feature one end that's lightly coated with a more sensitive ignitor. That end of the pellet is slightly darker and is easy to distinguish. When using these in a speed loader, insert the pellets into the loader so that the ignitor end drops into the bore first if the pellets are poured directly from the loader into the bore. The Triple Seven pellets are the same on each end, and it doesn't matter which goes in first.

The projectile of choice among most in-line rifle shooters is easily the saboted bullet. While there may be some differences of opinion about what bullet, bullet diameter or weight works best, it is estimated that close to eighty percent of all muzzleloading hunters today are shooting in-line rifles, and nearly eighty percent of them are loading and shooting modern bullets with a plastic sabot. These bullets have a lot going for them, but also have one major downside: The sabot that grips the projectile is loaded without any lubrication at all.

As clean as Pyrodex and Triple Seven may be when compared to good ol' black powder, both propellants still leave noticeable residue or fouling behind when a charge burns down the barrel. And it doesn't take much of this fouling to totally destroy accuracy with a saboted bullet. For that reason, always take time to run a damp patch down the bore between shots. You want that second or third shot to be just as accurate as your first, and unless the fouling in the bore has been wiped with a damp patch on the cleaning jag, it's not going to be.

Even if the "smokeless powder" Savage Model 10ML II didn't shoot any faster, flatter or harder than any other modern in-line muzzleloader, it would still have one major factor in its favor. And that is the totally non-corrosive and non-fouling nature of the modern nitrocellulose-based powders that make this muzzleloader so darn lethal on big game. This rifle can be shot all day, without once having to wipe the bore.

You read right. Here is a muzzleloaded big-game rifle that can be shot twenty . . . thirty . . . forty or more times without worrying about fouling build-up or serious loss of accuracy because the bore was not wiped.

Now, when I am at the range, and I am striving for the one-inch quality groups my Model 10ML II rifles are fully capable of producing, I will take the time to wipe

Muzzleloader Hunting

When trying to negotiate thick cover like this, the last thing a muzzleloading hunter needs is a possibles bag snagging on every branch or bush.

the bore with a dry 28-gauge shotgun bore mop between shots. Nothing is sprayed on that bore mop. I simply push the mop down the bore with one of my auxiliary loading rods and pull it straight back out. This keeps the extremely light (non-building) skim of smokeless discoloration wiped from the rifling. By doing so, I can get the rifles to print tight clusters at one hundred yards that seldom open to more than one and a half inches. However, I can load and shoot any number of shots without wiping the bore, and still get the same loads to print around one and a half inches at that distance

So, when hunting with these rifles, I don't worry about wiping the bore between shots. After a shot, even if the target went down on the spot, I reload immediately. If I don't need to put in a finishing shot, the rifle is already loaded for the next morning's hunt . . . or next week's . . . or next month's. Thanks to the non-corrosive benefit of smokeless powders, I really don't even have to clean the rifle. In fact, I hunted one whole season, from early October on into early January, shooting the same stainless steel .50 caliber Savage muzzleloader. During the course of the season, I took fourteen whitetails with the rifle, and easily put fifty or more shots through it checking the zero when I traveled to a new state. In all of that time, I only cleaned the rifle twice—and that was after hunting in several torrential downpours.

Big country often means having to cover a lot of ground on foot. Keeping accessories to a bare minimum helps the hunter travel light.

Muzzleloader Hunting

The hunter who shoots the Model 10ML II rifle with 40- to 45-grain charges of powders like IMR4227, Accurate Arms 5744 or VihtaVuori N110 really doesn't need to use a speed loader with the capacity for 120-grain powder charges. So I simply use once-fired .308 center-fire rifle cartridge cases, which I can pick up free of charge at local rifle ranges. I weigh my smokeless loads on an RCBS electronic powder scale, use a powder funnel to get the powder into the case, then slip a small plastic cap I get from Brownell's over the neck of the case. These caps are for ⅜-inch diameter parts tubes, and the inside diameter fits around the .30 caliber neck very well. The lip that sticks down from the cap permits me to take a short piece of vinyl electrician's tape and wrap the cap flange and brass case neck with a very effective waterproof seal.

Four or five of these weigh nothing, and take up very little room in a jacket pocket. Then, in a separate sandwich-size zip-locked plastic baggie, I'll carry four or five sabots and bullets, plus a half dozen No. 209 primers. The only other thing I carry is a small bullet starter for getting a tight fitting sabot and bullet into the bore. Everything I need for any possible follow up shots weighs only about one half pound.

Now, just about every time I head out with one of my favorite modern in-line rifles and partial pocket full of speed loaders, I think back to the days of my old Dixie long rifle, and that huge bag of loading components and accessories I once packed out to my stand. I must have looked like a "Yankee Peddler" to anyone who might have spotted me. Life with a hunting muzzleloader has certainly gotten much nicer . . . and lighter! ■

8
The Muzzleloaded Whitetail Rifle

I n a way, we actually owe the muzzleloading seasons we now enjoy to the ability of the white-tailed deer to adapt to an ever-changing habitat, and how this remarkable animal bounced back from near extinction to record numbers. Of course, this is thanks to the hard work and dedication of the game departments that have been entrusted to oversee the welfare of our wildlife, and to manage species like deer through regulated harvest.

I can remember the first whitetail hunt I ever went on, back in 1963. At that time, my home state of Illinois had a growing herd of around 65,000 deer, and only about twenty counties were open to deer hunting. During that season, only about 35,000 hunters participated, and the harvest was around 6,000 deer. Today, Illinois' herd has grown to right at one million deer, and hunters who bowhunt can literally harvest all the antlerless deer they want to buy tags for. Plus there are opportunities to hunt with modern shotguns with slug loads, large-bore handguns and muzzleloading

An estimated 3.5 million muzzleloading hunters head out to some species of big game each and every fall. Easily seventy-five percent to eighty percent of them are looking to hang their muzzleloader tag on a white-tailed deer. Special seasons and the opportunity to take bonus game are the draw.

rifles. Altogether, close to 250,000 deer are harvested annually in the state. But, that harvest really isn't enough to keep this herd from continued growth.

Game managers in every state where the whitetail is found are now pretty well faced with the same problem. While just forty or so years ago, game departments feared over-harvesting a fragile resource that was just bouncing back from all-time low numbers, today the concern is that we're simply not harvesting enough of the deer. From out of this bounty of whitetails has evolved our modern muzzleloader deer seasons, often permitting the tagging of bonus game, but at the very least providing the deer hunter additional time to put some venison in the freezer.

Fewer than ten percent of today's muzzleloading crowd still hunt with a truly traditional rifle. While the rifle this hunter used to bag his buck may be of traditional side-hammer design, it's doubtful that stainless steel and plastic were around during the 1840s.

With every sport or interest, there's always one group or another wanting to take credit for its widespread success. With muzzleloader hunting, it's certainly no different. Traditionalists like to argue that the special *"muzzleloader-only"* hunts or seasons were established solely to allow historically-minded shooters an opportunity to experience what it was like to go after big game with an old-fashioned smokepole. On the other side of the debate, we find those modern in-line percussion rifle shooters who claim that without their involvement and the growth in muzzleloading hunter numbers, we would not enjoy the expanded seasons most states have adopted. Well, neither side is entirely right . . . or wrong.

The truth is, the muzzleloader seasons we now enjoy are all part of an overall game-management plan. I can remember some of the early muzzleloading seasons in Arkansas. The low number of hunters who use muzzleloaders kept the game department there from establishing a state-wide muzzleloader season. The early hunts were limited to specified wildlife management areas. But as the deer herd continued to grow, as well as the interest in hunting with a muzzleloader, the Arkansas Game & Fish Commission realized that they had a great management tool in place and eventually established early and late state-wide muzzleloader seasons. There are now about 150,000 muzzleloading deer hunters in the state.

In Missouri, the first state-wide muzzleloading season wasn't much more than a token offering to appease the small number of muzzleloading hunters who hounded the Department of Conservation for a special season of their own. But, much to that department's surprise, the number of hunters participating in the short weekend hunt continued to grow year after year. Eventually, hunters were given the choice of buying either a modern-gun tag or a muzzleloader tag. If they went the latter route, they could hunt the regular nine-day November modern gun season (using a muzzleloader), and if they failed to fill their tag, those hunters with "muzzleloader-only" permits got an additional nine-day "muzzleloader-only" season in early December.

Muzzleloading hunter Todd Lust of Iowa left little to chance when going after this bruiser. He relied on all the modern technology and performance his rifle and load could muster.

All of this took place during the mid 1980s through the 1990s. At the same time, the deer herd in Missouri grew from about 600,000 deer to nearly one million deer. To encourage more harvest during the "muzzleloader-only" season, the Missouri Department of Conservation relaxed the regulations to allow anyone who failed to fill a tag during the modern-gun season to participate in the December muzzleloader hunt. The number of muzzleloading hunters in this state has been on the rise ever since, and so has the number of deer harvested with rifles of muzzleloaded design.

Throughout most of its range, whitetail numbers are still at all-time highs. In many states, 100,000 to 200,000 hunters are now taking full advantage of the special muzzleloading hunts, whether it's to take additional game, to finally bring home some venison or to keep on pursuing a trophy-class buck. Choice of muzzleloader style is now entirely personal. In most states, today's hunter can go as traditional or as modern as he or she desires. So, in the remainder of this chapter, we will look at both the traditional and modern rifles, plus the loads that are effective on whitetails and similar-size game.

Then...

Just when the first whitetail was harvested with a muzzle-loaded firearm was not documented. However, early explorers to the Americas brought with them the early matchlock muskets of the period, and we can be assured it was with one of those that the first deer was taken. From about the turn of the 16th century on up until the development of the conical bullet during the early 1800s, the only known muzzleloaded projectile in the Americas was the patched round ball. During those three hundred years, numerous whitetails were surely taken with the round ball to provide sustenance for explorers.

While many of the early flintlock guns that began showing up in North America by the late 1600s featured the huge .60 to .70 caliber bores favored back home in Europe, the long, slender "Pennsylvania" and "Kentucky" rifles that replaced them were built with considerably smaller bores-sizes. The muzzleloading historian will find that most of these rifles were originally made with .40 to .44 caliber bores. And quite honestly, when loaded with a patched round ball, such rifles would be marginally effective on game the size of the whitetail deer.

It's doubtful that many of these rifles were commonly loaded with much more than the equivalent of 70 grains of FFFg black powder. When this charge is loaded behind a tightly patched 90- to 128-grain round ball, the load would generate just 800 to 1,000 f.p.e. at the muzzle. And that is with today's improved black powders. At fifty yards, the knockdown power of the American long rifle was likely reduced to only about five hundred foot-pounds at best . . . meaning that was about the maximum effective range.

Today's muzzleloading deer hunter looking to cleanly harvest a whitetail with a patched round ball should not consider a rifle any smaller than .50 caliber. Dixie Gun Works' .50 caliber "Tennessee Mountain Rifle" is an excellent example of an authentically-styled long rifle that makes a great deer rifle—as long as the hunter realizes the limitations of the round ball projectile.

The Dixie rifle, which is available in flintlock or percussion ignition, comes with a lengthy forty one and a quarter inch octagonal barrel. I've hunted with one of the rifles several times, and found it to shoot well with an eighty grain charge of FFFg black powder behind a 178-grain .490-inch round ball tightly gripped by a .010-inch lubricated cotton patch. The load pushes the ball from the long barrel at 1,850 f.p.s., generating 1,360 f.p.e. at the muzzle. At one hundred yards, the load would hit a whitetail with about 450 foot-pounds of remaining energy. When I hunted with the rifle and load, I limited my shots to about seventy-five yards, and cleanly took every deer shot at.

If I were to go after deer, or other game of similar size, with a patched round ball today, I would likely look at going with a rifle of .54 caliber. When loaded with a full one hundred grain charge of FFFg black powder and a tightly patched .530-inch round ball, the thirty two inch barreled Lyman "Great Plains Rifle" would get the 224-grain lead sphere out of the muzzle at just over 1,660 f.p.s. This translates into right at 1,350 f.p.e. Due to the heavier weight of the ball, at one hun-

Through the 1970s, the Thompson/Center Arms "Hawken" rifle was the most popular muzzle-loaded deer rifle on the market.

dred yards it would retain just over five hundred foot-pounds of energy. Again, I would limit my shots to seventy five yards at most.

The traditionally minded hunter looking to get a taste of what it was like to hunt with a rifle and load from the past would be better prepared for the task of cleanly harvesting a deer when using a conical bullet rifle. One of my favorites has always been the good ol' Thompson/Center Arms "Hawken." For several years way back when, I used one of the .50 caliber half-stocks for most of my deer hunting and took quite a few deer with the rifle, shooting a ninety grain charge of FFg black powder behind one of the big 370-grain T/C "Maxi-Ball" bullets. The load was good for only about 1,475 f.p.s. at the muzzle, but due to all the mass of the bullet, it generated around 1,780 f.p.e. At one hundred yards, it would still hit a whitetail with around 900 foot-pounds of remaining energy. In other words, so loaded, this twenty-eight-inch .50 caliber rifle delivers the big bullet with twice the remaining energy at one hundred yards than possible with the round ball load shot from the long-barreled

.50 caliber Dixie "Tennessee Mountain Rifle."

No matter what traditional style or caliber rifle you may hunt with, or whether you load and shoot the patched round ball or heavier conical bullet, research the load enough to insure that it delivers adequate energy for taking game as big as deer. For most .50 or .54 caliber round ball rifles, the maximum effective range is likely around seventy five yards. And any .45 thru .54 caliber rifle that will shoot a heavy 240- to 400-grain conical bullet with enough velocity to generate 1,500 to 1,800 f.p.e. at the muzzle should still deliver the projectile with enough force at one hundred to one hundred and twenty five yards to be considered a reliable whitetail hunting rifle.

Now... ▪▪▪ It has been at least twenty years since I've gone after a big buck

with any of the loads just covered for traditionally styled muzzleloading rifles and projectiles. And when I compare the velocities and energy levels to the ballistics possible from today's extremely advanced in-line rifles, modern powders and saboted projectiles, the difference is almost hard to believe. Through the 1970s and 1980s, most of us were striving for one hundred yard effectiveness, and any hunter who boasted of taking shots out to one hundred and fifty or one hundred and seventy five yards was generally considered either a liar or foolhardy!

Most of today's major in-line ignition muzzleloading riflemakers are now touting the 200-yard effectiveness of their rifles. If one of the modern primer ignited rifles cannot get a bullet out of the muzzle at more than 2000 f.p.s., it seems that the performance-minded big-game hunter just isn't interested. Top game-taking performance is the name of the game when it comes to selling hunting muzzle-loaders these days.

In recent years, Thompson/Center Arms has advertised the performance of their Encore 209x50 Magnum as *"the most powerful .50 caliber muzzleloader in the world."* The company boasted that the rifle produced *"muzzle energy equal to a 7mm Remington Mag."* Not to be out-marketed by such performance claims, Knight Rifles, Connecticut Valley Arms, Winchester Muzzleloading and a few others jumped in with some chest-beating and bragging of their own.

Now, the load that was supposed to make the twenty six inch barreled .50 caliber T/C Encore muzzleloader the top performer on the market consisted of 150 grains of Pyrodex pellets behind a saboted 240-grain jacketed hollow-point bullet. The velocity T/C claimed was 2,207 f.p.s. According to my calculations, that equates to 2,590 foot-pounds of energy, which is a long way from the 3,100 to 3,200 f.p.e. produced by most 7mm Remington Magnum factory loads with 150- to 160-grain bullets.

Author Toby Bridges with the very first whitetail he ever took with a modern in-line ignition Knight rifle. He shot the deer during the fall of 1986, while hunting with Tony Knight on his family's farm in northern Missouri.

When looking at the purchase of a new high performance muzzleloaded whitetail rifle, don't be fooled by perfomance claims. Take these ballistics for what they really are: promotional copy. Every major in-line muzzleloading riflemaker is just a little guilty of making such unfounded brags. So, what kind of performance can you expect from some of today's hotter in-line rifles and loads? A whole lot better than the loads shot out of early in-line rifles during the late 1980s and early 1990s.

My first modern in-line ignition whitetail rifle was a .50 caliber Knight MK-85. The first deer I ever shot with that rifle was taken with a 90-grain charge of Pyrodex "RS" and a saboted .44 caliber 240-grain Hornady jacketed hollowpoint bullet. It wasn't exactly a hot, long-range load. And the best I could get it to group was right at two-and-a-half inches at one hundred yards. But back in 1986, it was the best-performing big-game muzzleloader I had ever shot and hunted with. That first in-line harvested eight-pointer was shot at about seventy five yards, along a ridge just across the creek from Tony Knight's home in northern Missouri.

The load was good for right at 1,575 f.p.s. at the muzzle, generating just 1,320 f.p.e. The buck, standing at seventy five yards, was hit with about 1,000 footpounds of remaining energy—and dropped like a rock. At that instant, I knew I would, from that time on, hunt whitetails only with a modern in-line rifle loaded with a modern saboted bullet. But even then, I had no idea of where the future performance of such rifles and advanced loads would take us.

The rage today is shooting massive 150-grain powder charges made up of either Pyrodex pellets or Triple Seven pellets. The latter is the slightly hotter of the two powders, and the realistic velocity possible with a saboted 250-grain bullet and such a powder charge is around 2,025 f.p.s. from a twenty-four inch barrel. A slightly longer twenty six inch bore would bring velocity up to around 2,040 f.p.s. and the twenty eight inch .50 caliber barrels now found on a growing number of newer in-line rifle models would get muzzle velocity with a

Actually, most loads for whitetails would be overboard for game as small as the Indian blackbuck . . . until you factor in the distance of the shot, out where the energy begins to taper off.

saboted 250-grain bullet to about 2,060 f.p.s. While noticeably slower than the velocities some riflemakers are claiming, the loads still generate anywhere from 2,275 to 2,355 f.p.e. Now that's a significant increase over the early loads I first shot out of modern in-line muzzleloaded rifles.

By the early 1990s, I had upped the charges I was shooting out of any modern in-line rifle to one hundred grains, and I had switched to the premium "Select" grade of Pyrodex "RS." I also went to 250- and 260-grain bullets of .451/.452-inch diameter, since they proved noticeably more accurate out a of the .50 caliber bore I tended to favor. From a twenty-four inch barreled stainless steel Knight MK-85, the loads were capable of reaching 1,640 f.p.s., bringing energy levels up to around 1,500 foot-pounds.

One bullet I used frequently was the 250-grain Hornady .452-inch XTP. It has a ballistic coefficient of just .147, which means that it is about as aerodynamic as a brick! The hollowed-out, flat frontal shape of this squat jacketed bullet causes it to slow quickly, and with the loss of velocity comes a dramatic loss of retained energy. At one hundred yards, a bullet that leaves the muzzle at 1,640 f.p.s. slows to about 1,200 f.p.s. and plows home with only about 800 foot-pounds of remaining energy. Out at two hundred yards, the velocity of the load will be just around 1,000 f.p.s., and the amount of remaining knockdown power is reduced to a little more than 500 f.p.e. Honestly, the maximum effective range of my "favorite deer-hunting load" during the early 1990s would have been around one hundred and twenty five to one hundred and forty yards—and that would have been pushing it.

The same 250-grain Hornady XTP that leaves the muzzle at just over 2,000 f.p.s., with around 2,300 f.p.e., would still be flying at a little more than 1,500 f.p.s. at one hundred yards, cleanly taking any whitetail buck with more than 1,250 foot-pounds of retained energy. In fact, these loads would still have more than 900 f.p.e. all the way out at two hundred yards. Isn't it amazing what an extra 500 f.p.s. will do for muzzleloading performance?

The full two hundred yard potential of modern in-line rifles can only be tapped when the shooter loads and shoots a modern aerodynamic saboted bullet that's of the same advanced technology as the rifle and powder charge. The Hornady SST (Super Shock Tip), Precision Rifle "Dead Center" and Barnes all-copper "Spit-Fire" spire-pointed bullet designs are the ones that will take muzzleloader performance into the future. The sleek shape and high ballistic coefficient of these newer saboted bullets actually turn most of the hotter in-line rifle models into honest two hundred and fifty yard deer rifles.

Outdoor writer and renowned muzzleloading hunter Jim Shockey with a nice pronghorn he took with a prototype of the Knight .50 caliber DISC Rifle. He dropped the buck at close to two hundred yards with a saboted 300-grain Barnes "Expander MZ"—and a month later used the same saboted bullets to take a 1,000-pound plus Kodiak brown bear.

Muzzleloader Hunting

A Thompson/Center Arms .50 caliber "Omega" loaded with three fifty grain (black-powder equivalent) Triple Seven pellets and one of T/C's own versions of the 250-grain Hornady SST (they call it the "Shock Wave") will give a shooter an honest 2,060 f.p.s. muzzle velocity. At the muzzle, that load is good for 2,355 f.p.e. Thanks to the vastly improved aerodynamics of this polymer-tipped jacketed spire-point, this load retains velocity and energy much better than the same powder charge shot behind a jacketed hollow-point bullet. In fact, at two hundred yards, the 250-grain bullet would still be zipping along at around 1,450 f.p.s., and would take down any whitetail with almost 1,200 foot-pounds of punch.

Precison Rifle Custom Muzzleloader Bullets of Manitoba, Canada, offers some of the highest ballistic coefficient muzzleloader bullets available today. While the firm's line of poly-tipped swaged lead "Dead Center" saboted bullets includes an impressive selection of .451-inch bullets of various weights for the .50 caliber rifles, it is the two hundred and sixty grain saboted .400-inch diameter bullet that most likely holds the most promise for today's .50 caliber in-line shooting deer hunter. It is an exceptionally aerodynamic spire-pointed projectile that has an unbe-lievably high .375 b.c., and does it ever retain energy down range!

This bullet is loaded into a .50 caliber bore using a new kind of sabot that features petals or sleeves designed to actually break away instead of peel back from the bullet. When loaded into a twenty-six inch barreled rifle like the Knight DISC Extreme or T/C Encore, a 120-grain charge of FFFg Triple Seven will get the bul-let out of the muzzle at nearly 2,100 f.p.s., with right at 2,550 f.p.e. Now, thanks to the extremely high .375 b.c. of this bullet, it slows little at one hundred yards. In fact, it is still flying at more than 1,800 f.p.s. at that distance, hitting anything in its way with around 1,870 f.p.e. At two hundred yards, this sleek .40 caliber bullet is still moving along at more than 1,600 f.p.s., driving home with close to 1,500 f.p.e. All the way out at three hundred yards, the 260-grain "Dead Center" would still retain a velocity of around 1,450 f.p.s. and have about 1,200 foot-pounds of knock-down power remaining.

Precision Rifle offers the two hundred and sixty grain "Dead Center" in a .45 caliber sabot for rifles in that caliber as well. And as far as this muzzleloading hunter is concerned, it is the absolute best bullet for use in the so-called "Super" .45 caliber in-line rifles. With one of the hotter one hundred and fifty grain Triple Seven pellet or Pyrodex pellet charges behind it, it makes some of these .45 caliber models very lethal two and fifty yard deer rifles. However, with most of the loads being promoted by the riflemakers, the bullets they tend to recommend deliver about 1,200 f.p.e. at two hundred yards.

Any load that can deliver a good expanding bullet with more than 900 f.p.e. at two hundred yards should be more than adequate for harvesting whitetails and other game of about the same size, no matter if the rifle is .45 or .50 caliber. Personally, I have strongly favored the .50 caliber in-line rifles simply because there is a much greater selection of saboted bullet available for rifles of that caliber. As this book was written, the .45 caliber bores still only accounted for less than ten percent of all in-line muzzleloaders sales. The .50 caliber, on the other hand, now accounts for more than eighty percent of all muzzleloaders sold, especially modern

Open country like this requires a flat shooting rifle and load. The author used one of the smokeless powder Savage 10ML II rifles to take this buck at two hundred and fourteen yards.

in-line big-game rifles. And the bullet makers are going to market to the majority.

Since 2000, I have done quite a bit of my muzzleloader deer hunting with one frontloaded rifle—the smokeless powder .50 caliber Savage Model 10ML II. The overall easier maintenance and stepped-up performance with its smokeless loads has had me shooting it more than any other in-line rifle. I liked being able to stay at the range all day, shoot fifty or so shots, then head home and not have to worry about cleaning that rifle until the next day . . . or the next week, if I wanted. This is due to the totally noncorrosive nature of the nitrocellulose-based powders that can be shot out of the Model 10ML II.

However, I am not totally convinced that the powers of smokeless powder have been safely harnessed. As this book was being written, I've learned of several 10ML II rifles damaged by the high pressures of the smokeless loads, and even experienced a failure of the system myself when a charge of Accurate Arms 5744 detonated rather than burned, resulting in a ruptured barrel.

But thanks to the much hotter smokeless powders that perform well out of this rifle, the old ballistics of the early loads I shot out of in-line rifles like the Knight MK-85 now seem a thing of the past. With just forty five grains of *medium-burn rate* smokeless powders like IMR4227, Accurate Arms 5744 and VihtaVuori N110, the Savage can claim that the Model 10ML II is the fastest .50 caliber muzzleloader on the market.

The load I've hunted with most during recent years has been 45 grains of VihtaVuori N110, loaded under a saboted two hundred and 50 grain Hornady .452-inch SST bullet. Now, this load develops close to 45,000 p.s.i. inside the barrel of the Model 10ML II, and to help better contain that pressure, I've found that the load is more consistent when a *Ballistic Bridge Sub-Base,* from Muzzleload Magnum Products, is loaded between the powder charge and saboted bullet. Not only will the rifle and load consistently print inside of one and a quarter inches at one hundred yards, but the combination is also good for an amazing 2,405 f.p.s., with 3,200 f.p.e. at the muzzle.

At two hundred yards, the polymer-tipped two hundred and fifty grain Hornady bullet is still moving at about 1,700 f.p.s., and will turn just about any whitetail upside down where it stands with right at 1,600 f.p.e. Since going to this rifle, the amazing down-range ballistics of the rifle and loads has astounded me. In fact, of the seventy five or so deer I've taken with the rifle, only two or three have actually left where they were standing when I squeezed off the shot. And those that did "run" went less than thirty yards. All others, including several 250- to 300-pound bucks, have gone down on the spot.

Muzzleloading and muzzleloader hunting have changed more than any other shooting sport over the past three decades. The rifles and loads have become so advanced that if a typical muzzleloading hunter from the early 1970s could time-travel to the present, he or she would not recognize the guns or their performance capabilities as "muzzleloading." However, the reason why most of us now hunt with a muzzleloader has changed since the '70s as well. Today, the vast majority of muzzleloading shooters are hunters looking to take full advantage of the bonus hunting offered by the special muzzleloader seasons. Their only real concern is that the buck they've just shot is lying on the ground when the smoke clears. Whether or not there's actually smoke in the air doesn't seem to matter any longer. ■

9

Going for Larger Game

ithin the limitations of the projectile, the muzzleloaded rifles and loads for hunting whitetail deer will also double nicely for any other North American game of basically the same size. This primarily means game such as mule deer and pronghorn. Likewise, some of the hotter loads that are capable of generating energy levels above 2,000 foot-pounds at the muzzle can most often be used successfully to harvest caribou and the average-sized black bear—but again, within the limitations of the projectile.

To take game as large as buffalo with a patched round ball, western hunters of the 1830s and 1840s had to use large-bore muzzleloaders and hefty powder charges. Getting as close as possible insured a greater level of retained energy.

Through the more than forty years I have hunted with a muzzleloading rifle, several times I have set out to find one rifle and load that could take anything from pronghorn antelope to moose. For a while, each time, I always felt that I had found the rifle I would hunt with for the rest of my life—until I discovered something

Truly large game such as this can absorb a lot of energy. This 1,200-pound bull walked away after a solid heart shot, only to drop in its tracks several hundred yards away.

better. But it has been this search for the *"Ultimate Muzzle-Loaded Hunting Rifle"* that has brought me, and countless others, from shooting the old patched round ball rifles of the 1960s to shooting and hunting with the fastest shooting, hardest-hitting, most efficient modern in-line rifle and load currently available. And, I'm sure my search will continue on into the future.

In this chapter, ***Muzzleloader Hunting: Then and Now*** will take a look at the guns and loads, both traditional and modern, that can be relied on to cleanly harvest game that may top nine hundred to one thousand pounds.

Then ...

Thirty years ago, about ten years after I had harvested my first muzzleloader whitetail, I got the urge to hunt something bigger . . . and began looking at making an elk hunt in Colorado. I had just made the switch from .45 to .50 caliber for my deer hunting, looking for the added knockdown power for cleaner kills. But I still had not gotten the accuracy I was looking for with the big, heavy Thompson/Center 370-grain .50 caliber "Maxi-Ball" out of the percussion T/C "Hawken" rifle I had purchased, plus that rifle did not shoot all that great with a patched round ball when loaded with any more than ninety grains of FFg black powder behind a patched 178-grain .490-inch lead ball. So, I decided to build my own .50-caliber round ball elk rifle.

I started with a 15/16-inch diameter octagonal Douglas "Premium" barrel, which I think was forty inches in length, and shortened it to thirty four inches. I wanted something longer than the twenty eight inch barrel found on the T/C "Hawken," but I wasn't necessarily looking for a long "Kentucky" rifle either. I chose to build a somewhat thicker and shorter full-stock design that sort of looked like an original full-stocked Leman rifle. What emerged was something else, but it did shoot, and shoot well.

I found that the high-quality .50 caliber Douglas barrel (one-in-sixty-six inch twist) was fully capable of handling up to one hundred and twenty grains of FFg black powder behind a patched .490-inch ball with good accuracy out to one hundred yards. In fact, I sighted the rifle to print pretty well "dead on" at that distance, and even with the rugged non-adjustable (other than filing and tapping) sights on the barrel, my *"Bridges Kentucky-Leman Hybrid"* consistently printed the load inside of four inches, which I felt was more than adequate for keeping hits in the kill zone of an animal as big as an elk.

I knew the load had a lot more "oomph" than I was getting with the ninety grain charge of FFg and same diameter and weight ball out of the shorter "Hawken" rifle. Only back then, I didn't know how much better the ballistics were. Now I realize that the Hawken load was producing a muzzle velocity of about 1,685 f.p.s., with only about 1,120 f.p.e. Out of the longer thirty-four inch Douglas barrel, the heavier one hundred and twenty grain charge of FFg was getting the one hundred and seventy-eight grain ball out of the muzzle at around 2,000 f.p.s., with nearly 1,600 f.p.e.

My first-ever elk hunt, a self-guided affair, was a success, while the performance of the load used in my new .50 caliber *"really big game"* muzzleloaded hunting rifle was nearly a failure. On the fifth day of my hunt, I was working a pocket of aspens at about 9,000 feet when I spotted the antlers of a bedded 5x5 bull. I carefully, and slowly, inched to within sixty yards of the animal, then gave a light cow call. The bull stood and offered a perfect broadside shot. I held just to the rear of the front shoulder and squeezed back on the trigger. The rifle kicked back and I heard the ball smack home, but I could no longer see the target through the huge cloud of white smoke that hung in the still morning air.

While I realized that I was shooting at possibly a seven-hundred-pound animal, I honestly expected to see it lying on the ground as the smoke cleared. Then I heard the unmistakable sound of a heavy animal running, and when I could see through the self-inflicted smoke screen, there was my bull—running at full tilt for a pocket of cover nearly a mile away. I scrambled to a slightly higher advantage point just in time to see the elk disappear into the thicket, which wasn't more than a couple of acres in size. Now, I could see all exits from that aspen patch, and during the course of the next hour, nothing came out. So, using cover to hide my approach, I went to see if that elk was down.

I was easing along the edge, looking into the tangle of dead and live aspens, when I spotted the bull standing, watching me. The shot was again about sixty yards. I could see my first hit, and it looked good. So I held for the same spot and shot again. Once again that elk took out of there as if he hadn't been touched. This time, his exit was all down hill. A few minutes later, he began to slow as he reached a stand of dark timber. As soon as the elk was out of sight, and with my rifle reloaded, I pursued.

Once into the cover, the elk hadn't gone too far. When I slowly worked into the heavy conifer growth, I saw something move thirty yards away and froze immediately. I could see the bull's legs, but not enough of his chest cavity to shoot again. So I eased down into a sitting position, and was able to get a good shot at the heart area—low and to the rear of the front leg. At the shot, the bull lurched, walked twenty yards and flopped down. Was I ever relieved.

My first two shots, both from only about sixty yards, had hit within two inches of each other, and both had passed through both lungs. Even so, that elk had covered more than two miles. Fortunately, my third shot had found its mark and pretty well centered the heart. Ever since that hunt, I have many times wondered how many elk are lost to the inefficiency of the patched round ball loads so many hunters still use in Colorado, where very antiquated muzzleloader regulations prevent the serious performance-minded muzzleloading hunter from using the best-possible rifle and load.

On the long drive back to my home in Illinois, with a winter's supply of great eating in the back of my pickup, I came to the realization that whenever the muzzleloading hunter is headed out for game as large as elk, really big bear or moose, the best advice is to *USE SOMETHING BIG!* When shooting a patched round ball for game this size, the .50 caliber is marginally effective at best. A much better choice for the patched round ball fan is to use a rifle of at least .54 caliber, or maybe even a .58 caliber.

During the early 1980s, I purchased the component parts needed to build a true, authentically-styled .54 caliber *Samuel and Jacob Hawken* half-stock percussion rifle. A rifle that had all of the qualities and knockdown power of the originals that were the number-one choice of the 1830s to 1850s *mountain men* of the West. Almost a year of love and sweat went into that project, and the finished product was very likely the finest of only a dozen or so custom rifles I have ever built.

This rifle had a top-quality, thirty-four inch long, one-inch diameter .540-inch bore Green River barrel. And when this beefy half-stock was finished, the rifle weighed in at about eleven pounds. With that kind of weight, I didn't mind stoking it up with a truly "magnum" charge of FFg black powder. In fact, the charge I finally settled on was a full one hundred and forty grains of the sulfurous propellant. When loaded under a very tightly patched (.015-inch-thick patch) .535 round ball, the massive powder charge pushed the two hundred and thirty grain sphere of soft lead out of the thirty four inch barrel at just over 1,950 f.p.s., developing nearly 1,950 f.p.e.

Now, for a young man with limited income who lived in the farm country of

The late Turner Kirkland with a Botswana bull elephant he took with an original 1850s four-gauge double rifle that weighed twenty pounds. The load: three hundred grains of FFg and a 1,097-grain ball.

Illinois, opportunities to hunt elk were far and very few in between. I did pack that heavy Hawken rifle around on several elk hunts, but only had the opportunity to shoot one elk with it—a cow that weighed around four hundred and fifty pounds. When hit with that big ball from forty yards away, that elk went down practically on the spot. The shot placement had been pretty much the same as with the bull I had taken a few years earlier with my custom-built .50 caliber full-stock rifle.

For several years, I hunted with a dedicated flintlock shooter who had contracted a well-known custom riflemaker to build him a thirty eight inch barreled .58 caliber full-stock rifle—specifically for his annual elk hunting. I don't recall the barrel maker, but I do remember that he was shooting a hefty one hundred and forty grain charge of FFg as well behind a patched .570-inch diameter ball. That ball weighed in at 278 grains, and with the heavy charge of black powder, this rifle was capable of getting the ball out of the muzzle at around 1,700 f.p.s. Now, with the much lead, the load is good for about 1,800 f.p.e. The added weight of the ball and larger burning chamber of the larger bore was actually less efficient than the same powder charge behind a forty eight grain lighter ball shot out of the thirty four inch barrel of my custom .54 caliber Hawken rifle.

The largest round ball rifle I ever had the opportunity to shoot was a massive twenty pound original 1850s side-by-side four-gauge percussion elephant rifle. The rifle belonged to Dixie Gun Works founder Turner Kirkland, who actually used it to take a bull elephant in Botswana, Africa during the mid 1970s. The load he shot, and which I also duplicated in the big rifle, consisted of three hundred grains of FFg black powder behind a patched .900-inch diameter round ball that weighed a whopping 1,097 grains! When you pulled the trigger on this one, you knew it.

So what kind of ballistics was this behemoth producing? Would you believe around 1,350 f.p.s.? Not impressed by the velocity? Well, at that speed, a ball weighing that much generates an astounding 4,400 f.p.e. at the muzzle. That is basically the same energy as a .458 Winchester Magnum loaded with a 500-grain bullet.

Turner's son, Hunter Kirkland, used that big double on a Nebraska bison hunt he and I went on one cold, snowy January. I watched as he swung on an 1,800-pound bull as it shot past him at about fifty yards. Hunter swung on the bull and touched off the shot. And when that huge, slow ball drove home, it rolled that nearly one-ton animal much like a cottontail rolls when hit with a load of shot from a twelve gauge shotgun. I used a .62 caliber full-stock Leman I had built specifically for the hunt, and while it did the job with a one hundred and sixty grain charge of FFg behind a patched 340-grain .610-inch ball, the performance wasn't nearly as impressive as that of the big four-bore rifle Hunter Kirkland used to take his bull.

Once improved conical bullets were developed during the early to mid 1840s, few American gunmakers continued to build rifles with slow-twist barrels for shooting the old patched round ball. Oh, a few backwoods mountain gunmaking operations may have still hand-rifled barrels for the easy-to-produce round ball projectile, but well-established gunmakers such as Edwin Wesson, Horace Warner, Nelson Lewis, William Billinghurst and Norman Brockway realized the superiority of the elongated bullets. The rifles produced by these master gunsmiths remain some of the most accurate muzzleloaded rifles of all times.

Here and there in this book, we have discussed the type of rifling required for shooting a bullet that can be two or more times longer than its diameter. Such long bullets require a fast-twist bore in order to stabilize the long projectiles in flight. While true round ball rifles of .50 to .54 caliber will have a slow one-in-60- to 72-

inches rate of rifling twist, true conical bullet rifles of the same caliber will generally feature rifling that spins with a one-in-twenty four to forty eight inches rate of twist.

My first "bullet rifle" was the old .50 caliber Thompson/Center Arms "Hawken" I bought to replace my original .45 caliber Dixie long rifle. I hunted with the T/C half-stock for the first time during the 1972 season, but instead of the big, long 370-grain "Maxi-Ball" I had bought the rifle to shoot, I ended up shooting a patched .490 round ball. This particular Hawken, with the factory one-in-48-inches rate of rifling twist, simply would not shoot the long T/C bullet, but did well with the round ball ahead of a moderate charge of FFg black powder. Through the 1970s, I tried repeatedly to get various other rifles with a similar rate of twist to shoot the old Maxi conical, but never could get the degree of accuracy I demanded.

So in 1982, I built my first true-bullet rifle. I had salvaged the lock, trigger, trigger guard and a few other parts from my old factory Hawken, and installed all of these on a semi-custom modern stock, complete with pistol grip, a high Monte Carlo butt stock and a flat modern-style butt plate. Then, I had the now long-out-of-business H&H Barrel Works cut me a .50 caliber barrel with rifling grooves that rotated with a fast turn-in-twenty-four inches. I found that with a 100-grain charge of FFg, I could get big 350- to 400-grain bullets out of the muzzle at around 1,450 to 1,500 f.p.s. Even with open sights, I could keep most hits inside of three inches at one hundred yards. So I replaced the rear sight with a 4x Redfield long eye relief handgun scope, and discovered true long-range muzzleloader accuracy for the first time.

One of my favorite bullets for the rifle during the early 1980s was the then brand-new 385-grain Buffalo Bullet Company conical. This was a semi-modern looking bullet, with the soft-swaged lead knurled nearly lengthwise with a quilted pattern, plus several slightly over-sized bearing bands that had to be lightly engraved by the rifling during loading. With a hot 100-grain charge of Pryodex "P," the rifle would get the big bullet out of the muzzle at around 1,550 f.p.s. This translates into right at 2,050 f.p.e.

While I never did get the opportunity to hunt elk or anything nearly that large with the custom half-stock .50 caliber hunting rifle, I did take quite a few great whitetail bucks, a few mule deer bucks and several pronghorns. In fact, I pulled off the greatest "off-hand" shot of my life with that rifle while hunting antelope in Wyoming one fall. The nice fifteen and a half inch horned buck was sauntering past my sagebrush blind one morning at what I figured was just over two hundred yards. I stood and the buck stopped—perfectly broadside. I locked into as steady a hold as I could, positioned the crosshairs about eighteen inches over the pronghorn's back and eased back on the front trigger of the double-set trigger arrangement. That big ol' 385-grain hollow-pointed Buffalo Bullet soft-lead conical plowed home perfectly, just to the rear of the front shoulder. The antelope never knew what hit him!

My calculations are that at 1,550 f.p.s., big bullets like the 385-grain Buffalo Bullet would still hit an elk at one hundred yards with around 1,000 foot-pounds of retained energy. Properly placed, such loads would be more than sufficient. Now, let's go back and look at the "hot" round ball load I was shooting out of my custom .54 Hawken rifle. While my 140-grain charge of FFg would get the 230-grain ball out of the muzzle at 1,950 f.p.s. with 1,950 f.p.e., by the time that ball gets to one hundred yards, retained energy has dropped to only about seven hundred foot-pounds. If a hunter miscalculated the distance by just twenty five yards, and an elk was actually only that much farther away, the load would hit with just about 600 f.p.e. And that, for an animal the size of an elk, as often as not could prove to be *NOT ENOUGH!*

When hunting game as large as elk or moose with a rifle of traditional design, shooting a traditional load with either a patched round ball or bore-sized conical bullet, the challenge should be *getting close* and making a good shot. Taking a shot at game this large at one hundred and fifty to two hundred yards with a load that may not even retain 500 f.p.e. is nothing to boast about—even if the hunter is successful at harvesting the game. However, getting to within fifty to seventy-five yards of an elk, and making a clean shot with a rifle and load that could have been used one hundred and fifty to two hundred years ago, gives any muzzleloading hunter real bragging rights.

NOW ∎∎∎ Well, that's the way muzzleloader hunting for really big game

use to be. Things have certainly changed in just the past ten to fifteen years, and the big game-taking performance of today's modern in-line rifles and loads is nothing short of astounding. I'm not just talking about harvesting an annual whitetail or two. You see, with some of the hotter loads, a few of today's hardest working in-line rifle models are fully capable of producing the same level of really big game-taking performance as well accepted center-fire elk-rifle cartridges, like the old .35 Whelen or .444 Marlin.

The first time I ever got within shooting range of a bull moose, I was looking at the animal through the scope of my .50 caliber Knight MK-85. Inside that rifle was a 120-grain charge of Pyrodex "P" behind a saboted 300-grain jacketed .451-inch Speer flat-nose bullet. I was less than eighty yards away, waiting for the bull to turn perfectly broadside to allow me to slip that lethal missile right through the vitals of the chest cavity.

Slowly, the bull moved a few yards through the belly-deep undergrowth. I tried my darnedest not to look at that head of horns that had lured me all the way from a ridgetop nearly five miles away. Then my opportunity presented itself. The bull stopped, and lowered its head to feed. I held just to the rear of the front shoulder, about a third of the chest cavity up from the bottom of the brisket, and touched off the shot.

As the smoke cleared, the bull still had his head down, munching away on the low-growing grasses. Then, ever so slowly, the bull raised its head and looked in my direction. Without a falter, the huge animal turned and, at a half-walk, half-trot gait, crossed the narrow clearing and disappeared into the heavy growth of stunted spruces along the opposite side. All the while, I stood there in disbelief. Had I just missed something as huge as a bull moose at seventy-five or eighty yards? I was just about to reload when I heard a tremendous crash. When I looked up, I saw the top of a spruce tree two hundred and fifty yards away rocking back and forth. With the rifle reloaded, I went to investigate . . . and found nearly 1,400 pounds of moose laying there stone-cold dead!

When I field-dressed the bull, I discovered that the bullet had done everything one could ask of it. It had expanded well and passed through both lungs, coming to rest just under the shoulder of the opposite side. At the muzzle, that load was good for around 1,700 f.p.s., meaning that when the 300-grain jacketed flat-nose bullet

The author double-lunged this older near nine-hundred-pound bull at sixty-five yards, and the elk traveled just fifty yards before going down.

left the muzzle, it did so with 1,920 f.p.e. At one hundred yards, the bullet would have hit with around 1,400 foot-pounds of retained energy, and my bull was closer than that.

On an elk hunt a few years later, I was using another .50 caliber in-line rifle loaded with 110 grains of Pyrodex "P" and the then-new Barnes saboted all-copper 300-grain Expander MZ. The rifle was a primer-ignited model, and thanks to the hotter initial burn of the powder charge, I found that I was nearly duplicating the ballistics of the load I had used to take my moose. So when my outfitter, Fred John of Wasatch Outfitters (Morgan, Utah), bugled-in a truly magnificent older 6x5 bull to within sixty yards, I wasn't surprised that my double-lung shot resulted in that 900-pound bull going down within fifty yards. In fact, by that time I had so much confidence in the modern rifles and saboted bullet loads, I actually expected that kind of performance!

What a difference twenty years of hunting-muzzleloader development had made in the performance of .50 caliber rifles. That Colorado bull taken during the early 1970s had required two nearly identical hits through both lungs, plus a third heart shot to bring down—after a nearly two mile pursuit.

Punched through both lungs with a modern all-copper hollow-point bullet that had been propelled by thirty grains less powder, from basically the same distance, my big Utah bull was down for the count within fifty yards. The following season, I returned to the same area and took another 6x6 bull at just fifteen yards, shooting the same load, and that bull went down on the spot.

Today, even the early performance of the saboted bullet and Pyrodex loads has been greatly eclipsed, thanks to the introduction of Pyrodex pellets, granular Triple Seven and Triple Seven pellets—plus an ever-growing selection of modern bullets that do a much better job of retaining energy down range. With just about any of the current No. 209 primer ignited in-line rifle models, the muzzleloading elk hunter can now get a saboted 300-grain bullet out of the muzzle at more than 1,900 f.p.s., generating a whopping 2,400 f.p.e. And thanks to newer, aerodynamic and high-ballistic coefficient designs, these bullets are now delivering far greater retained energy for cleanly taking down even game as big as elk and moose all the way out at two hundred yards.

Out of a 28-inch barreled Thomspon/Center Arms .50 caliber Omega drop-action in-line rifle, I have found that with three 50-grain (black-powder equivalent) Triple Seven pellets, I've gotten a 300-grain bullet to actually leave the muzzle right at 2,000 f.p.s. The load, with any saboted bullet of that weight, is good for just over 2,600 f.p.e. at the muzzle. Now, with one of the big jacketed hollow-point 300-grain bullets, like the .452-inch Hornady XTP, the load will hit home at two hundred yards with about eight hundred foot-pounds of energy left.

However, if the shooter loads the same charge behind one of the newer 300-grain .452-inch Hornady SST polymer-tipped spire-point bullets, the retained

When pursuing a bear as big as this five-hundred-plus pounder taken by Tony Knight, a hunter needs to be shooting something with a little more punch than what's needed for the average-size whitetail.

energy at two hundred yards would be a little more than 1,300 f.p.e. Why the big difference? It all has to do with the ballistic coefficients of the two different bullets. So what is ballistic coefficient? Well, it is the relationship of the bullet weight . . . length . . . diameter . . . and shape. The higher the b.c. number, the more aerodynamic the bullet. The 300-grain XTP hollow-point has a b.c. of .181, while the sharp-pointed SST has a b.c. of about .230. In this comparison of two different bullets that leave the muzzle at the same velocity, it is easy to see how important a high b.c. is to maintaining velocity and knockdown power down range.

Precision Rifle Custom Muzzleloader Bullets currently offers some of the highest ballistic coefficient saboted muzzleloader bullets available. While the company lists a great variety of bullet styles and weights, several should really interest the elk, moose or big bear hunter looking for all the retained energy a modern .50 caliber muzzleloader can muster. The bullet maker's 340-grain .451-inch diameter "Dead Center" saboted bullet has a published b.c. of .376. When loaded in front of a 110-grain charge of FFFg Triple Seven, this sleek polymer-tipped cold-swaged lead bullet leaves the muzzle of a twenty six inch barreled T/C Encore 209x50 Magnum barrel (twenty five inch actual bore length) at 1,795 f.p.s. and develops 2,432 f.p.e. Thanks to the extremely high ballistic coefficient, this bullet loses velocity slowly. At one hundred yards, it's still moving at 1,616 f.p.s., and hits with 1,971 foot-pounds. Then, when it reaches two hundred yards, the bullet still has 1,455 f.p.s. of momentum and delivers some 1,598 foot-pounds of wallop.

Muzzleloader Hunting

It is largely due to this kind of performance that the .50 caliber rifles now dominate the hunting-muzzleloader market. It's just next to impossible to get a .45 caliber in-line, even with a really hot load, to even come close to duplicating these kind of ballistics. The selection of sabots and bullets for the .54 caliber bores is hardly ten percent of the variety now offered for the popular half-inch bore.

Likewise, the number of hunters loading and shooting big, heavy bore-sized conical bullets continues to dwindle more and more with each new season. However, there are a few states with some pretty antiquated regulations still in place that don't permit the use of saboted bullets. One such state is Colorado. The Division of Wildlife there seems to be living in the dark ages, and apparently doesn't have a clue

Caribou can top four hundred pounds on the hoof, but aren't all that difficult to bring down. Often, the key is being able to properly place the bullet where it needs to go at two hundred or more yards.

about muzzleloader performance. Their regulations still require the use of a patched round ball or bore-sized lead conical. Isn't it time for performance-minded muzzleloading hunters to get busy there and get the regulations changed? And if the regulations can't be changed, maybe it's time to help those who stand in the way of progress to find a new job.

One modern bore-sized conical bullet that is widely used in Colorado is the Power Belt, which features a plastic skirt at the base to both help keep the loose-fitting bullet in place over the powder charge and to seal the bore at the moment of ignition. For the popular .50 caliber, Power Belt Bullets offers several different weights and styles, but the two that seem to offer optimum performance are the 295- and 348-grain copper-washed bullets with a polymer-type tip the company refers to as their Aero-Tip. This enhances the aerodynamics of the big bullets for better retention of velocity and energy down range.

Loaded ahead of two 50-grain Pyrodex pellets (100-grain charge), the 295-grain bullet will leave the muzzle of a twenty six inch barrel at 1,610 f.p.s., with 1,700 f.p.e. With a three-pellet powder charge (150 grains black-powder equivalent), the same bullet is good for 1,865 f.p.s. at the muzzle with 2,270 f.p.e. Now, this bullet has a b.c. of about .190, and at the higher muzzle velocity, it will still have about nine hundred and forty foot-pounds of knockdown left at two hundred yards.

When the 348-grain Power Belt is stuffed down a twenty-four inch barrel over a 100-grain charge of FFg Triple Seven, the bullet will exit the muzzle at around 1,625 f.p.s., with in the neighborhood of 1,635 f.p.e. Switching to 100 grains of FFFg Triple Seven, the velocity is pushed to 1,815 f.p.s., and energy jumps to 2,540 foot-pounds. This bullet has a b.c. of around .205, meaning that at the higher velocity just given, it would still have close to 1,100 f.p.e. remaining at two hundred yards. Either of these two bullets should work well on elk-sized game. However, the copper-looking "jacket" is actually just a very thin copper wash. The bullets are a butter-soft pure lead, and flatten very easily. Direct shoulder shots should be ruled out.

Now we'll take a look at the ballistics of the smokeless Savage Model 10ML II with loads that are well suited for taking elk, moose and other really big game. While some may

say we've saved the best for last in this chapter, others still feel that the smoke-less loads fired out of the Savage muzzle-loader have no place in today's muzzle-loader hunting. Either way, it is one hard-hit-ting muzzleloaded big-game rifle.

One of the hard-est-shooting big-

An excellent elk and similarly sized game bullet is the three hundred grain Hornady .452-inch "XTP." The big hollow-point is especially lethal on shots within one hundred yards, where a one hundred-plus-grain charge of Pyrodex or Triple Seven churns a lot of energy.

game loads I've shot out of the .50 caliber Savage Model 10ML II has been a forty-five grain charge of VihtaVuori N110, loaded with a saboted 300-grain .452-inch Hornady SST. This one gets out of the twenty four inch barrel at 2,285 f.p.s.— and generates a tremendous 3,480 f.p.e.! Now, that's knockdown power. Thanks to the .230 b.c. of the 300-grain SST, this load will clobber a bull elk at two hundred yards with more than 1,850 foot-pounds of wallop.

No matter if you're going after elk, moose or a sizeable bear, with either an older-style rifle and load or one of the hot new in-line rifles and saboted spire-point bullets, just make sure the load you are shooting develops the energy needed to get the job done. Remember, it is the amount of energy that the game is hit with that determines how well the load performs, not only how fast the bullet is flying. ∎

Why the **"Big Bore"** Rifles Died

The transition from .45 caliber to .50 caliber during the late 1960s and early 1970s was purely due to the added fire-power of the slightly larger bore. Back then, the old patched round ball was still the most widely used hunting projectile, so it shouldn't come as any surprise that through the 1970s and early 1980s, the still larger .54 caliber continued to grow in popularity. And likely would have been the number one caliber today, if only improved conical hunting bullets and eventually saboted bullets had not been introduced.

The heyday of the .54 bore was during the late 1970s. Many hunters who had enjoyed great success with a .50 caliber rifle and round ball for whitetails began to look at elk hunting. And it didn't take long for them to realize that a patched 224-grain .530" ball out of a .54 caliber bore could deliver more wallop on larger game than a patched 178-grain .490" soft lead ball out of a .50 caliber rifle. By the early 1980s, very likely 40 percent of all muzzleloading rifles sold were of .54 caliber.

But, with the development of improved conical bullet designs, like the 385-grain Buffalo Bullet for the .50 caliber rifles, and the introduction of saboted jacketed handgun bullets during the mid 1980s, the .54 quickly declined in popularity. Muzzleloading hunters found that the new bullets could deliver greater energy levels with better accuracy from a .50 caliber bore than the old patched round ball out of a .54 rifle.

The rise of in-line rifle popularity and shooting saboted bullets really marked the end of the .54 caliber rifles. Shooters found a much larger selection of bullets and sabots for the .50 than the .54, and that the slightly smaller bore would deliver superior performance with less load development. Today, rifles of .54 caliber actually represent less than five percent of all muzzleloading rifles manufactured and sold in the U.S.

Knight Rifles, of Centerville, Iowa, has more recently tried to introduce something of an *in-between* caliber—a modern .52 caliber bore. I have had the opportunity to do some shooting with one of the Knight DISC Extreme rifles in this caliber, and have found it to be one of the most accurate in-line muzzleloaders ever shot. The company has developed new sabots for the .52 bore - one for shooting .458" bullets the other for shooting .475" diameter bullets. Likewise, they have introduced an all-copper 350-grain .458" addition to their "Red Hot" bullet line, plus a 275-grain and a whopping 375-grain .475" bullet for the .52 as well.

Shooting with the company's new "Power Stem" breech plug (designed for more complete burn of heavy loose grain Triple Seven charges) and a full 150-grain charge of FFFg Triple Seven, I found that I could get the saboted 275-grain bullet out of the 26-inch barrel at around 2,120 f.p.s. for 2,750 f.p.e. And the rifle grouped this load inside of one and a half inches with regularity.

With the huge 375-grain .475" diameter all-copper semi-spitzer bullet and 150-grain charge of FFFg Triple seven, this rifle rocks on both ends. The bullet leaves the muzzle at just under 1,950 f.p.s., with 3,175 f.p.e. Now, we're talking about a rifle and load for *really big game*. Several of the hundred yard groups shot with the rifle and load stayed inside of one and a half inches.

The shooter looking for a more economical load for the Knight .52 caliber DISC Extreme could use the Knight .458x.52 sabot and the jacketed lead core 300-grain .458" Barnes "Original" semi-spitzer soft point. This is a great all-around big game bullet that performs well at around 2,000 f.p.s.—and it's a darn sight cheaper than the all-copper Barnes produced Knight "Red Hot" bullets.

Only time and an improved selection of bullets will determine whether or not the Knight .52 meets the same demise as the old .54 caliber muzzle-loaded big game rifles.

10

Small-Bore Muzzleloaders for Small Game

J ust twenty years ago, there were quite a few well-made, deadly-accurate small caliber frontloaded rifles available to the muzzleloading hunter who enjoyed potting a few squirrels, rabbits and other similar-size game as much as taking an annual whitetail or two. These were, for the most part, .32 and .36 caliber rifles that could be loaded with a light charge of fine black powder or Pyrodex to produce ballistics similar to a .22LR rimfire rifle. For just a few cents per round, the rifles provided a lot of shooting and hunting enjoyment.

Unfortunately, the number of squirrel hunters in this country has definitely been on the decline in recent years. Before the explosion of the whitetail populations just about everywhere this great animal is found, any woods-savvy hunter worth his salt hunted squirrels. Fall bushy-tails are a true test of a hunter's ability to slip undetected beneath a towering hickory or oak and tumble out a squirrel of two that may be

Hunting small game like squirrels with a muzzle-loaded rifle means a small bore—and accurate shot placement.

feeding in the canopy above. To make the hunt even more challenging, a few would rely on a small-bore muzzleloader.

Today's hectic world often leaves us with too little time to traipse around in our favorite stands of hardwoods. When the muzzleloading hunter can steal time from a busy schedule to escape for a hunt, that time is now usually devoted to hunting more glamorous game, such as the white-tailed deer. Because of this obsession with hunting whitetails, we now enjoy the finest selection of top-quality muzzleloaded big-game rifles ever available. However, since fewer and fewer of us can now find the extra time to chase squirrels, or other small game, the selection of muzzleloading small-bore small-game rifles has definitely dwindled.

Still, there are a few new-made modern reproduction .32 and .36 caliber rifles available that are ideal for sniping at a few squirrels or rabbits. And the hunter who makes the effort just might find one of the older "gems" that were

The Hopkins & Allen underhammer .36 caliber rifles, available from about 1963 on through the mid 1980s, could be loaded to be deadly accurate. With a light charge of powder and patched .350 ball, they were great for sniping at sunning cottontails.

available through the 1970s and 1980s. And in this chapter, we'll look at loading and shooting these pipsqueak-bored muzzleloaders, and how to tap their performance for small game.

Then...

Some of the superb reproduction small-bore muzzleloaders of the past include the .36 caliber Thompson/Center Arms half-stock "Seneca"; that same firm's short and fast-handling "Cherokee" in .32 or .36 caliber; Dixie Gun Works' .32 caliber version of their long 40-inch barreled Tennessee Mountain Rifle; the unique "Mule Ear" percussion side-slapper Navy Arms offered in .32 and .36 caliber; and even the simple old Hopkins & Allen .36 caliber underhammer "Buggy Rifle." Some of these rifles were produced in fairly large numbers at one time, and the hunter who frequents gun shows and gun shops that deal in used guns may eventually come across one of them. Most out-of-production muzzleloaded reproduction rifles still have not reached real collector status, and one can often be picked up in excellent condition for a few hundred dollars.

The long-barreled .32 caliber version of the Tennessee Mountain Rifle that was once available from Dixie Gun Works was a fine small-game muzzleloader.

Some of the current small-bore muzzleloading rifles available include the Italian-made "Blue Ridge Rifle" imported by Cabela's, and a pair of "Kentucky"-styled rifles that Dixie Gun Works also imports from the same Italian manufacturer—Pedersoli. The 39-inch barreled full-stock "Blue Ridge Rifle" is offered in a choice of .32 or .36 caliber, in flintlock or percussion ignition. Dixie's .32 caliber "Kentucky" rifle comes with a thirty-five and a half-inch barrel, and is also offered in either flint or percussion ignition. The small-game hunter looking for a slightly faster-handling rifle with a shorter barrel might find the .32 caliber Dixie "Scout Carbine" handier in the woods. This one likewise comes in choice of flintlock or percussion ignition.

The criterion for a great small-game muzzleloading rifle is pretty simple— a small-bore rifle that propels a light sphere of lead with a light powder charge. Unlike choosing the best-suited muzzleloaded rifle for hunting big game, which is one that will shoot accurately with lots of energy, the small-game hunter is actually looking for just the opposite. After all, the idea of hunting small game is to turn it into edible table fare! And this is generally best accomplished with a small caliber projectile that is delivered with just enough energy to cleanly harvest the squirrel, rabbit or whatever the target may be.

At one time, quite a few shooters tried to promote the .45 caliber rifles as "do-it-all" muzzleloaders, capable of being loaded hot enough for deer or loaded down with light charges for shooting a few squirrels. Truth is, the .45 caliber is not a great choice for either use. Even with light 20- to 25-grain charges of FFFg or Pyrodex "P" behind a patched .440-inch ball, rifles of this bore-size are simply too destructive for small game, and unless the shooter is an excellent marksman and can pull off a "head shot" every time, not much is going to be left of the target for feeding the family.

Even the .40 caliber rifles are still way too destructive for harvesting small game intended for the table. It has always been the rifles with .32 and .36 caliber bores that have been favored by experienced muzzleloading squirrel hunters. And with the loads required to tap the true accuracy of some small caliber frontloaders, even rifles in these two tiny bore-sizes can result in a great deal of meat loss.

So, which is best for shoot-

Noted black-powder authority Mike Nesbitt and nice pair of cottontails headed for the stew pot, thanks to the accuracy of a good-looking custom small-bore muzzleloader.

ing game this small—the .32 caliber or the .36 caliber? Let's take a look at some of the benefits and inherent problems associated with loading, shooting and hunting with each. Then you can make that decision for yourself.

First of all, small-bore muzzleloading rifles are known for being finicky. Simply put, the smaller the bore, the faster it tends to foul. In order to maintain pinpoint accuracy with either the .32 or .36 caliber, the small-game hunter will have to run a lightly dampened patch down the bore between each and every shot. Just the fouling left from one shot will cause the next to create higher pressures, and the slightest difference from one shot to the next is enough to move point of impact an inch or two at just twenty five yards.

When loading and shooting larger .50 and .54 caliber rifles, volume measured 90- or 100- or 110-grain charges of black powder, Pyrodex or Triple Seven can actually vary as much as one to five grains from charge to charge. The difference really doesn't affect all that much where a heavy 178- to 230-grain ball hits. But when we're talking about loading and shooting a tiny ball that weighs just 45 to 65 grains, a powder charge that varies as little as one or two grains can mean the difference between a *clean hit* or a *clean miss* on targets as small as a bushytail and cottontail.

So when it comes to being "finicky," it's pretty safe to say that loading the smaller .32 caliber bores requires more attention and finesse than stoking the slightly larger .36 caliber rifles. The smaller bore definitely fouls quicker,

The small-bore muzzleloading rifle and load that can best duplicate the ballistics of a .22 long rifle proves to be the best suited for hunting game as small as bushytails and cottontails.

and the light 45-grain .310-inch round ball loaded into most .32 caliber rifles is more affected by slight variations in the powder charge than a 65-grain .350-inch ball shot out of a .36 caliber bore. But, what about the destructive nature of the slightly larger bore and projectile?

One of the most accurate percussion .36 caliber rifles I've ever shot and hunted with was the twenty-seven inch barreled T/C Seneca half-stock rifle. With its brass furniture and cap-box, it was also one of the nicest looking. Unfortunately, this rifle featured a relatively slow (for such a small bore anyway) one-turn-in-forty eight inches rate of rifling twist. To get this rifle

Small .32 and .36 caliber muzzleloader bores are easily fouled by even light charges of powder. To maintain accuracy and to keep the rifle capable of being loaded, it is necessary to run a damp patch through the barrel after every shot.

After a long snowy stretch, cottontails will often come out to sun themselves, offering the patient small-bore muzzleloader shooter an opportunity to collect some fine eating.

to deliver its best accuracy required stoking it up with at least thirty grains of FFFg black powder or Pyrodex "P" grade powder. The load would push the sixty-five-grain patched .350-inch ball from the muzzle at just over 1,700 f.p.s., with close to 500 f.p.e. Now, this is nearly one-and-a-half times the energy levels produced by the .22 Winchester Magnum Rimfire. A soft-lead ball that hits any small edible target with this much wallop isn't going to leave much for the frying pan! Even when the charge was reduced to twenty-five grains, the rifle still produced energy levels that were simply too destructive.

My favorite muzzleloaded small-game rifle of all time has been the percussion T/C Cherokee in .32 caliber. This light little half-stock rifle was built with a short and fast handling twenty-four inch barrel that was rifled with a fast one-turn-in-thirty-inches rate of rifling twist. Thanks to the faster twist, the rifle still shot great with charges of FFFg as light as fifteen grains. With that much powder, the ball was pushed from the muzzle at around 1,100 f.p.s., generating just 120 f.p.e. And this is right on par with the ballistics of standard velocity .22LR ammunition fired from a rifle barrel. Even if a shot from the Cherokee so loaded was off an inch or two, it still did not totally destroy edible portions of a bushytail.

While I do tend to favor the smaller .32 caliber bores for gathering up the makings for a good squirrel stew, I have to admit that I have taken more squirrels with my old long-barreled semi-custom percussion .36 caliber "Hatfield Squirrel Rifle" than any other small-bore rifle I have ever owned and shot. It features a lengthy thirty-nine inch barrel, and when I first got the rifle back in 1983, I found it to shoot wonderfully with a twenty-five grain charge of FFFg black powder and a .015-inch-thick patched .350-inch round ball. However, the combination of the powder charge and the lengthy bore means the load is getting that ball out of the muzzle at around 1,600 f.p.s., for about 375 f.p.e. If you hit a squirrel anywhere other than in the head means, you'll be losing some fine eating.

For a couple of years, I played around with FFFg and Pyrodex "P," but just could not get either of those powders to shoot well out of this rifle with anything less than twenty five grains. Back then, I also did some flintlock shooting, and one day tried loading the .36 Hatfield rifle with just fifteen grains of the super-fine FFFFg priming powder for my flintlocks. Accuracy was excellent at twenty-five yards, and when I ran a couple of the tightly patched .350-inch balls across the chronograph, I found the load was doing just 990 f.p.s., which translates into 140 f.p.e.—or about the same as a high velocity .22 long rifle. Through the years, I have taken more than one thousand bushytails with that rifle and load.

The .32 and .36 caliber Italian imports now offered by Dixie Gun Works and Cabela's feature a one-turn-in-forty-eight-inches rate of rifling twist. Right out of the box, the guns are going to produce best accuracy with anywhere from twenty-five to thirty-five grains of FFFg black powder or Pyrodex "P" grade. Likewise, the energy levels generated will be higher than desired for taking most small game. Hodgdon's new FFFg Triple Seven is noticeably hotter than black powder of the

The author prepares to knock another bushytail from the branches above, using the short and light .32 caliber Thompson/Center Arms percussion "Cherokee." He feels this little rifle is one of the best small-game muzzleloaders ever offered.

same granulation. A lighter fifteen-or-so-grain charge of the new FFFg propellant should tame down the velocities and energies to make these rifles better suited for busting a few bushytails.

In the race to have the most efficient, fastest-shooting and hardest-hitting muzzleloaded big-game rifle on the market, even when riflemakers do offer a muzzleloader with a bore small enough to use for small game, they seem to have forgotten that for this type of hunting, less is best. And when the rates of rifling twist are as slow as a turn-in-forty-eight inches and slower, it generally takes a hotter charge to make the rifles shoot accurately. I, for one, would like to see Thompson/Center Arms reintroduce the .32 and .36 caliber Cherokee percussion half-stock rifle—and keep the faster one-turn-in-thirty-inches rate of rifling twist—or see anyone else offer a similarly-styled rifle.

So, there are the basic choices—the more finicky and less destructive .32 caliber, or the less finicky and more destructive .36 caliber. While the current crop of small-bore muzzleloaders may seem less than "optimum" for hunting squirrels and other small critters, just about any of them can be loaded to perform well enough for most hunting situations. The hunter just has to learn to cope with the limitations of his or her choice.

Now, it's not unusual to ease in under a nut tree to discover four . . . five . . . six . . . or more squirrels gluttonously feeding in the limbs above. To take full advantage of these opportunities, it pays for the muzzleloading squirrel hunter to be organized. Since these small-bore frontloaders are finicky about powder charges, it's best to pack them pre-measured in small plastic tubes. Not only does this allow you to load the same exact amount of powder for each shot, it eliminates the time it takes to measure out a charge.

Carrying pre-patched round balls in a handy loading block can really speed up reloading as well. A loading block is nothing more than a half-inch or so thick piece of wood drilled through with a number of holes near the size of the rifle bore. Into each of these holes, the hunter can push a ball already wrapped in the proper patching. In use, the loading block is often carried on a lanyard of some sort, and when it's time to get another ball down the bore, it takes only a few second to center one of the pre-patched balls over the bore and shove it on into the barrel with a short starter. Then the projectile is pushed on down the bore with the ramrod. The use of pre-measured powder charges and a loading block with pre-patched balls can cut loading time in half.

The small diameter wooden ramrod that comes standard with just about any small-bore rifle is extremely fragile. It doesn't take much to snap it in half, and this is pretty common when trying to reload quickly to get a shot at another squirrel.

Outdoor writer Gary Clancy with a fine winter-prime coyote harvested with the same MK-85 he used all through the deer season.

For actual hunting, replace the wooden ramrod with one of the tough synthetic rods, such as those available through Mountain State Muzzleloading Supplies (Williamstown, West Virginia). Remember, one good morning of squirrel hunting often produces more action, and more reloading, than an entire season of hunting whitetails. And with an unbreakable ramrod, you won't be forced out of the hunt.

Whether you're after a brace of bushytails that are feeding on hickory nuts or a limit of cottontails that are out sunning themselves after being holed up during a week-long snow storm, there is no more challenging way to do it than with a small-bore muzzleloading rifle. And, if you want to just hone your shooting and loading skills, all the action this hunting provides can have you more than ready for any upcoming big-game hunt.

NOW... ∎∎∎ Let's face it, since the in-line ignition rifles hit the market back in the 1980s, all of the interest has been in using these rifles to hunt deer and other big game. During the early 1990s, Knight Rifles did offer, for a very limited time,

Small-bore .32 and .36 caliber rifles may be a little on the light side for coyotes. The author used one of the .40 caliber Dixie Gun Works "Cub" rifles to take this yodel dog that came in to the sounds of an electronic game call.

a .36 caliber version of the MK-85. Likewise, during the mid 1990s, Thompson/Center Arms offered an optional .32 caliber barrel for their System One "interchangeable barrel" in-line rifle. But other than those modernistic two, small-bore muzzleloaders have remained pretty well a traditional thing.

Quite a few modern in-line rifle owners very often use their rifles to take some varmints and predators, but since "eating" these targets is the last thing on their minds, no one seems to worry about meat loss. Consequently, most continue to use the same powder charges and bullets they use to hunt the big game for which they bought the rifle. The varmint or predator "targets of opportunity" simply allow the hunter to practice with the rifle and load under actual hunting conditions. If the intended target happens to be a valuable furbearer, such as a bobcat or fox, it's only a matter of finding a saboted bullet that won't expand and destroy the pelt. ▪

11

Managing the Muzzleloading Shotgun

Then...

Since rifling didn't show up until nearly two hundred years after the first firearms were in use, the chances are better than just "good" that the first flying or running game ever harvested with a load of shot fired from a muz-zleloader was accomplished with an early matchlock. Even so, "fowlers" did not become widely used until the development of the flintlock ignition system. And by the late 1600s, European sportsmen had already discovered a fascination with the challenge of "shooting flying."

Ever since, the shotgun has been popular with shooters, primarily because it was developed as a *hunter's tool* and does not require any great deal of skill to master. Unlike a muzzleloaded rifle, the so-called *scattergun* isn't a precision instrument capable of amazing accuracy at longer range. The truth is, shotguns were developed as a close-range gun that could take game with a fast, often haphazardly aimed shot.

The majority of muzzleloading

The originals of this big .75 caliber British "Brown Bess" smooth-bored flintlock musket probably saw more use as a flintlock shotgun than as a military musket. Being .75 caliber makes the gun an eleven gauge.

guns built on through the 1700s continued to feature a smooth-bored barrel. Rifles with spiraling grooves actually did not see large-scale use until after the turn of the

19th century. Through the 1600s and 1700s, hundreds of thousands, maybe even millions, of large caliber smooth-bore flintlock muskets were in use by major military powers, such as England and France. Despite the popular misbelief that the American Revolution was won thanks to the unparalleled accuracy of the early "Kentucky" rifles,

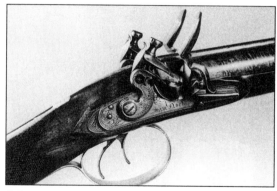

This extremely high-quality Samuel Nock flintlock dates from about 1800, and with the right loads, could still produce game-getting patterns. However, its collector's value is more the $10,000.

the vast majority of battles were fought with smooth-bore muskets.

The two most commonly used long guns of the Revolutionary War were the .75 caliber British "Brown Bess" and the French .69 caliber Charleville muskets used by most Continental soldiers. During the war, these big flintlocks were loaded with a hefty paper or cloth patched ball that could weigh up to almost six hundred grains (for the .75 caliber Brown Bess). Still, most of these big smooth-bore guns probably saw greater use following the war as a fowler loaded with a handful of bird shot.

The heyday of muzzleloading shotguns was likely from about 1820 until around 1860. Even here, at the end of muzzleloaded-shotgun development, gunmakers still didn't fully understand the effects of a choked bore. However, a few had realized that smooth-bores built with a slight constriction at the muzzle did tend to produce patterns that kept more shot toward the center. A few original guns from the later percussion era had bores that were gradually tapered from one end to the other. A premium-quality percussion Manton side-by-side I was privileged to own at one time had 36-inch-long twin barrels that were right at eight-gauge at the breech end, then tapered all the way down to ten gauge at the muzzle.

Most original 19th-century muzzleloaded shotguns, as well as most of the early reproductions of these guns that have been offered since the 1970s, featured cylinder-bored barrels. Choking a shotgun barrel that must be loaded through the muzzle more often than not results in difficult loading. A few of the later original smooth-bores were built with what was referred to as a *jug choke.* This was nothing more than a short section near the muzzle that had been expanded or polished out to be slightly larger than the rest of the bore. The idea was that the pellets of a shot charge would follow the barrel walls, and when the charge passed through the short section that was larger, the pellets would move outward. Once the jug choke returned to actual bore-size, the pellets were then redirected inward, toward the center of the shot string.

Most original muzzleloading shotguns and modern-made close copies are built with a bore that is exactly the same at both ends of the barrel, without a choke of any sort. The secret to getting the cylinder bore barrels to perform acceptably lies in loading near-equal volumes of powder and shot—plus using the proper sequence of wads.

Let's look at the wad sequence. Ideally, wads for a muzzleloading shotgun should fit just snug enough in the bore that they stay in place when any downward pressure on the ramrod stops. Wads that fit so loose they practically fall down the bore when inserted through the muzzle most likely won't provide the proper seal. Blow-by from the burning powder charge can really open patterns and leave huge areas void of shot. Also, much needed power can be lost.

On the other hand, a wad that must be driven through the muzzle and down the bore will normally shoot well enough, but once the bore begins to cake with fouling, loading these can become next to impossible. Herein lies the trouble with choking a muzzleloading shotgun barrel. Once a proper diameter *over-powder wad* is inserted through the constriction of a choke, it no longer fits the bore tight enough to insure a proper gas seal. And once the shotgun has been fired several times, just getting the wad through the choke at the muzzle becomes extremely difficult.

As already stated, the amounts of powder and shot that tend to produce the best patterns from a cylinder-bore muzzleloading shotgun will be fairly equal in volume. The amount of one should never be greatly out of proportion to the other. For instance, a 75- to 80-grain charge of FFg black powder is about equal *volume wise* to a one and an eigth-ounce charge of shot; ninety grains of the propellant is nearly equal volume to one and a quarter ounces of shot; and a one and a half-ounce charge of shot should be teamed up with a 100- to 110-grain charge of powder.

One of my favorite muzzleloading shotguns of all time is one that Dixie Gun Works sells as their "Magnum Ten Gauge Double." The thirty-inch barreled gun features a right barrel that is a true cylinder bore. However, the left barrel has a very slight choke to it. The company says it is modified, but it loads and performs more like an improved-cylinder choke. At any rate, a little more time and effort is required to load the barrel with the slight constriction.

The beauty of loading almost any ten or twelve-gauge muzzleloading shotgun is that every load is, in essence, a custom reload. Most of the time, these smooth-bores can be loaded and effectively used on a wide variety of upland game, from speedy bobwhite quail to tough-to-down wild turkey gobblers. It is this versatility that has made the Dixie ten-gauge one of the most-used muzzleloading shotguns I've ever owned.

Muzzleloader Hunting

For the wide-open right barrel, I have always simply loaded with the card-and-fiber shotgun wads also available from Dixie Gun Works (of Union City, Tennessee). Directly over the powder charge, I'll push down one of the .125-inch-thick heavy card *over-powder wads.* Then, directly on top of that, I will seat one of the half-inch *fiber cushion wads.* The shot charge is then dumped in and the whole load topped with a thin, but tight-fitting, .025-inch-thick card *over-shot wad.* The left, slightly choked, barrel is loaded in basically the same manner, but right on top of the fiber cushion wad, I usually slide down just a plastic ten gauge shot cup, such as those offered by Ballistics Products (Corcoran, Minnesota). Then the load is topped with a thin over-shot wad.

The author used his favorite old Dixie Gun Works "Ten-Gauge Magnum" to take this boomer sage grouse.

The left barrel of this shotgun tends to throw extremely even patterns when the shot cup is used. However, when I've tried loading this barrel with an entire one-piece plastic ten-gauge shotgun wad, the patterns really open up. I've used the Dixie ten-bore double to harvest a half-dozen turkey gobblers, mostly relying on the left barrel. And when going after such a tough-to-down target with a muzzle-loading shotgun, the load favored consists of one hundred grains of FFg black powder and a one and a half-ounce charge of No. 4 shot. The only other charge I actually used in this double has been ninety grains of FFg behind a one and a quarter-ounce charge of shot, usually No. 6s. And with that load, I have hunted everything from cottontails to pheasants.

Both Dixie Gun Works and Cabela's import from Italy a great little twenty-gauge percussion double that is lightweight, fast handling and one heck of a lot of fun to hunt with. I've used one of the Pedersoli-manufactured side-by-sides to hunt rabbits, squirrels and pheasants. The load that has worked very well for me consists of seventy grains of FFg and a one and an eighth-ounce charge of No. 6 shot. The left barrel on this small-gauge muzzleloading smooth-bore also has a very slight constriction at the muzzle, but it doesn't seem to hamper loading or make that bore perform much better than

The rewards of a great morning hunt with a classic side-by-side percussion 20-gauge Pedersoli muzzleloading shotgun.

the right barrel. I always load it as if loading twin-cylinder bore barrels.

The beautiful Mortimer twelve-gauge, also produced by Pedersoli, is another muzzleloading smooth-bore that may be of special interest to the shooter looking to master an early flintlock fowler. It has to be one of the finest, most authentically styled reproduction guns available today. The gun comes with a thirty one-inch tapered round cylinder-bored barrel, and many other features that were common to the high-quality English-built muzzleloaders of the late 1700s and early 1800s.

This flintlock shotgun even features a nicely checkered stock, beautiful case-colored furniture and an externally mounted sliding safety on the lock. Mortimer guns were high quality two hundred years ago, and Pedersoli's modern copy of this great smooth-bore is as well. For percussion-ignition fans, Dixie Gun Works offers the same gun in that ignition. The manufacturer recommends loading eighty grains of FFg black powder and a one and an eighth-ounce shot charge.

Just about any adjustable powder measure works fine for measuring both powder and shot charges, as long as you are loading shot sizes No. 6 and smaller. The relatively small internal diameter of most measures tends to crowd large shot sizes too much, preventing an honest or accurate measurement. However, if you are loading with No. 6 or No. 7½ shot, you can set one of these measures for say 90 grains, measure out the powder charge and dump it on into the bore. Then insert the over-powder and cushion wad. With the measure at the same setting, you'll find that

Behind that wall of smoke is a shattered clay pigeon. This competition muzzle-loading shotgun has been custom-built with removable screw-in chokes that produce modern shotgun performance.

it will allow you to measure the smaller shot sizes fairly accurately. And when set at ninety grains, with No. 6 or No. 7½ shot, it will accurately give you right at one and a quarter ounces of shot. Dixie Gun Works catalogs a fine selection of flasks and shot bags for the serious muzzleloading shotgunner.

Off and on over the past several decades, several companies importing reproduction muzzleloaded shotguns have offered models that came with a tighter choke at the muzzle. One that comes immediately to mind was a side-by-side 12-gauge once offered by Navy Arms. The gun was known as the "T&T" model, which stood for "Turkey & Trap." As you may have already guessed, this 30-inch barreled smooth-bore featured twin "full-choke" barrels. Loading these in the manner already discussed was next to impossible.

I used one of the doubles for several years for turkey hunting, since it did throw noticeably tighter patterns than any of the more open-bored muzzleloading shot-guns on the market. I overcame the problem of getting wads through the tight choke

A leisurely stroll along a small waterway is a great way to pick up a few bushytails while after teal with a slow-to-load muzzleloading shotgun. This over/under percussion twelve-gauge was once offered by Berretta.

constriction by simply steering away from using the traditional wad sequence. Instead of loading a card over-powder wad and a half-inch-thick cushion fiber wad over the powder, I simply used three or four of the quarter-inch lubed felt wads available from Ox-Yoke Originals (Milo, Maine). These were flexible enough to be inserted through the choke constriction one at a time, then pushed down over the pow-der charge with the ramrod. I picked up a "wad punch" from Dixie that allowed me to cut out .750-inch diameter thin styrofoam over-shot wads that also could be pushed through the choke, and which fit the smaller twelve-gauge bore extremely snug.

So, what kind of performance can someone expect from any of today's muzzleloading scatterguns? It all depends on the individual gun and the load it prefers. Even so, here is a look at the performance you should be looking to achieve.

All too often, very light or very heavy loads fail to produce the best patterns out of a cylinder bore. Powder and shot charges that could be considered medium loads tend to turn in the most uniform patterns. Out of the popular twelve-gauge bores, this usually equates to a one and an eighth- to one and a quarter-ounce shot charge ahead of a three and a quarter-dram (eighty-nine grains) or three and a half-dram (ninety-six grains) load of FFg black powder—or the volume equivalent of Pyrodex "RS" or "Select." Smaller twenty gauge bores commonly show a preference for seven eighths- or 1-ounce shot charges and two and three-quarters-dram (seventy-five grains) or three-dram (eighty-two grains) powder charges. Shooters who are looking for more knockdown with a bigger ten-gauge often opt for loads consisting of three and three-quarters-dram (one hundred and two grains) to four and a half-dram (one hundred and twenty-three grains) charges of FFg or Pyrodex "RS/Select" behind one and a half to two ounces of shot.

Out of a cylinder bore barrel, these loads should produce patterns of about fifty percent at thirty yards. Or, in other words, the load should keep approximately half the pellets in a given shot charge inside a thirty-inch circle at that distance. If the barrel is choked improved-cylinder, the pattern should tighten slightly to keep nearly sixty percent of the pellets in the circle, around seventy percent if it has a modified choke constriction, and close to eighty percent if the barrel features a full choke. (A one-ounce charge of No. 4 shot contains 132 pellets, No. 5 contains 168 pellets, No. 6 contains 218 pellets, and No. 7½ contains 388 pellets.)

If you have been considering the purchase of a muzzleloading shotgun for hunting and feel you will demand tighter, more-uniform patterns, then concentrate on those models now available with removable screw-in chokes. (Covered in more detail in the last part of this chapter, and in the following chapter on "Taking The Muzzleloader Turkey Challenge.") No matter how hard you work at developing your loads, you'll never get a cylinder bore barrel to turn in full-choke patterns. But then, you'll never find a full-choke barrel that loads as easily as a cylinder-bore muzzleloading shotgun either.

If muzzleloading shotguns were as easy to tame as a modern breechloading shotgun, what would be the challenge of hunting with them? It is custom-tailoring a load for one of these smooth-bores that makes the effort so rewarding. There is a lot of satisfaction in taking upland game up close and personal with an old-fashioned smooth-bore design dating from the late 1700s or early 1800s. If you haven't given these smooth-bores a try, you're missing one of the more enjoyable and rewarding aspects of muzzleloading.

Caution:

Any time that you are loading any percussion shotgun, always make sure that there is not a cap on the nipple. And this doesn't mean just on the barrel you may be "reloading." If you've taken a shot with a double gun, and one barrel must be reloaded, before ever sitting the butt of the gun on the ground and beginning the reloading process, first remove the live percussion cap from the unfired barrel. It is just a good safety practice to get into.

Now . . .

When it comes to muzzleloading, adding a little modern technology isn't always such a bad thing—especially if you're looking for improved performance, anyway. Fortunately, the muzzleloading shotgunner who wants the looks, handling and basic challenge of loading, shooting and operating a very traditionally styled muzzleloading shotgun—that can nearly shoot right along with modern breechloading smooth-bores—can have just that. Several modern reproduction scatterguns are now available with screw-in chokes that will help keep the "scattering" more manageable.

From time to time, Cabela's (Sidney, Nebraska) offers a Pedersoli-built side-by-side that comes with the removable and interchangeable choke system. The gun is offered in ten and twelve gauge, and comes with improved cylinder, modified, and extra-full screw-in chokes. When time is taken to load these guns properly, the patterns they produce will rival the patterns possible with many of today's shotshell-taking breechloaders.

I had the opportunity to play around with one of the 28½ barreled twelve-gauge versions a few years back, and used it to take a variety of game, from rabbits to pheasants and even turkey. While the handling and shooting of the gun was not really any different than with any other percussion double I've used in the past, loading the choked barrels did take just a bit longer than loading a gun with true open-bored barrels.

Muzzleloader Hunting

As with any unfired percussion muzzleloader, the shooter should first insure that the gun is not already loaded, then snap a cap or two on each nipple to blow out any oil left from the previous cleaning. Next, a measured ninety-grain charge of either FFg black powder or Pyrodex "RS/Select" is poured into each barrel. Then, in preparation to inserting the wads, each of the screw-in chokes must be unthreaded and removed. With the chokes out of the barrels, they become "cylinder bored" and can be loaded the same as the reproductions that come without a choke. However, thanks to the constrictions of the screw-in choke system, this side-by-side percussion twelve-bore performed very well with the one-piece plastic wad units.

Directly over the powder charge, I would seat one of the lubed Ox-Yoke Originals one quarter-inch-thick felt twelve-gauge wads. Then I would run down a one-piece Remington "Power Piston" plastic wad, pour in one and a quarter ounces of shot and top with a thin card over-shot wad. And after all of that had been loaded into each barrel, I would thread the chokes of choice back into the muzzles of the two barrels. The Cabela's double was then capped and ready to be shot.

The reason for leaving the chokes in place when pouring in the powder charge is to keep the fine granules of powder from getting into the extremely fine threads inside the bore of the barrel. To keep these chokes "removable," it's necessary to keep the tube threads lubed with a high-temperature choke-tube lubricant. This tends to leave a sticky film on the threads. If the chokes were removed and then a charge of powder dumped in, quite a bit of the powder would stick to the threads or lube, and make threading the choke tube back in extremely difficult.

The patterns produced by the twelve-gauge double were impressive, and not all that different from patterns produced by a breechloading shotgun barrel with the same choke constriction. I was especially impressed by the tight pattern produced by the "extra-full" choke tube. At thirty yards, I found that I could get a one and a quarter-ounce charge of No. 6 shot to print near ninety percent patterns. And the "modified" tube would deliver nice, even seventy-five percent patterns, while the "improved cylinder" choke consistently put about sixty-five percent of the pattern inside a thirty-inch circle at thirty yards.

Anyone wanting to hunt waterfowl with a muzzleloaded shotgun should take a closer look at this double, especially in the big thirty-inch barreled ten-gauge package. While steel shot loads should not be loaded into and shot out of any current muzzleloading shotgun, and certainly no orignal with soft Damascus steel barrels, the Italian-made doubles Cabela's now offers are ideal. The choke system in these guns will allow the use of other non-toxic shots, such as Bismuth. And when time is taken to work up a great buffered load, these old-fashioned frontloaded smooth-bores can be used to take ducks and geese in this modern world. ■

12

The Muzzleloader Turkey Challenge

Taking a big twenty-five pound wild turkey gobbler with a muzzleloading shotgun could prove to be the greatest challenge the muzzleloading hunter can tackle. Season-wise, older gobblers possess the uncanny ability to give a hunter the slip, making this big bird as much a trophy as any big-game animal. Those who have spent a number of years pursuing this great upland bird often refer to the wild turkey as *"America's Big Game Bird."* One thing is for certain, the hunter who has matched wits with this bird . . . and lost . . . will quickly learn to give it the same respect given to a trophy-class whitetail buck or bull elk.

Any hunter who underestimates the survival instincts of a wily older wild turkey gobbler is generally destined to go home empty handed. Accept it, the wild turkey is no dummy. It takes a hunter with woods savvy to be consistently successful season after season, especially when going after this tremendous game bird with a close-range muzzleloaded scattergun.

Success with a muzzleloading rifle for whitetails and other big game has encouraged an ever-growing number of hunters to turn to muzzleloading guns for hunting other species as well. And thanks to continually growing wild turkey populations, this big bird is high on that list. In this chapter, we will take a look at

There is a lot of satisfaction in walking out of the turkey woods with a fine muzzleloaded gobbler thrown over your shoulder.

the guns and loads, both old and new, that are up to the task of cleanly downing a huge bird that can run thirty m.p.h. and fly fifty m.p.h.

Then... Thirty or

so years ago, many states offered very limited turkey hunting opportunities. Hunters often had to enter into a special lottery drawing for one of a few thousand permits that were to be issued. Today, in many of these same states, the turkey hunter can easily purchase a permit right across the counter. Plus, in quite a few states, the hunter can now harvest two or three turkeys during the course of the season, and many hunters are turning to the challenge of hunting with a muzzleloading shotgun to harvest at least one of those birds.

There is something special about taking a wild gobbler with a muzzleloaded shotgun, as twelve-year-old Zack Opel experienced. It's doubly rewarding when it's your first turkey.

Get a gobbler close enough and you can cleanly take the bird with just about any muzzleloading shotgun and load. I once dumped a big Texas Rio Grande gobbler at just twelve yards with an extremely small twenty eight-gauge muzzleloader! But I most definitely wouldn't recommend it as the ideal choice for hunting an adult bird that can easily top twenty pounds. Even at thirty or forty yards, a wild turkey may seem far too large to miss. However, keep in mind that a big gobbler can be a tough target to put down. You see, the target isn't the whole turkey—but rather just the head and neck. In other words, the "kill zone" the muzzleloading shotgunner has to go for measures roughly two inches wide by ten inches tall. A shotgun and load that can put a dozen or more pellets into this zone will better increase your chances of that turkey laying there flapping his last as the smoke thins.

Taking my first muzzleloader turkey was every bit as important to me as taking my first muzzleloader whitetail. That first spring with a muzzleloader, I was hunting the rough Ozarks hill-country of south-central Missouri, and by the third morning of the season, I had enjoyed several close opportunities. But for one reason or another, I felt the birds were just a little farther than I cared to shoot at with the circa 1850s original English built "William Moore" twelve-gauge percussion double I carried for the hunt.

The shotgun was a favorite of mine, and threw nice even patterns when stuffed with a 95-grain charge of FFg black powder and a one and three eigths-ounce charge of No. 5 shot. Now, since the thirty-four-inch barrels did not exhibit the first hint of choke constriction, the patterns were far from being tight. But by carefully loading the big double with near equal volumes of powder and shot, plus the proper combination of traditional muzzleloader shotgun wads, the patterns were very evenly dispersed. At twenty-five yards, I found that I could easily keep ten or so of the No. 5 pellets on a 2"x10" strip of construction paper, used to duplicate the target I would be going for if and when I got a big gobbler within that range.

At the first crack of daybreak on the fourth morning, a roosted gobbler answered back to my owl hooting. The bird was just one hundred and fifty yards away. Slowly and quietly, I cut the distance in half and

Toby Bridges with the first gobbler he ever took with the Dixie ten-gauge double, a fine tom from Missouri.

settled down next to an old logging road. The tom continued to gobble on his own, and just before I felt it was time for him to fly down, I gave a very light hen yelp on my slate call. I heard the bird leave the roost and hit the ground, so sat the call on the carpet of leaves and rested the big double on an upraised knee. I had just drawn the right hammer to full cock when I spotted the gobbler coming on at a half walk, half run. At twenty yards, the bird stopped, raised its head and started looking around. When the hammer fell, the nearly one hundred and seventy-five-year-old shotgun roared. That gobbler was floored by the load.

Father and son double—author Toby Bridges, right, and son Adam enjoy a little conversation about the morning turkey hunt. Bridges' muzzleloading twelve-gauge Knight MK-86 performed every bit as well as his son's three-inch magnum twelve-gauge pump.

I took several more gobblers with that old shotgun before retiring it. The gun was replaced with a modern ten-gauge reproduction percussion double Dixie Gun Works still offers today, sold as their "Ten-Gauge Magnum." Shooting a hefty 100-grain charge of FFg black powder and one and a half ounces of No. 6 shot, this gun performed well on wild turkey. However, it still threw relatively open patterns, limiting shots to twenty to twenty-five yards. So, I played around with developing a wad (of sorts) that would help maintain tighter patterns at thirty and maybe thirty-five yards.

Back then, I did a lot of modern shotgunning as well, and reloaded my own 20-, 16- and 12-gauge shot shells. I discovered that a crimped sixteen-gauge hull would slip right into the muzzle of the Dixie ten-gauge, and the experimenting began. The version of the homemade wad that produced the best patterns was made by filling a fired sixteen-gauge hull with shot, then running it under the crimper of my reloader. Once the hull had been crimped, I would take a sharp knife and cut the plastic hull all the way around just above the brass head. And once the plastic had been cut free, I would dump out the shot, then take the cup produced and cut three evenly spaced one-inch cuts at the open end. This formed the petals or sleeves needed to pull the homemade shot cup back from the shot charge.

I worked my load up to 110 grains of FFg black powder. Over the powder charge, I would seat a single .125-inch *over-powder* card wad, and top that with a half-inch-thick *fiber cushion wad.* Right on top of that, I would set the homemade plastic shot cup, then poured down the one and three-quarters ounces of No. 6 shot it took to fill it. The entire load was then topped with a .030-inch-thick over-shot card wad. So loaded, the Dixie ten-bore proved to be a very effective thirty- to thirty-five-yard turkey gun. At the longer distance, the gun and load would consistently keep ten or twelve pellets on the 2"x10" strip of construction paper I used for my target.

Muzzleloading shotgunners today don't have to go to this much effort to work up such a turkey load for any open-bored frontloading shotgun. Ballistics Products (Corcoran, Minnesota) now offers several different twelve- and ten-gauge shot cups that come without any slits for forming the petals, or sleeves. These can be loaded the same as my old homemade shot cup, allowing the shooter to determine the length of petal or sleeve that results in the best patterns from a particular smooth-bore. And if you go this route, just be sure to slit the cups, because without the sleeves to pull the shot cup away from the shot charge, at under twenty yards a still shot-filled cup can hit an old turkey gobbler with the same devastating effects as a rifled slug!

Now ■ ■ ■

Just as the modern-day muzzleloading big-game hunter has taken to the futuristic in-line muzzleloading rifles and top-performing loads, the serious turkey hunter looking to use a frontloaded smooth-bore is now turning to similarly styled muzzleloading shotguns. Like the modern rifles, these guns are built with an efficient in-line percussion-ignition system that greatly reduces any chances of a misfire—as long as the hunter has snapped a cap on the ignition system before loading, and loaded the shotgun properly.

Introduced in the early 1990s, the Knight MK-86 was the first of these in-line muzzleloading smooth-bore wonders. Aside from the modern in-line ignition system and modern safety system found on this shotgun, the one other feature that has made this front-loading twelve-gauge so effective on wild turkey is the .665-inch *"extra-full"* screw-in choke that came standard on this shotgun. When a shooter takes the time to build a precise load, this modern muzzleloading shotgun is fully capable of matching the performance of a modern three-inch magnum breechloading shotgun.

Tony Knight with a big twenty-seven pound Iowa tom taken with a 12-gauge MK-86 and a healthy load of No. 5 shot.

The muzzle of the twenty-four-inch Knight MK-86 barrel is threaded to accept screw-in interchangeable chokes of the *"Rem-Choke"* variety. The one Knight shipped with the gun was a .665 Hastings choke, which immediately lets everyone know that this was intended to be one serious turkey gun. Another feature I really liked about the modern smooth-bore was that the receiver came drilled and tapped for easy installation of a low-power scope, or a simple rear peep sight. That first season with an MK-86, I relied on a 1X scope that allowed me to adjust the center of my pattern to print dead on a gobbler's head and neck. Since then, I've replaced the scope with a William's receiver sight. Both approaches sure take the guesswork out of aiming.

The extremely tight constriction of the .665 Hastings choke requires that the choke be removed in order to get properly fitting wads into the barrel. However, it took only once for me to learn that you should first dump in your powder charge, then remove the choke for the remainder of the loading sequence. If the choke is removed and a powder charge dumped in, quite a few powder granules will end up in the threads for the choke found inside the bore. This makes threading the choke back in place after the shotgun has been loaded extremely difficult.

The Knight MK-86 that I have hunted with since the gun was first offered seems to perform best when loaded with a hefty 110-grain charge of Pyrodex "RS/Select." Over that, I load a .125-inch heavy *over-powder* card wad and two of the one quarter-inch thick lubed Ox-Yoke Originals felt shotgun wads. Next, I push down one of the Ballistic Products "Turkey Ranger" twelve-gauge shot cups, and fill this with a one and three-quarter-ounce charge of No. 6 lubaloy copper-coated lead shot. The load is topped with one of the twelve-gauge styrofoam Knight overshot wads. Now, the "Turkey Ranger" wad is one of the Ballistics Products shot cups that comes non-slitted. I usually slit mine down about a half-inch, which is enough to form an airfoil that will pull the cup away from the shot charge shortly after leaving the muzzle.

Once the loading process is completed, the extra-full choke tube is threaded back into the muzzle. And so loaded, this shotgun will keep nearly one hundred percent of the shot load inside that magic thirty-inch circle at thirty yards. At forty yards, the load is good for around ninety percent patterns. At fifty yards, the MK-86 so loaded has proven capable of hitting with right at eighty percent of the pattern inside a thirty-inch circle. And while I don't really condone "long-range" shooting at wild turkey gobblers, I can remember one stubborn old Iowa bird that refused to come any closer, and the MK-86 reached out and tapped him at nearly fifty yards. The gobbler turned out to be the largest I've ever taken—a twenty-eight and a half pounder!

The Ballistics Products "Turkey Ranger" 12-gauge shot cup shown with a one-and three-quarters-ounce charge of No. 4 shot and buffering compound.

Knight Rifles has more recently replaced the MK-86 with an all-new in-line model known as the TK-2000. For this very modern in-line percussion shotgun, Knight actually reverts back to some very old technology. Instead of a constricted choke, the company installs a new "screw-on" jug choke. Other than the fact that this choke screws on, the concept is not all that different than the jug chokes that showed up in some shotgun bores during the second half of the 19th century.

The TK-2000 is a true twelve-bore, and is still loaded pretty much the same as the old MK-86—except the shooter now does not have to remove the choke to get proper fitting wads into the gun. The jug choke found in the screw-on choke tube actually opens up larger than true twelve gauge, then returns to the actual bore-size of the barrel a little more than an inch from the muzzle. This allows the shot charge to move along parallel with the bore all the way to the choke. Then the expanded

164

internal dimension lets the shot follow the surface, outward and away from the center of the shot load. However, as the surface turns back in and returns to actual bore size, the shot is then redirected in toward the center of the shot charge. Many shooters who have hunted with this shotgun report exceptional turkey-taking patterns out to forty or more yards.

Another of my personal favorite muzzleloading shotguns is the Lenartz "Turkey Taker" produced by Lenartz Muzzleloading, a small semi-custom gunmaking operation located near Alto, Michigan. The gun is actually a twelve-gauge version of the Rdi-50 (Radial Drop Ignition) in-line ignition rifle also produced by this company. Both feature an effective, easy-to-use ignition system that utilizes a hot No.

Muzzleloading gun maker Tim Lenartz with a fine Illinois gobbler he took at forty yards with one of his own twelve-gauge "Turkey Taker" in-line shotguns. This one features a .665-inch extra-full screw-choke.

209 primer. To prime, the shooter simply lifts a small handle on the gun's "primer cover," exposing a primer-shaped opening. A .209 primer is dropped in, and the handle pushed back down to enclose the primer.

The "Turkey Taker" I've used now for a number of seasons is a great performer with the same load I shoot in my old Knight MK-86, and loaded in the same manner. The feature I like about this light six and a half pound in-line muzzleloader is its short, easy-handling length thanks to the short receiver and twenty-two-inch barrel. Lenartz also installs a set of great Williams adjustable rifle sights on the barrel, allowing a shooter to sight the center-density of a load to print right where the gun is aimed. The Lenartz muzzleloader is a delight to carry all day in the turkey woods, and really performs when its time to pull the trigger.

The turkey hunter who likes a blend of modern performance and a bit of old-fashioned tradition should look at the Cabela's twelve- and ten-gauge doubles that also come with screw-in chokes. These great side-by-sides allow the turkey hunter to have a "modified" choke in one barrel for those birds that often run in almost too close for the tight pattern of the "extra-full" choke—in the other barrel for those stubborn old birds that won't step an inch closer than thirty yards. Like the in-lines with constricted chokes, the tubes must be removed for loading proper-fitting wads.

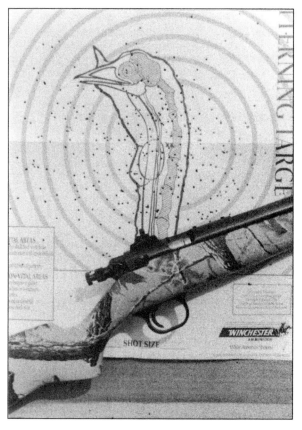

It's hard to believe that a muzzleloading shotgun can throw a thirty-yard pattern such as this. However, the Knight MK-86 shown here comes with a screw-in "extra-full" choke tube that will outperform many three-inch magnum-pump and semi-auto 12-gauge turkey guns.

My most memorable morning of hunting wild turkey was one I hunted with one of the Cabela's twelve-gauge doubles. Work had kept me from hunting the last week of the Missouri season, but as daybreak broke that last Saturday of season, I was standing in a pasture only a mile or so from my home. I waited to hear the first gobble of the morning, and when a gobbler greeted the coming day from a ridge a half-mile away, I hooted like an owl. And another gobbler answered less than one hundred yards away.

I eased down next to big white oak and called once very lightly with my old Rohm Borthers box call, and that gobbler went ballistic. It had rained through the night and that bird was apparently very lonely. I heard him fly down, and called lightly again. The turkey cut me off with a gobble before I ended the third note. I sat the call down and waited. Only a couple of minutes passed and there he was, just fifteen yards away. I waited for the tom to move behind a tree, then corrected the direction of the muzzles of the Cabela's double. When the big bird stepped out, I putted lightly on the diaphragm call in the roof of my mouth and up came his head—and back came the trigger. Ten minutes later, I was back home with a beautiful twenty-four-pound gobbler and the sun wasn't even all the way up yet.

The short, easy handling length of the Lenartz "Turkey Taker" has made the shotgun one of the author's favorite muzzleloading turkey guns.

Well, I had an Iowa tag in my pocket as well, and lived only fifteen miles from the state line. The season was open and I knew a farm I could hunt, so I jumped in my Jeep and made the twenty-minute drive. As I climbed out of the vehicle, I could hear two birds gobbling back and forth to one another. A few minutes later, I slipped in between them and did some excited calling. When I first sat down to call, I was about one hundred and fifty yards from each of the birds. But after a few series of cuts and clucks, and a few excited yelps, both were coming to me. And they were coming fast. I reached up and cocked back the hammer of the left barrel, and waited. Both showed up almost simultaneously,

This Iowa tom was taken with a Thompson/Center Arms muzzleloading 12-gauge in-line, topped with a scope for easy centering of a pattern on a gobbler's head and neck area.

and in range. When the better of the two stepped clear of the other gobbler, I centered the bead on the base of the tom's waddles and brought the trigger back. At thirty five yards, the "extra-full" choke tube and 100-grain charge of FFg black powder behind one and a half ounces of No. 5 shot dumped that bird where he stood. The turkey was almost identical in every respect to the one I had taken just forty five minutes earlier in Missouri with the right barrel.

A two-state double in less than an hour. And it was done with a slow-to-load muzzleloading shotgun. ▪

Weather-Proofing the Muzzleloading Turkey Shotgun

Spring turkey seasons just happen to take place during what is usually the wettest time of the year. In fact, many short two-week long seasons are often cut nearly in half due to inclement weather. And if you've ever hunted turkeys, you know what it's like to get really soaked.

Unfortunately, the number one reason for a misfire with any muzzleloaded gun is due to rainy weather. So, when faced with hunting during damp weather, what precautions can the muzzleloading turkey hunter take to insure that when the opportunity presents itself that a muzzleloading shotgun, whether of traditional or modern design, will belch fire, smoke, and a healthy charge of shot when the trigger is pulled?

Easily the most vulnerable part of a load is the percussion cap that produces the fire for ignition. This is especially true with the traditional side-hammer guns, where the cap is right out in the open, and most vulnerable to wet weather. The solution is actually pretty simple. Just run down to the local archery shop and pick up a tube of bowstring wax. Then take a few seconds to rub down the cone of each nipple. And once a percussion cap has been pushed down onto the waxed surface, rub a little more wax around the base of the copper cap. This really seals the ignition primer inside from the weather. Now, RWS percussion caps are some of the most waterproof on the market, but even when using these, I still use the bowstring wax to insure that moistures stays out. And getting to the nipple of an in-line rifle does take a little more effort, but the time spent to coat the nipple and base of the cap with wax could mean the difference in just the hammer falling or the shotgun firing.

Another good loading habit to get into when going after spring gobblers with a muzzle-loaded smoothbore is to squirt a dab of grease-based black powder lube onto the bottom of the fiber cushion wad. Then, when this wad is seated down over the heavy over-powder card wad, this lube will be "squished" into as thin protective barrier that will keep moisture from reaching the powder charge. Plus, when the shotgun is fired, the lube will help keep the fouling from the burning powder charge soft, making the reloading of that barrel easier.

Some muzzleloading turkey hunters also stretch something thin over the muzzle, to keep rain and dampness out of the barrel altogether. I've seen everything from a small balloon to several strips of vinyl electrician's tape used. All such precautions will keep the load dry from the weather, and the muzzleloaded turkey shotgun as close to 100-percent sure-fire as a muzzleloader can get.

13
The Frontloading Sidearm

f I were to ask everyone reading this book, "How many of you hunt with a muzzleloading pistol or cap-and-ball revolver?" not many hands would go into the air. Oh, lots of these guns have been sold over the years, and a few shooters have actually used a handgun of frontloading design to take some game, but for the most part, these pistols are now shot just for the sheer enjoyment of shooting a 19th-century and earlier design sidearm.

Only a handful of states permit the use of these guns for hunting large game.

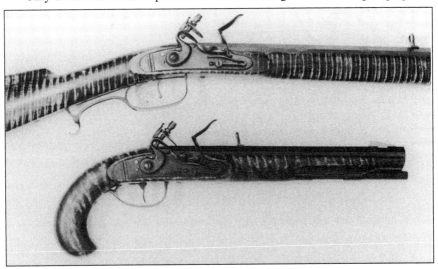

When early hunters and trappers carried a single-shot muzzleloaded sidearm, it was often of the same caliber as the rifle they relied on. Shown is a pair of custom flintlocks built by riflemaker Jack Garner.

The reason why is simple: Few of them can develop the needed energy to insure a good, clean harvest of anything the size of a white-tailed deer. There are a few of these guns that can be loaded with more than enough knockdown power to handle the job, but they generally require quite a bit of load development to tap their full potential with accuracy. On the other hand, some of the smaller bore cap-and-ball revolvers are ideal for packing along on a day's rabbit hunt for taking a few shots at sitting targets.

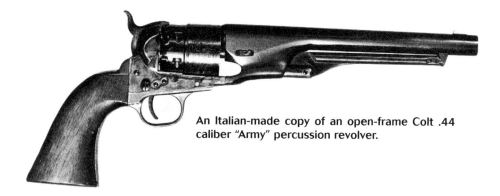

An Italian-made copy of an open-frame Colt .44 caliber "Army" percussion revolver.

Then...

Since the introduction of the first new-made Navy Arms reproduction of the Colt Model 1851 Navy percussion revolver during the late 1950s, literally millions of various percussion revolvers and single-shot muzzleloading pistols have flowed into the U.S. from manufacturers in Italy and Spain. Today's black-powder revolver makers have easily doubled or quadrupled the number of originals ever produced by makers like Colt or Remington. In fact, during the late 1980s, one Italian manufacturer alone claimed to have exported some 900,000 percussion revolvers to this country over a ten- to fifteen-year period.

While all of the steel-and-brass framed modern copies of the various cap-and-ball revolvers from the past can be found with a wide range of importer names on the barrel, including Navy Arms, Dixie Gun Works, Euroarms of America and others, most of these guns are actually produced by only a few different companies. During the late 1970s and early 1980s, Lyman imported from Italy a line of very high quality percussion revolvers, which included near exact copies of the .36 caliber Colt Model 1851 Navy and the .44 caliber Colt Model 1860 Army, plus .36 and .44 caliber copies of the closed-frame Remington revolvers that were used during the Civil War.

Generally speaking, the Lyman revolvers commonly retailed for ten dollars to twenty dollars more than comparable models from many of the other importers at the time. Truth is, many of these guns came from the very same factories in Italy. However, Lyman paid a premium price for their guns to sport a higher-quality finish, including a deeper blue on the barrel and better color case-hardening of the Colt frames. Internally, the Lyman revolvers and the revolvers offered by a number of other importers were basically the same. Externally, the Lyman revolvers better

This shooter is using the ram of the loading lever to force a slightly oversized lead ball into the chamber of a big .44 caliber Colt "Walker" reproduction revolver.

duplicated the finish of an original Colt or Remington percussion revolver—and that look costs a little extra.

For the past thirty or so years, Sturm, Ruger and Company has offered their extremely well-built percussion .45 caliber *"Old Army"* model, which is basically a frontloaded black-powder version of the company's revered line of *"Blackhawk"* single-action cartridge revolvers. Had breechloading firearms not been developed, this percussion wheelgun would likely represent the pinnacle of revolver development. The Old Army incorporates an internal working mechanism that is far superior to original circa 1850 to 1860 percussion-revolver designs. Modern coil springs and refined engineering not only make the action of the revolver much more reliable, but also smoother and noticeably more positive. Such quality has its price, generally nearly double the cost of most reproductions of .44 caliber Colt- and Remington-design handguns.

No matter whose name appears on the gun, or whether it is of original open-frame Colt or closed-frame Remington design, or even if it is of modern design like the Ruger Old Army, all percussion revolvers basically load in the same manner. Starting the loading sequence means first checking to make sure that none of the five or six chambers of the cylinder is already loaded. It's impossible to get any load into the relatively limited chamber space without the projectile being very visible near the mouth of the chamber. Once a shooter is sure there are no loads in the revolver, it's time to begin the actual loading sequence.

The revolver is first placed at half-cock to allow the cylinder to rotate freely, enabling the shooter to manually turn the cylinder with his fingers, and place a percussion cap on each of the nipples at the rear. These are fired to blow out or burn any oil in the nipple or chamber. The revolver is now ready to be charged.

Most .36 or .44 caliber black-powder revolver chambers won't allow loading very heavy powder charges. *Maximum loads* are pretty well dictated by how much powder can be gotten into the chamber, leaving enough room to seat the projectile below the chamber opening. As a rule, the heaviest charge you can get into a .36 caliber Navy Model Colt is about twenty-nine grains of FFFg (or the volume equivalent of Pyrodex "P"), while the slightly larger .44 Army models can be stoked with up to about thirty seven grains of the same powder. Even so, best accuracy with most of these guns is achieved with powder charges that are thirty percent to forty percent lighter.

The easiest and fastest way to get a charge of powder into one of the chambers is to use a powder flask with an appropriately sized spout screwed in place. Simply place your forefinger over the open end of the spout, then hold the flask upside down and work the spring-powered lever with your thumb. This allows the spout to fill with powder, and when the lever is released, the flask can be turned back upright and the spout will hold one full charge of powder. Most importers of these revolvers also offer a flask with the appropriate-sized spout standard. Several muzzleloading gun suppliers, such as Dixie Gun Works, offer a variety of spouts that will measure set charges from twenty to all the way up to two hundred grains. (Dixie also offers spouts for the little .31 caliber "Pocket Model" revolvers that measure charges as light as twelve grains.)

With the powder charge poured into a chamber, place the projectile into the mouth of the chamber; it should not freely drop in over the powder charge. Black-powder revolvers are most commonly loaded with a round ball. However, some shooters have preferred short conical bullets in these guns. Many original Colt revolver bullet moulds dating from the 1860s featured two cavities—one for casting an appropriately sized round ball, the other for producing a squat conical bullet for the same caliber revolver.

Whether you choose to load with the round ball or conical, the projectile must be slightly larger in diameter than the chamber to fit properly. With the projectile setting at the front of the chamber, rotate the cylinder until the ball or bullet is in alignment with the rammer of the loading lever. Using the lever, force the projectile into the smaller diameter chamber. A thin ring of lead should peel away from the outside circumference of the projectile as it is pushed into the chamber, creating the tight fit necessary to keep the projectile in place until it is fired.

The author and hunting partner Ben Burton, right, teamed up to take this old Tennessee tusker with their percussion revolvers.

The chamber of most .36 caliber percussion revolvers will measure right at .375 inch from wall to wall, while the chambers of most .44 cap and ball handguns will measure right at .450 inch. Traditionally, the .36 caliber revolvers have been loaded with a .376-inch diameter ball, and .44 revolvers stuffed with a .451-inch ball. Many percussion-revolver shooters feel that .001-inch is not sufficient to insure that a ball fits tight enough to guarantee that recoil from shooting adjacent chambers won't cause it to work forward, catching onto the rear of the barrel as the cylinder rotates. Many .36 caliber handgun shooters now rely on slightly larger

.380-inch balls and .44 shooters often load with .454-inch diameter balls. The chambers of the Old Army measure out at .453 inch and Ruger recommends loading with .457-inch diameter projectiles.

Once the projectile has been seated over the powder charge in one chamber, repeat the process with another, then another and another until all are loaded. Some shooters first charge all of the chambers of the cylinder, then seat each of the projectiles. Loading in this manner could create one of several problems. First, while it is virtually impossible to double-charge a chamber, it is possible to skip a chamber and forget to pour powder in at all. When more than one charge of powder is poured into a chamber, it will usually overfill, letting the shooter know instantly what's happened. Plus, if a chamber is skipped, you could have a projectile seated down into that uncharged chamber. Likewise, with really tight-fitting projectiles, the shooter may have to wrestle with the loading lever just a bit, and some powder could be jostled out of one chamber and into another. Loading one chamber at a time tends to produce the most consistent, most trouble-free loading of these revolvers.

After all chambers have been loaded with powder and projectile, top each with a generous dab of grease, black powder or even good ol' Crisco. This serves two purposes. First, and foremost, the grease forms a seal that prevents the fire in one chamber from seeping around the projectile in another chamber and setting off that charge as well. The condition is known as a *"chain fire."* When a revolver is loaded with ill-fitting projectiles and without lube at the front of the chambers, it's possible that every chamber could ignite almost simultaneously—possibly injuring the shooter and damaging the revolver. Another benefit of the grease is to keep powder fouling soft, in the barrel and at the face of the cylinder. When built-up fouling becomes hard and crusty, it can be impossible to rotate the cylinder . . . or to get any degree of accuracy when the bore is filled with heavy fouling.

Ox-Yoke Originals (Milo, Maine) packages and sells dry lubricated felt wads, known as "Wonder Wads," which can be loaded between the projectile and powder charge. These do an excellent job of preventing multiple chambers from firing at once. Even so, the *dry lube* really does not do much to keep fouling soft. The shooter who uses these wads and still places a bit of lube over the loaded chamber generally enjoys the most trouble-free shooting and best accuracy.

Loading these revolvers really isn't the hassle it may sound like. After a few tries, just about anyone can get the hang of loading the guns. And once each chamber has been charged and topped with a seated projectile and lube, all that's left to do is place a percussion cap on each of the nipples at the back of the cylinder. Some revolvers use No. 10 caps, others No. 11 caps. Just be sure to use one that fits nice

Larry Weishuhn and renowned Texas wild-hog hunting guide Maurice Chambers with a good razorback that Larry dropped with a single shot from a Knight "Hawkeye" in-line muzzleloading pistol.

and snug. A loose cap that falls off the nipple can find its way under the cylinder and hamper its rotation, often requiring the shooter to slip the cylinder out of the revolver frame to get rid of the stray cap.

So, what kind of performance can you expect from one of these old-fashioned wheelguns? Well, as already pointed out, probably not enough energy, even at close range, to be considered adequate for taking anything larger than a groundhog or fox. But they are still fun to shoot.

Loaded with 29 grains of FFFg black powder, a seven and a half-inch barreled .36 caliber Colt Navy will get an eighty-one-grain .376-inch ball out of the muzzle at around 1,100 f.p.s. While not a bad velocity for such an old revolver design, the load is good for only 217 f.p.e. A .44 caliber Army Model loaded with a chamber filling 37 grains of FFFg and 138-grain .451-inch soft-lead ball is good for right at 1,000 f.p.s. at the muzzle of an eight-inch barrel. And that load generates 325 f.p.e. at the muzzle. So, as you can see, these guns are hardly adequate for serious big-game hunting. However, where legal, some hunters carry them to put in a quick finishing shot when needed.

Watch enough old movies about the early frontier days, both east and west, and the viewer would begin to think that just about every grown male settler, trapper, hunter or adventurer carried a muzzleloaded sidearm as a backup to the long-barreled "Kentucky" or shorter barreled "Hawken" they also packed. Truth is, most rarely carried such a "belt" pistol. They avoided packing anything that wasn't absolutely necessary for survival. Even though most probably wished they had a quick second shot more than once, they generally put their trust in the long gun they packed and, especially, in their woodsmanship to see them through hard times.

Those who did pack a sidearm generally relied on a pistol that was basically of the same caliber as his rifle, allowing the use of the same ball and patch (or bullet) for loading. Except for the amount of powder loaded into the shorter-length barrel, these muzzleloaded handguns were stuffed in the same basic manner as the rifles. Which means first making sure the handgun was not already loaded, then snapping a cap or two to clean the nipple of oil. A measured charge of powder was poured through the muzzle, the projectile was started into the bore and seated over the powder charge with the ramrod. All that remained then was to either cap the nipple of a percussion pistol or prime the pan of a flintlock handgun.

Typically, most pistols of this design are loaded with a patched round ball. And thanks to the fact that more powder can be loaded into these than into most percussion revolvers, the ballistics are a little better. Dixie Gun Works offers a clean-looking copy of the basic plain "Kentucky" pistol, in flint or percussion ignition, that comes with a ten and three-eighths-inch octagonal .45 caliber barrel. With a thirty-five-grain charge of FFFg black powder, the single-shot handgun gets a patched 128-grain .440-inch round ball out at around 750 f.p.s., which is only good for 160 f.p.e.

Moving up to the nine-inch barreled .50 caliber percussion Lyman Plains Pistol really doesn't increase game-taking performance all that much. When loaded with a forty five grains charge of FFFg black powder and a patched 178-grain .490-inch round ball, this great-looking single-shot handgun is good for about 800 f.p.s. at the muzzle for administering the *"coup de grace"* at close range with about 250 f.p.e. The same gun in .54 caliber, with the same powder charge and 224-grain .530-inch round ball, slows velocity down to about 750 f.p.s., but has about 280 f.p.e. at the muzzle.

With some practice, a shooter can learn to hit a six-inch or eight-inch target at twenty-five yards with some regularity with these handguns, but long-range guns and loads they are not. In fact, their only true practical use is to put in the humane finishing shot on deer-sized game—and from up close. The extremely low energy levels at the muzzle definitely rule them out as primary big-game hunting guns. But, as with all muzzleloading guns, they are fun to shoot.

Now ...
One of my favorite muzzleloading handguns during the mid 1990s was the Knight Rifles "Hawkeye" in-line pistol—truly a "two-hand" gun with a lengthy fourteen-inch .50 caliber barrel. The bore was rifled with a fast one-in-twenty-inches rate of rifling twist, and the big in-line percussion pistol shot very well with 70 grains of Pyrodex "P" and a saboted 260-grain Speer .451-inch JHP.

The Kahnke Model 82 is an accurate, hard-hitting in-line ignition-hunting handgun capable of delivering plenty of punch for taking deer-sized game at reasonable distances.

Scoped, I found I could keep groups inside of two and a half inches at one hundred yards. I took one big whitetail doe with the gun at about eighty yards, nearly dropping the deer where it stood.

The most enjoyable hunt I ever made with the "Hawkeye" was a trip down to south Texas to chase wild hogs with my good friend and fellow outdoor writer Larry Weishuhn. In three days of hunting, we chalked-up about a dozen wild hogs, several with the big "Hawkeye," which held its own right along with the in-line .50 caliber rifles we were also shooting. Unfortunately, there just was not enough demand for Knight to keep the handgun in their line-up.

In my opinion, there are currently only two muzzleloading handguns available today that can deliver sufficient energy down range to be considered adequate as the primary arm for hunting some big game. Those two pistols are the Thompson/Center Arms Encore 209x50 Magnum Pistol and the Kahnke Model 82 single-shot muzzleloading pistol. When time is taken to work up the hottest load each will shoot with accuracy, they are fully capable of delivering a saboted bullet with enough energy to get the job done on deer-sized game out to around one hundred yards.

The Kahnke Model 82 is available with either a twelve- or fourteen-inch barrel in .45, .50 or .54 caliber. And like modern in-line ignition hunting rifles, this nicely balanced percussion single-shot in .50 caliber is the best-selling version. When loaded with a seventy-grain charge of Pyrodex "P" behind a saboted 250-

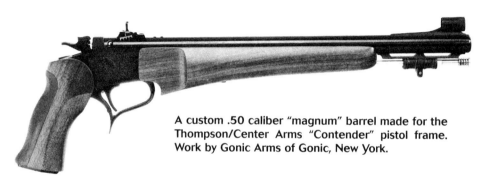

A custom .50 caliber "magnum" barrel made for the Thompson/Center Arms "Contender" pistol frame. Work by Gonic Arms of Gonic, New York.

grain Hornady XTP, the fourteen-inch barrel model is capable of getting the bullet on its way at almost 1,300 f.p.s., which translates into just about 940 f.p.e. at the muzzle. At fifty yards, the bullet would hit a whitetail with about 700 f.p.e., and with a well-placed shot, should do the job.

The magnum of today's muzzleloading handgun world is the fifteen-inch barrel T/C Encore 209x50 Magnum break-open pistol. Thanks to hot No. 209 primer ignition, this short companion to the Encore 209x50 Magnum rifle is fully capable of digesting eighty grains of FFFg Triple Seven—with accuracy. One of my regular hunting buddies uses one of these handguns and can punch impressivetwo and a half inch one hundred yard groups, thanks to the fast one-turn-in-twenty-inches rate of rifling twist. With the 80-grain charge of FFFg Triple Seven and saboted 250-grain T/C spire-pointed "Shock Wave" bullet, this handgun develops right at 1,500 f.p.s. at the muzzle. That's 1,250 foot-pounds of muzzle energy from a muzzleloaded handgun. Thanks to the .240 (T/C's figure) ballistic coefficient of this bullet, it is still moving at around 1,260 f.p.s. at one hundred yards, and hits with around 860 f.p.e.—and that's pretty darn good one-hundred-yard performance from a muzzleloading handgun. In fact, it's almost the performance of a .50 caliber in-line muzzleloaded rifle loaded with the same powder charge and bullet.

And it is this kind of retained down-range performance that has convinced a slowly growing number of game departments to allow some of the modern in-line pistols to be used during certain big-game seasons. If you decide to give it a whirl, first check to make sure it's legal in the state where you plan to hunt. Then take the time to work up as accurate a load as that handgun can muster, and never sacrifice any degree of accuracy for just a few more feet-per-second velocity or foot-pounds of energy. ■

14
Keeping Muzzleloaders Clean

E asily the number-one apprehension among shooters looking to buy their very first muzzleloading gun is the thought of all the cleaning associated with a muzzleloader. Often, shooters will play around with a historical muzzleloader design for a while, then hang it on the wall and never shoot it again. The lure of the special muzzleloading seasons keeps them looking at the new in-line rifles. But even though these guns are noticeably easier to clean, just the thought of the smell and filthy fouling associated with black powder and some black-powder substitutes is enough to keep some shooters from coming back into the sport.

Across the country, thousands of expensive and once deadly-accurate muzzle-loading rifles are lost to neglect each year. Many of these guns are victims of the residue and fouling left from the last "accurate" round that was ever fired out of the frontloader—a shot that probably took a whitetail buck . . . a bull elk . . . or maybe a spring black bear. Once that game was down, all attention was given to getting it dressed, out of the woods and to the check station, locker plant or onto the meat pole back in camp. If it's warm, the meat must be attended to quickly to keep it from spoiling, so it's not uncommon for the hunter to totally forget there's a dirty rifle that needs care, too. By the time he does get to the rifle, it may be too late.

It does not matter if a muzzleloading gun is fired just once or a dozen times, if it was shot with black powder or one of the black-powder substitutes—the gun has to be cleaned. These propellants leave behind a very corrosive fouling or residue when they burn. The fouling produced by just a single shot is enough to totally ruin the bore of any muzzleloader that is left dirty for very long. Under damp and humid conditions, the future accuracy of a rifle can be lost in as little time as overnight. Ideally, once a muzzleloader has been shot, it should be cleaned well before the day is over.

When headed for the range, many shooters now take along all of their cleaning gear and cleaning solutions in order to give their muzzleloader or muzzleloaders a thorough cleaning before heading back home. This is a good habit to get into. If a dirty muzzleloader is ever slipped back into the case, there is simply a natural reluctance to pull it out and clean it once back home. At the range, your hands are

Black powder, Pyrodex, and Triple Seven fouling are all extremely hygroscopic, and can pull moisture right out of the air on a frosty morning like this.

already a little soiled from loading and shooting . . . so what the heck?

There are a number of excellent black-powder cleaning solvents available that can make cleaning even the dirtiest muzzleloader bore a cinch. But in a real crunch, did you know that black-powder fouling (as well as Pyrodex and Triple Seven fouling) can be cleaned from a muzzleloader bore with

A good habit to get into is carrying a plastic baggie with a small supply of cleaning patches and a cleaning jag. It takes only a few minutes to eliminate the vast majority of fouling from the bore with just saliva-dampened patches—right in the field.

nothing more than plain ol' water? That's right, H_2O. Even plain saliva-dampened patches can be used to get the vast majority of fouling out of a rifle bore.

Black powder, Pyrodex and Triple Seven fouling are all very hygroscopic. That means the layer of fouling left in the bore by these powders can literally draw moisture right out of the air. And it only takes a shot or two for the hot-burning charges to totally burn away any protective lubricant that may have been applied to the bore after the last cleaning.

Now, very similar ingredients are used to make black powder and Pyrodex. Both are made with sulfur, which can be extremely corrosive when left in contact with nonprotected steel surfaces. This is especially so when compounded by the presence of moisture.

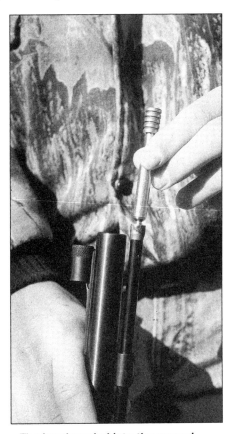

The jag threaded into the ramrod . . .

Muzzleloader Hunting

And I don't just mean rain or snow. When humidity levels are relatively high, leaving a muzzleloader bore dirty for twenty-four hours is about as bad as dunking it in water! Fortunately, Triple Seven does not contain sulfur, making it less likely to cause corrosion problems. However, the fouling is still somewhat hygroscopic, meaning that a rifle shot with Triple Seven charges might buy you until morning (with a few precautionary procedures), but the fact that the powder contains no sulfur doesn't mean the rifle does not have to be cleaned. It does.

A patch lightly dampened with saliva . . .

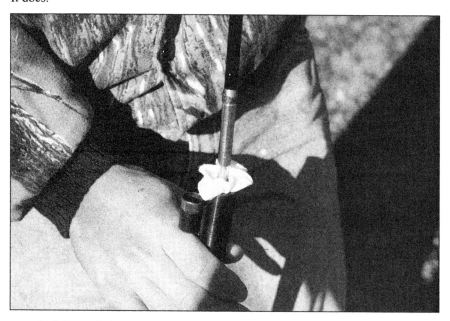

And the majority of fouling wiped from the bore with five or six patches.

If you intend to do your muzzleloader cleaning at home, at least take the time to run five or six lightly solvent-dampened cleaning patches down the bore before leaving the range to get the vast majority of fouling wiped out. If the rifle is an in-line model, break the breech plug loose. Fouling tends to dry or set-up within a couple of hours after the rifle has been shot, making it harder to get out of the bore, even with a really good solvent. Also, the longer a shooter leaves a dirty breech plug tightly threaded into the rear of the barrel, the harder it often is to break loose. With your last shot of the day, wipe the bore pretty clean and loosen the breech plug. Believe me, it's time well spent.

Likewise, another good cleaning habit to get into is to always pack along a dozen or so cleaning patches and a cleaning jag (if your rifle ramrod does not feature one) every time you head out for a hunt. These will all easily fit right into a sandwich-sized zip-locking plastic baggie. And if you are lucky enough to get in a lethal shot on that buck or bull you've been hunting, before even field dressing the animal, take four or five minutes to wipe the bore with saliva- or water-dampened patches to get as much of the powder fouling out as possible. When you get back home or to camp, loosen and remove the breech plug. Then douse down the bore and other lightly-fouled metal parts with a good moisture-displacing spray lubricant, like WD40. Those five or six minutes spent on the rifle will buy you the time you need to put off a complete cleaning until well into the next day.

Hot Soapy Water or Solvent?

Despite all of the great muzzleloader-cleaning solvents on the market today, the most widely used solution for getting the fouling out of a rifle's bore and from the surfaces of other metal parts is simply good ol' hot soapy water. This is usually no more than tap water with a healthy squirt of dishwashing detergent. For camp use, some hunters develop their own "special blends" . . . such as getting a gallon of windshield washer fluid, then adding a little detergent. But it simply boils down to soapy water!

The fouling left behind by black powder, Pyrodex or Triple Seven charges can be easily cleaned from the bore with water alone. However, a little soap speeds up the cleaning process. And if the load is built around a grease-lubed bullet or a heavily lubed patched round ball, the detergent will help break down any grease residue left behind.

Many of the old-timers who have been shooting muzzleloaders for several decades believe the hotter the water, the better. It heats the metal of the barrel, and once the bore has been cleaned of fouling and several dry patches run through to get out most of the moisture, the barrel can be set aside muzzle down. This allows any remaining moisture to drain out, while the heated barrel prompts drying. In about five or six minutes, several more dry patches can be run the full length of the bore, followed by several lubricated patches. That barrel is then clean—until the next time it is shot.

There are many times when it is impossible to have access to a sink full of hot soapy water, plus there are also many shooters who simply cringe at the thought of dunking a prized muzzleloader in water—soap or no soap. Fortunately, there are now some excellent black-powder solvents (for Pyrodex and Triple Seven also) available that can and will thoroughly clean the dirtiest muzzleloader bore and make it spotless.

Hodgdon's "EZ Clean" has been formulated to quickly and easily break down Pyrodex fouling and residue, but works just as well for black powder or any other substitute.

Knight Rifles offers one of the best black powder-Pyrodex-Triple Seven cleaning solvents I've ever used. It is a strong detergent-based solution that removes fouling from metal parts quickly. At the beginning of a cleaning session, the in-line rifle owner can drop the dirty breech plug (and nipple if the rifle still relies on No. 11 or musket caps for ignition) into a small container of this solvent, and by the time the bore has been wiped free of fouling, the residue can be wiped quickly and easily from those parts. Knight Rifles also offers a very complete line of cleaning equipment and components, including wire bore brushes, cleaning patches, auxiliary loading/cleaning rods, bore swabs, patch pullers, you name it. The aerosol Knight Oil is one of the best on the market, and contains DuPont Teflon and rust inhibitors.

Thompson/Center Arms also offers a complete line of cleaning gear for the muzzleloading shooter and hunter. This includes their "Number 13" black-powder cleaning solvent, which makes short work of a black powder-, Pyrodex- or Triple Seven-fouled bore and other metal parts. Connecticut Valley Arms offers yet another strong muzzleloader cleaning solution known as "Barrel Blaster" solvent. Like most everyone in the muzzleloading gun business these days, this importer also offers an extensive line of cleaning supplies and gear. Other notable black-powder solvents include Birchwood Casey "No. 77," Shooter's Choice "Black Powder Gel," Hoppe's "No. 9 Plus" and Dixie Gun Works "Black Solve." All will get the cleaning job done fast.

Cleaning the Different Muzzleloaders

When talking about *traditional muzzleloaders,* you're basically talking about guns that feature a *fixed breech,* and have a barrel that is either *pinned* in place or attaches to the stock assembly using what is known as a *hooked breech.* A muzzle-

Muzzleloaders built with a "hooked breech" feature barrels that are commonly held in place by one or two "wedges" that pass through the fore-stock and a tennon attached to the bottom of the barrel.

loader with a barrel that is pinned will have to be cleaned with the barrel still attached to the stock assembly, while the design of a muzzleloader with a hooked breech allows the shooter to remove the barrel from the rest of the gun for cleaning. And when the topic today centers on modern *in-line ignition* muzzleloaders, it means that the gun features a *removable breech plug,* allowing them to be cleaned more easily all the way through a barrel that is open on each end.

Frontloading guns with a pinned and nonremovable barrel can prove to be the slowest to clean. These are generally your Kentucky-style rifles, with long barrels and long, slender forearms that reach to the muzzle. Most copies of early flintlock smooth-bore muskets are also of this type construction. While the pins can be tapped out, releasing the *tennons* attached to the bottom of the barrel and allowing the barrel to be removed from the stock, the fit of the pins becomes looser the more this is done. So, most fanciers of the older long, full-stock muzzleloaders simply

The "hooked breech plug" of this rifle fits snugly back into a recess of the tang that remains attached to the stock.

clean the barrel while it is still attached to the stock assembly.

The first step is to loosen the screws holding the lock mechanism in the lock mortise of the stock, and slide it out of the stock. Small amounts of fouling from the flash of a flintlock pan or the explosion of a percussion cap will spew fouling on the side of the barrel, lock and often down into the mechanism. These areas must be cleaned free of corrosive fouling as well.

To clean the bore, the gun should be propped slightly at an angle, with the butt on the ground. Using the ramrod or cleaning rod with a proper-sized cleaning jag

The White "Thunder Bolt" is a well-built, accurate and easy-to-clean in-line muzzleloading rifle. Like all in-line rifles today, this one features a removable breech plug.

at the end, five . . . six . . . seven . . . or so solvent-dampened cleaning patches should be run up and down the bore, until the last one comes out relatively clean. Then, the bore should be wiped dry with three or four dry cleaning patches and, after that, a couple of well-lubed patches. At that point the bore of the rifle should be pretty darn spotless.

Variations of today's removable breech plugs. The threads must be lubricated with a proper grease before being installed in the rifle to insure that they remain "removable."

Actually, cleaning the fouling from the barrel around the nipple area of a percussion rifle or where the pan of a flintlock butts up against the barrel can take about as long as wiping the bore free of fouling. For some reason, this fouling seems to get more baked on, and getting it off the metal surface may require using an old toothbrush or typewriter cleaning brush, plus some elbow grease. The hammers of both percussion and flintlock systems will require a good cleaning as well. And so does the fouling that will coat the frizzen and pan of the flintlock mechanism. When cleaning some of these "mechanical" parts, be sure you get all fouling removed and don't leave any moisture behind. This is especially true if you have to carefully clean some fouling that may have gotten into the lock mechanism.

Cleaning a hooked-breech muzzleloader barrel allows the shooter to tap out a wedge (or two) that runs through the fore-stock and corresponding tennon attached to the bottom of the barrel. The front of the barrel can be lifted and a hook at the rear of the barrel, extending from the breech plug, will disengage a recess on the separate tang, allowing the barrel to be quickly and easily removed from the stock assembly. This is a common feature on most "Hawken"-style half-stock muzzle-loading rifles and most reproduction double-barrel shotguns.

Once the barrel has been removed, the nipple is generally unthreaded from a percussion barrel and the breech end of that barrel is submersed in a bucket of hot, soapy water. A wet patch is then placed over the muzzle and pushed on into the bore with the jag at the end of the ramrod or cleaning rod. Once the jag and patch reach the bottom of the barrel, they're pulled back toward the muzzle, creating a vacuum that also pulls some of that hot, soapy water in through where the nipple threads (or

A breech plug and nipple removed from a Traditions "Lightning" model in-line rifle. The "wrench" at right, required to disassemble the rifle, comes as standard equipment.

the vent hole of a flintlock). When the ramrod is pushed back down, the solution is pushed back out that hole. A dozen or so strokes usually get that bore as clean as it is ever going to be.

Follow up with a few dry patches, then let the hot-water-heated barrel air dry for about four or five minutes. While it is drying, scrub the fouling from the nipple and from the lock surfaces. Once the barrel has dried for a few minutes, run one or two more dry patches down the bore, then spray down the outside of the barrel with a good aerosol lube, such as Knight Oil, and run a couple of lightly lubed patches down the bore as well. Before reassembling the gun, be sure to lubricate the surfaces of other metal parts.

Of course, some shooters don't like using soapy water to clean a muzzleloader, but the method just described is definitely the fastest way to clean any barrel with a hooked breech. Solvent-soaked cleaning patches can be run in and out of the bore, the same as with a gun with a fixed pinned barrel, but the process will take longer.

The removable breech plug of early in-line rifle designs was one of the biggest selling points of these rifles—for two reasons. First, if a shooter did not want to shoot his rifle to unload it, the breech plug could always be removed, the powder dumped out and the projectile pushed out the rear of the barrel. (Often, the powder that got stuck in some of the threads for the breech plug proved more difficult to clean out than if the rifle had just been fired and cleaned thoroughly.) Secondly, it

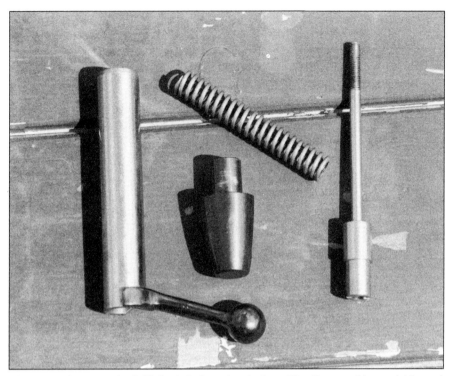

The bolt of an Austin & Halleck bolt-action in-line rifle disassembles quickly and easily for a thorough cleaning.

allowed these barrels to be cleaned all the way through, basically like a modern breechloader. This enabled the shooter to look through the barrel and visually determine that all fouling had been removed from the bore.

Most in-line rifle shooters don't like having to always remove the action and barrel from the stock for cleaning the rifle. And if the gun is positioned so the barrel and receiver are somewhat "upside-down" to keep dirty solvent from seeping into the trigger mechanism, there is actually no reason to remove the barreled action from the stock each time. Running five or six solvent soaked-patches through the bore is usually all it takes to get the fouling out, then a couple of dry patches to remove any moisture, followed by several lubed patches to protect it until it's time to shoot or hunt again.

Most of the modern "bolt-action" in-line rifle designs will also require stripping down the bolt and cleaning all fouling from internal and external surfaces. Each disassembles a little differently, but today's rifle manufacturers have made it all very simple to encourage shooter to clean this part as well as the rest of the gun. Even if the in-line rifle you shoot and hunt with isn't a bolt-action design, be sure to clean the fouling that accumulates inside the hammer nose if it uses any type of percussion cap.

The smokeless loads shot in this Savage Model 10ML II do buy the hunter some time, but during a cold, snowy hunt, that rifle will still require attention before the night is over.

One very important aspect of maintaining an in-line percussion muzzleloading rifle is to be sure to use the recommended lube on the threads of the breech plug. A removable breech plug is only a great feature when it remains removable. Unfortunately, not all greases or lubes are equal. It takes a really high-temp grease to keep the breech plug from getting stuck, and quite a few in-line rifle owners are now shooting a rifle with a breech plug that won't come out of the barrel. So, adhere to using the lubricant (grease) recommended by the maker of your rifle. Manufacturers tend to know what works best in their product.

One of the easiest-to-maintain in-line rifles available today is the Savage Model 10ML II. And that's only when shooting the recommended noncorrosive smokeless powder loads. The bore can be easily maintained using the same nitro-solvents used to keep modern center-fire rifles clean. When shooting any of the black-powder substitutes, the rifle's breech plug design contributes to the plug becoming frozen. It allows fouling to seep in around a long unthreaded snout, sets up and makes getting the plug difficult, if not impossible, to break free and thread out. Some shooters have remedied the problem by wrapping the snout with a couple of wraps of plumber's pink Teflon tape.

Due to the hot powder charges being shot in so many of the latest high-performance muzzleloaded rifles, saboted bullet are now leaving the muzzle of most at 2,000+ f.p.s. The high heat produced by these charges and the hyper speed of the plastic sabot inside the bore results in more plastic fouling left in the bore. If your in-line rifle has stopped giving the tight pinpoint accuracy it once did, simply run a good bronze-wire bore brush in and out of the bore fifteen or twenty times and follow up with a modern cleaning solvent like good ol' Hoppe's No. 9. A couple of dampened patches, followed by a dry patch, will restore accuracy to most rifles.

So how long does it take to give a muzzleloaded rifle a good, thorough cleaning? Generally about 10 minutes, once you've got the sequence down pat. It only seems much, much longer when you've got other things you would rather be doing than cleaning a dirty muzzleloader. But keeping your rifle clean is just part of the territory that goes along with shooting and hunting with a gun of frontloading design.

What about cleaning the "other" black-powder frontloaders, like the single-shot handguns and the percussion revolvers? Well, just think of a muzzleloaded single-shot handgun as a very, very short muzzleloaded rifle. Depending on whether the barrel is pinned in place or features a hooked breech, clean it just as you would a muzzleloaded rifle of the same basic design.

As for the percussion revolvers, each type has a basic procedure for disassembling into different major parts. Colts break down into three part groups—the barrel assembly, the cylinder and the frame. Remington revolvers break down into just two part groups—the cylinder and the rest of the gun. The instructions that come with each type should detail how to break the guns down for cleaning. With five or six different chambers to clean and the various recesses for the separate nipples at the rear of the cylinder, these early wheelguns often take a little longer to clean than the typical muzzleloaded rifle. Even so, most can be thoroughly cleaned in twenty minutes or less. So, if you're going to shoot one, you might as well shoot the living daylights out of it . . . because it is going to take just as long to clean it whether you've shot one cylinder full or ten cylinders full. ■

Other Outdoorsman's Edge Books Available

❏ **Mounting Your Deer Head at Home**
by Monte Burch

❏ **Blood Trails II**
by Ted Nugent

❏ **Hunting Rutting Bucks**
by John Trout, Jr.

❏ **Wildlife & Woodlot Management Handbook**
by Monte Burch

❏ **Finding Wounded Deer**
by John Trout, Jr.

❏ **Sure-Fire Whitetail Tactics**
by John Weiss

❏ **Moon Phase Whitetail Hunting**
by Jeffrey Murray

❏ **Advanced Turkey Hunting**
by Richard Combs

❏ **The Ultimate Guide to Planting Food Plots for Deer and Other Wildlife**
by John Weiss

❏ **The Complete Guide to Saltwater Fishing**
by Al Ristori

❏ **Complete Guide to Rabbit Hunting: Secrets of a Master Cottontail Hunter**
by David Fisher

- **Butchering Deer:**
  The Complete Manual of Field Dressing,
  Skinning, Aging, and Butchering Deer at Home
  by John Weiss

- **The Art of Whitetail Deception: Calling,**
  Rattling and Decoying
  by Kathy Etling

- **Predator Hunting: Proven Strategies that**
  Work from East to West
  by Ron Spomer

- **A to Z Guide to White-tailed Deer**
  and Deer Hunting
  by Dr. Randall Gilbert

- **Hunting Bears: Black, Brown, Grizzly, and Polar**
  Bears
  by Kathy Etling

- **Do-It-Yourself Gun Repair:**
  Gunsmithing at Home
  by Ed Matunas

- **Hunting Big Woods Bucks:**
  Secrets of Tracking and Stalking Whitetails
  by Master Guide Hal Blood

- **Antler, Bone, Horn and Hide:**
  Projects You Can Make at Home
  by Monte Burch

TO ORDER,

Call us at 1-800-652-7527, write to us at Woods N' Water Press,
P.O. Box 550, Florida, NY 10921 or visit us on the web at
www.fiduccia.com or www.outdoorsmansedge.com.